Judaism in North America

BLOOMSBURY RELIGION IN NORTH AMERICA

The chapters in this book were first published in the digital collection *Bloomsbury Religion in North America*. Covering North America's diverse religious traditions, this digital collection provides reliable and peer-reviewed articles and eBooks for students and instructors of religious studies, anthropology of religion, sociology of religion, and history. Learn more and get access for your library at www.theologyandreligiononline.com/bloomsbury-religion-in-north-america

Also available:

Islam in North America, edited by Hussein Rashid,
Huma Mohibullah, and Vincent Biondo

Christianity in North America, edited by Dyron D. Daughrity

Religion, Science and Technology in North America,
edited by Lisa L. Stenmark and Whitney A. Bauman

Religion and Nature in North America, edited by Laurel D.
Kearns and Whitney A. Bauman

Secularity and Nonreligion in North America, edited by Jesse M. Smith
and Ryan T. Cragun

New Religious Movements in North America, edited by Lydia Willsky-Ciollo

Latin American and US Latino Religions in North America, edited by Lloyd D. Barba

Judaism in North America

An Introduction

EDITED BY GARY G. PORTON

BLOOMSBURY ACADEMIC
LONDON · NEW YORK · OXFORD · NEW DELHI · SYDNEY

BLOOMSBURY ACADEMIC
Bloomsbury Publishing Plc
50 Bedford Square, London, WC1B 3DP, UK
1385 Broadway, New York, NY 10018, USA
29 Earlsfort Terrace, Dublin 2, Ireland

BLOOMSBURY, BLOOMSBURY ACADEMIC and the Diana logo are
trademarks of Bloomsbury Publishing Plc

First published online 2021
This print edition published 2024

A catalogue record for this book is available from the British Library.

A catalog record for this book is available from the Library of Congress.

ISBN: HB: 978-1-3504-0681-0
         PB: 978-1-3504-0682-7

Series: Bloomsbury Religion in North America

Typeset by Integra Software Services Pvt. Ltd.
Printed and bound in Great Britain

To find out more about our authors and books visit www.bloomsbury.com
and sign up for our newsletters.

Contents

Illustrations

List of Contributors

Ellie Ash is Postdoctoral Fellow with the Center for the Study of Religion and American Culture at IUPUI, USA.

Alan J. Avery-Peck is the Kraft-Hiatt Professor in Judaic Studies at the College of the Holy Cross, USA.

Elizabeth S. Berke is the Cantor Shenei at Anshe Emet Synagogue, USA.

Paul V.M. Flesher is Professor of Religious Studies at the University of Wyoming, USA.

Lewis R. Gordon is the Board of Trustees Distinguished Professor and Global Affairs and Department Head at the University of Connecticut, USA.

William Scott Green is the Fain Family Endowed Chair in Judaic Studies at the University of Miami, USA.

Alyssa A. Henning is an Independent Scholar in Rockville Maryland, USA.

Ellen LeVee died in 2021. At the time of writing she was Professor at Spertus Institute for Jewish Learning and Leadership, USA.

Ronen Dar Pink studies at the University of Miami, Coral Gables, Florida.

Gary G. Porton is Emeritus Professor of Religion, History, and Comparative and World Literature at the University of Illinois, Urbana-Champaign, USA.

Barry Scott Wimpfheimer is Associate Professor of Religious Studies at Northwestern University, USA.

1

Introduction to Judaism in North America

Gary G. Porton and Alan J. Avery-Peck

Before the seventeenth century, identifying a Jew and defining Judaism were easy. After the nineteenth century, describing Judaism and determining who is a Jew are more complex. Is Judaism a race, a nation, an ethnic group, or a religion? Do Jews adhere to a set of religious beliefs and practices, or does something else define them as a cohesive group, different from other people? Can one easily distinguish the Jews within any given location's population? Trying to compose a simple definition for "Jews" or for "Judaism" presents numerous difficulties. Not the least of these are significant differences between the ways in which Jews think of themselves and the ways non-Jews describe them.

Most Christians and Muslims today define Judaism as a religion and assume that all Jews share a common set of religious beliefs. Within this framework, Jews are most broadly defined as people who do not accept Jesus as the Messiah or Muhammed as God's ultimate prophet. To explain the Jews' failure to recognize these truths of Christianity and Islam, both Muslims and Christians argue that Jews do not understand the Jews' own scripture, the Hebrew Bible, commonly referred to by Christians and others as the Old Testament.

Defining Jews solely based on a set of beliefs is too narrow. While some Jews may describe themselves in terms of the divinity in whom they believe and by the way they understand the Hebrew Bible, others cringe at classifying Judaism as a religion and designate Judaism as "a way of Life." Still others call themselves secular—or, perhaps, cultural—Jews, whose Jewish identification derives only from some amorphous idea of "heritage" or "tradition." So, today, how should we classify Judaism and define Jew?

FIGURE 1.1 *Not all Jews dress the same when praying.* Source: *Boryak/Getty Images.*

The four common approaches to thinking about Judaism—religion, nation, race, and ethnicity—are modern concepts, and they are often shorthand for ways of marking differences. (1) A focus on religion privileges modes of differentiation created by firmly held concepts of suprahuman being(s) and a specific system of beliefs and practices connected to that divinity or divinities. (2) Nation infers political, economic, military, and social power held by people, who may occupy a defined geographic area. (3) Race stands for genetic or biological traits that are inherent and unalterable within a group. (4) Ethnicity points to any number of factors that separate populations into different groups.

None of these four categories on its own accurately describes Judaism or encompasses all Jews. Jews around the world exhibit diverse "genetic" traits, including skin color. Jews have lived in the past and still live within the boundaries of many nations, but they hold military, political, social, and economic power *only* in the modern State of Israel. Religion comprises a set of beliefs about a suprahuman entity, but Jews do not normally express themselves in terms of what they believe; rather, they generally prefer to define Jewishness in terms of "what they do." And ethnicity refers to a group distinguished by its language and certain cultural preferences, while Jews speak diverse languages and represent diverse cultures from around the world. Thus, none of these common labels adequately encompasses people who today call themselves Jews or whom others designate as Jews.

FIGURE 1.2 *Jews can pray anywhere.* Source: *tovfla/Getty Images.*

It is more useful to understand Jews as a group that, like other groups, has drawn borders, however porous, around itself to differentiate its members from other people to help them define who they are. Scholars have long understood that a primary method by which individuals and groups identity what they are is by first realizing what they are not. People, that is, understand that they are not "x" before they realize that they are "y" (Porton 1988: 288–9). Jews see themselves as different from other peoples among whom they live even if the two groups have much in common. Similarly, non-Jews view Jews as different from themselves even when the differences are not overtly apparent or even real. While this approach does not spell out specific traits of Judaism, it helps us to understand what Jewish identity has always accomplished for people who call themselves Jewish.

Before the modern era, "Jew" was not the usual term by which Jews named themselves. In the Hebrew Bible and most premodern Jewish texts, Jews called themselves *benei yisrael*, the Children of Israel—Israel here refers to Abraham's grandson, Jacob. The Greek for "Jew" originally designated a person from Judea, the southern kingdom of biblical Israel. Greeks did not employ "Jew" to designate an individual connected to the deity of the Hebrew Bible until the second century BCE (S. Cohen 1999: 69–105). Our modern understanding of "Jew" stems from the Christians popularizing the term as referring to the people mentioned in the Old Testament (Hebrew Bible), whom they held God had rejected in favor of the Christians. At about the same time, a Jewish tradition stated that Jews are known as the Children of Israel/Jacob, because every child of Jacob, in contrast to those of Abraham, who also fathered Ishmael, and Isaac, who also fathered Esau, accepted *only* the God of the Hebrew Bible as God (**Sifré Devarim** 31; Porton 1984: 120–2).

Beginning in the first centuries CE, the religious component of Jewish identity came to the fore. The biblical people of Israel, whom Jews consider their foundational ancestors, were originally a familial group. The aggregate are the descendants of Abraham, specifically through the line of Jacob. The story of the Hebrew Bible, from the Jewish point of view, emphasizes the singularity of Abraham and his descendants in terms of their special relationship to a single divine being (Gen. 12–50), the same deity who, according to the Hebrew Bible, created the entire world (Gen. 1–11).

YHWH, translated "Lord" in most English Bibles or as Jehovah in many other biblical translations, is *the name* of the Israelites' deity of the Hebrew Bible. The Hebrew Bible consistently maintains that Israelites are different from other peoples in the Near East because the former must worship *only* YHWH (**Deuteronomy**). The uniqueness of the Israelites, and the Jews after them, derives from the deity to whom they are bound. Whatever other meanings the term Jew had before the first centuries CE, Children of Israel was defined as a family whose distinctive nature derived from their special relationship with YHWH.

In the ancient Near East, the Hellenistic Near East, and the Roman Near East, Jews were defined as those who *do not* worship the divine beings of most of the population but paid allegiance to YHWH, whose shrines *did not* contain images. Jews' daily lives reflected their commitment to YHWH. Jewish differentiation manifested itself in the Jews' resting on the Sabbath, not drinking wine offered as a ritual libation to other divine beings, not eating the same foods that others ate, not participating in many community events concerning local deities, paying to support a Temple in Jerusalem, and perhaps making pilgrimages to that Temple at least once a year. If one queried the Jews about their distinctive practices, they would have responded that they are following YHWH's demands as expressed in YHWH's revelation to their ancestors, contained in a document called the Torah, roughly signifying what we today call the Pentateuch or, more generally, the Hebrew Bible as a whole.

While Christians argued that the Israelite God, YHWH, was the Father of the Messiah, Jesus, and the Muslims claimed that YHWH was their God, Allah, Jews did not often agree with those claims. But even during the rare periods prior to modern times when the Jews acquiesced to the assertions that others in fact worshipped the biblical God, such as in fourteenth-century Provence (Katz 1961: 36, 63), the Jews maintained that they *alone* correctly followed God's dictates expressed in the Hebrew Bible.

To this point, designating Judaism as a religion and defining Jews as those who are members of that religious community seem correct. However, especially as we move into modern times, the matter is much more complicated. The complexity is created in part by Jewish law's understanding of how one becomes a Jew, which does not require religious belief at all. Since the first century CE, Jewish law has maintained that children born to Jewish women are Jews, without regard to the identity of their fathers and without regard for what they believe or what rituals they perform. While certain birth rituals (e.g., circumcision) have been normative, neither they nor any prescribed faith-statement has ever been required for a person born to a Jewish mother to be considered a Jew. In line with these facts, especially in contemporary times when freedom of religion—or *from* religion—is a dominant social ideology, within the Jewish community it becomes possible for someone to say "I am Jewish, but I do not believe in God," or "I am Jewish, but I don't observe the Sabbath."

"I am Jewish but … " may perhaps be one of the most common Jewish declarations in the modern world. But it is a confusing assertion to those who profess almost any religion other than Judaism. To be a Christian, for instance, is to believe in Jesus and the message of Christianity. For someone to claim that she is a Christian but does not believe in the divinity of Jesus, or for a person to say he is a Muslim but does not believe that Allah is God makes no sense. Members of these religions therefore are likely to question how a Jew can say "I am Jewish, but I don't believe in God," and yet be considered by the Jewish community and by other Jews to be a Jew.

One way that Jews have responded to this issue is by distinguishing Jews, that is, people born of Jewish mothers, from those who additionally behave Jewishly, by following the beliefs and practices of the religion Judaism. Thus, we can imagine the claim that so-and-so is a Jew but not "Jewish," insofar as she does not practice the religion, Judaism. A Jewish mother, by definition, bares a Jewish child (S. Cohen 1999: 263–306). But if Judaism is "a way of life," to be Jewish, one must be active in that way of life. Birth, we might say, ascribes an identity ("Jew") but not a status ("Jewish").

Two more factors add to the complexity of defining contemporary Jews. First, in the twentieth century, Reform (1983) and Reconstructionist Judaism (1968, reaffirmed in 1969) have accepted as Jews individuals with one Jewish parent, *either* mother *or* father. Within a people who have always agreed, if on nothing else, on who is a Jew, this stance creates the unprecedented situation. For the first time there are individuals—those with a father, but not a mother, who is Jewish—being counted as Jews by some Jews but not by others.

The second complication emerges from the fact that a person who was not born to a Jewish mother can convert to Judaism and become a full member of the Jewish community. Furthermore, the children she bares after she converts are also deemed to be Jews and, like all people born to all other Jewish mothers, require no ritual of conversion or proclamation of faith (Porton 1994). Since the medieval period, converts have been referred to as the child of Abraham and Sarah, making clear that one's biological mother does not necessarily determine one's status within the Jewish community. Additionally, today disagreement exists in the Jewish community regarding the validity of conversions carried out by non-Orthodox rabbis. As a result, conversion, like patrilineal descent, significantly complicates all discussions of who, as much as what, is a Jew.

FIGURE 1.3 *Ethiopian Jews, Falashas, became Jews at the beginning of the Middle Ages.* Source: *Photograph by Yoram Biberman, courtesy of the photographer.*

Jews view themselves as the direct descendants of Abraham-Sarah, Isaac-Rebecca, Jacob-Rachel/Leah, as a unique family created through their special relationship with YHWH. That connection to YHWH sets off the Jews from the peoples among whom they lived. In the premodern world, Jews worshipped a God whom they argued was *not* Jesus's Father, *nor* was Muhammed that divinity's prophet. In much of the premodern world in both Christian and Muslim countries, in response to Jews' pronouncements, Christian and Muslim leaders imposed special taxes on Jews even as they restricted Jews' choices of occupation, the locations in which they could live, the real estate they could own, and the public display of their religious practices. In the premodern world, determining who was a Jew was simple. In Europe, there were Christians and people, including Jews, whom the Christians wished to convert. But, while the Christians succeeded in converting most other European peoples, they converted only a comparatively few Jews. In the Middle East and North Africa there were Muslims and there were Jews and a small number of Christians, whom some in Islam wished to convert or destroy (M. Cohen 1994).

FIGURE 1.4 *Interior of Turo Synagogue, Newport, Rhode Island.* Source: *Courtesy of the Loeb Visitors Center.*

The modern world is much more complex, and it is now much more difficult to define a Jew because birth alone no longer suffices as a definition. Many Jews can of course still be defined by the fact that they believe in the God of the Hebrew Bible and practice the Jewish rituals that emerged over time from biblical law. But there are others, self-identified and recognized as Jews by other Jews simply because of their Jewish lineage and/or some other aspect of their lifestyle or self-declaration. In a world in which religion is not a dominant political force, the nonreligious Jew is commonplace.

In the modern world, most of the limitations placed on Jews by Christian and Muslim governments and local rulers have disappeared. In terms of language, culture, dress, and values, most Jews in the modern age live and look exactly like the non-Jews among whom they live. American Jews are difficult to distinguish from other Americans, just as French Jews are an integral part of the French population. British Jews are like non-Jewish Brits, and Mexican Jews are generally indistinguishable from other Mexicans. In most cases, no matter which country we examine, Jews and non-Jews speak the same languages, attend the same schools, engage in the same occupations, watch the same TV shows, listen to the same music, read the same books and magazines, and equally participate in the country's cultural institutions. Jews can be found across the political, economic, and social spectrums and have the same fears and dreams as non-Jews in the countries in which they live. If a person born a Jew wishes to stand apart from her Jewish community, she is free to do so.

Even in terms of individuals who are religiously Jewish, much has changed in the modern world. While there certainly are religious differences between Judaism and the non-Jewish religions of the countries in which Jews live, the similarities in how religion is practiced, and the purposes religion serves are remarkable. While Jews continue to use Hebrew as a language of prayer, at least parts of their worship activity also occur in the same vernaculars as their non-Jewish neighbors; Jews and non-Jews employ similar theological terms in their country's language; many Jews compose Jewish religious works in the vernacular languages, and Christians and Muslims express their ideas in these same vernaculars. Frequently, the same theological term occurs in the vernacular—salvation, revelation—and the different meaning the term bears in each religion might not even be apparent to the religion's practitioners. Jewish social and political attitudes are often shaped not by Judaism but by the ethos of the country in which they happen to be living. *In many areas of their lives*, Jews have more in common with their non-Jewish compatriots than they do with Jews who live outside of their country's borders or who lived in the past centuries.

These similarities do not mean that Jews are entirely assimilated into an undifferentiated population of Americans, Brits, Mexicans, or any other population. Despite the vast likenesses today between Jews and the people among whom they live, and even considering the increasing numbers of Jews who do not identify as Jewish at all, after the Second World War and especially since the 1960s, many Jews around the world have become more interested in expressing what is uniquely Jewish about themselves and what they have in common with other Jews, whether in their

FIGURE 1.5 *Wilshire Boulevard Temple, a.k.a. "Temple of the Stars."* Source: *Kirkikis/Getty Images.*

own area or in other countries, including in Israel, and with past generations of Jews. These connections, which distinguish Jews from the people among whom they live, might revolve particularly around the Jewish sacred calendar and other ritual practices, or they might simply express solidarity with Israel or with the Jewish people. Even in the face of continuing modern open expressions of anti-Israel and anti-Jewish sentiments, some Jews want to express their unique identity through anything from their choice of foods—which may or may not adhere to Jewish dietary restrictions—or travel, going to Israel while others native to America might travel to their "ancestral homelands" in Europe, Asia, Africa, or the Far East. Finally, some Jews may be more comfortable among Jews, who they perceive to be like themselves, than among non-Jews, leading them, for instance, to a Jewish Community Center rather than to a YMCA or YWCA that offers the same programs.

Modern attempts to assert the cultural and religious unity of Jews and Christians, especially in the United States, have not reduced many Jews' feelings of being different. Many originally religious celebrations in America and in other places throughout the world have been redefined as public cultural events in which their religious significance is downplayed. In educational and social settings, "winter festivals" replace Christmas celebrations; Christmas carols no longer make up the *entire* program, and a menorah is placed near the Christmas tree equating the two holidays and attempting to include everyone. Spring festivals that replace Easter pageants with rabbits and candy also encourage everyone's participation.

FIGURE 1.6 *Menorah in front of store on main shopping street in Playa Del Carmen, Mexico.*
Source: *anouchka/Getty Images.*

But many Jews recognize that the celebration of Jesus' birth (Christmas) and the commemoration of the Maccabees' rededication of the Temple in Jerusalem about 165 years earlier (Hanukkah) have nothing to do with each other. Many Jews feel uncomfortable participating in a setting in which any Christian religious music is performed or ideas are expressed. In the same way, Jews recognize that Easter marks the crucifixion and resurrection of Jesus and so has an underlying religious meaning that is not pertinent to them, no matter how Easter is denoted in the public sphere. The result is that Jews often choose to stay away from civic gatherings, or even to feel unwelcome in shopping malls festooned for Christmas or Easter, for reasons not comprehensible to those who imagine there to be an at best limited religious significance to these celebrations.

In addition to the desire of many Jews not to participate even in Christian holidays that today do little more than manifest American civil identity, Jews are kept separate from their non-Jewish neighbors by the annual Jewish holidays that have no corollary to Christian celebrations. These are central Jewish holidays—the Jewish New Year (Rosh Hashanah) and Day of Atonement (Yom Kippur), for instance—that fall on days of the week and during times of the year at which non-Jews mark no holidays at all. The result is that Jews appear to be, and might themselves feel as though they are, living a life that is quite separate and different from that of non-Jewish Americans. This is particularly an issue as non-Jews often have no comprehension of the nature of these Jewish holidays or of why their Jewish neighbors sometime require special consideration, whether at their place of work or in public schools.

For these reasons, in the modern world, Jews both belong to their home country's culture and, at the same time, often stand out as disconnected from public aspects of that culture. The Jews' belonging and not belonging arise from the fact that, for most of their history, they have comprised a minority in the countries in which they have resided. Even if from time to time they were the largest segment of the population in small towns or villages, since the first centuries CE, they normally have not wielded political, economic, military, or social power in the countries in which they were located. The exceptions were few and far between. At times, for their own financial or political reasons, Christians and Muslims would grant Jews limited power and self-determination. But these "rights" could be and were revoked at the whim of those who controlled the country. Except for the modern State of Israel, Jews are still a small fraction of the population of the other countries throughout the world.

The estimated number of Jews in the United States in 2015 was between 5,250,000 and 6,500,000, and the number of Jews throughout the world in that same year was estimated to be 14,500,000 and 15,000,000. Jews make up about 0.2 percent of the world's population, and they comprise 1.7 percent of the US population. If we subtract the approximately 5,500,000 Jews in the United States and the approximately 6,500,000 in Israel, we discover that only 2,500,000 to 3,000,000 are spread throughout the rest of the Americas, Europe, Africa, Asia, outside of Israel in the Middle East, Australia, and New Zealand.

In America, 57 percent of the Jews reside in New York City, Los Angeles, Chicago, Boston, San Francisco, Washington, DC, Philadelphia, Atlanta, and Miami. This distribution means that if one does not live in the northeast, southeast, or southwest in America, the likelihood that one will encounter a significant presence of Jews or Jewish practices is minimal. Throughout the rest of the world, most Jews reside in a country's largest cities. Jews are primarily an urban population and, except in the modern State of Israel, are not evenly or widely dispersed throughout a country. Many contemporary individuals learn about Jews and Judaism *only* from books, magazines, or from a large variety of public and social media. Many people throughout the world either do not meet living Jews or they do not know that they have met them.

Given the sources of their information about Jews, most Christians—even if conscious of the diversity of people who call themselves Christians—are somewhat baffled by the variety of Jews, the diversity of Jewish observance of the same holiday, the multiple ways Jews perform the same lifecycle events, and the Jews' wide-ranging explanations of Jewish theological concepts. Even though virtually all Jews before the modern era accepted the same corpus of sacred literature, the same ritual calendar, a common outline of religious rituals and prayers, and the same theological vocabulary, in their daily activities, Jews then as today expressed this underlying unity in diverse ways. The multiplicity of Jewish practices and variety of ways Jews explain the core ideas of Judaism have been a constant feature of the Jewish people.

FIGURE 1.7 *Jews and Christians buried together in a military cemetery in the United States.*
Source: *Joel Carillet/Getty Images.*

The diversity in practices and understandings was promoted by the Jews' lack of a centralized authority, comparable to the pope in Catholic Christianity, and by the lack of a significant international bureaucracy, along with the geographical and cultural diversity of Jewish communities. Jewish diversity goes back at least as far as the first century, when, within the Land of Israel, there were multiple modes of Jewish identification: Pharisees, Sadducees, Essenes, Christians, Zealots, Jews who practiced baptism, even Jews who paid homage to Roman deities; and these are merely the Jews about whom we have information. Jews regularly disagreed over the meaning of the Hebrew Bible and how to perform Jewish rituals and recite Jewish prayers. We discover that some Jews followed a lunar calendar, while others counted time in terms of a solar year.

When we move to Jewish communities in Asia Minor, Egypt, Rome, Greece, and North Africa, we find even more variety. After the Roman destruction of the Jerusalem Temple in 70 CE, there were two major centers of Jewish power and creativity: Ancient Palestine and Babylonia, that is, present-day Iraq. Although these two Jewish communities had much in common, they also were quite different in many ways. As we move into the period after the fall of Rome and the rise of Islam, we find Sephardic Jews—under Islam—Ashkenazic Jews and Provence Jews—both under Christianity—each group easily subdivided into geographical variations, not to mention important centers of Judaism in North Africa. No single rabbi held authority over any other rabbi, and no one controlled the Jewish world. In addition, there was no mechanism for a rabbi to enforce his opinion on anyone other than those near him who accepted his authority. Today this diversity is symbolized by the State of Israel's *two* chief rabbis: one for the Sephardic community and one for the Ashkenazic community.

The differences among diverse communities of Jews are also accounted for by the fact that, although Jews and Jewish communities have frequently been located at the metaphorical, as well as the physical, edges of most countries, the borders between Jews and non-Jews have always been porous. Part of the variety we witness in Judaism derives from the locations in which the multiple Jewish communities have resided. Jews have been in India since perhaps the sixth century, and Indian Jews, reflecting their Hindu environment, perform rituals differently from other Jews around the world. The rituals of Jews in Muslim countries or from North Africa reflect the local practices in those areas. In addition, each group of Jews can decide how to do many things: what foods are acceptable on Passover; the melody to which the Torah is chanted; styles of synagogue décor and architecture; type of head covering used by men and women; languages that are spoken (Ladino vs. Yiddish)—all of these matters reflect local tastes and customs (Dobrinsky 1986).

We need to be clear, however, that *this diversity overlays an extensive common foundation.* Jews from as far back as the second century BCE have accepted the same twenty-four books of the Hebrew Bible as their foundational text. The words of the Hebrew Bible, especially the Torah—**Genesis, Exodus**, Leviticus, Numbers, Deuteronomy—were understood to contain everything Jews needed to know about God, humanity, the natural and animal worlds, human activity, and the final redemption of the world. God had revealed God's words through a select number of individuals— Moses, Aaron, **Joshua**, the Prophets, David, Solomon, Job, Daniel, Ruth, and Esther, to name the most important. All Jews had to do was to figure out what the words that composed the Revelation meant and how they should be applied. Judaism's foundational texts and ideas led to much that was shared. The potential for variety in interpretation allowed for diversity.

Until the modern world, beginning in the seventeenth century, virtually all Jews accepted what they saw as the basic tenants of the Bible: (1) God exists. (2) God created the entire world according to a careful plan. (3) God established a covenant with Abraham and his descendants, through the line of Jacob. (4) God revealed how the parts of the world should relate to one another and revealed that to the Jews, who then affirmed their acceptance of the covenant. (5) Eventually, God will bring the world to its successful completion. These are the central Jewish principles of Creation, Revelation, Covenant, and Redemption.

It bears noting that Jews were not the only ones who believed that the Pentateuch— the Jew's Torah—was the true and revealed word of God. Before Barukh Spinoza (1632–77), Christians, Muslims, and Jews agreed that the Torah was revealed, and Christians along with Jews accepted the Hebrew Bible as an accurate account of God's interaction with biblical Israel. At the same time, Jews, Catholics, Greek Orthodox, the varieties of Protestant Christianity, and the varieties of Muslims each maintained that they *alone* had the correct understanding of what those words in the Hebrew Bible

FIGURE 1.8 *Beth Shalom Synagogue in Elkins Park, Pennsylvania.*
Source: *Universal Images Group/Getty Images.*

mean. In general terms, before the seventeenth century one could argue that Jews, Muslims, and Christians agreed about the text of the Hebrew Bible, but each claimed to possess the *only* accurate tradition of interpretation that uncovered what the words meant. Our interest here is how the Jews understood God's message to them.

Jews understand what the Torah means through the eyes of the rabbis of late antiquity, first to eighth centuries CE, as summarized and understood by the European and Middle Eastern-North African sages who flourished in the tenth through the seventeenth centuries. They maintain that the Hebrew Bible lays out the blueprint upon which Judaism is to be built. The late antique rabbis built the structure upon their understanding of the blueprint—they constructed the rooms, the hallways, and set in place the doors and the windows. The sages of the tenth through the seventeenth centuries decorated the rooms according to the standards of the locations and times in which they lived. The plan was biblical; the overall structure was rabbinic; the details were contemporary to an age and place. Today, modern sages, rabbis, philosophers, and academics continue to modify the initial plan by, to use our metaphor, redecorating the rooms and, as they feel is necessary and appropriate, even rethinking the blueprint itself, modifying the number and shape of the rooms as is required by their modern sensibilities.

How did the rabbis and sages prior to the modern era understand the Bible, especially the Torah and its conception of the relationship of God to the world? The opening of

Genesis, the first book in the Hebrew Bible, assumes that God exists, that God created order out of chaos, that in six days God created everything and everyone that inhabit the world, that humans are created in the "image and likeness" of God (Gen. 1:26) to rule the world, and that creation is "very good" (Gen. 1:31).

The rabbis, in a fifth-century document, recorded that when God got ready to create the world, God consulted the Torah, exactly as an architect employs a blueprint (**Genesis Rabbah** 1:2). The rabbis thus understood that God, using an already thought-out plan, created an ordered and structured world, in which events did not happen randomly or even according to the momentary whims of God or any other divine being. Perhaps more importantly, seeing the Torah as the plan for that world, Jews understood that, by studying God's words in the Torah, they could conform their behaviors to exactly what was expected by God and reflected in the cosmic order. To live as a Jew was to make the personal choices to live the ordered and structured life that conforms to the mandates of the Torah. This path was how God from the beginning intended humans to interact with one another and with the other parts of creation.

God *did not* create human beings as an afterthought or only to cater to the needs and whims of the divine being. God created human beings "in the image and likeness" of God to rule the world in accordance with God's plan for the world. However, reading the stories of the creation of human beings in Genesis 1 and in Genesis 2 as two views of the same event, the rabbis never tired of exploring the complex nature of human beings. Humans were in the "image and likeness" of God; but they were not God. The merging of the divine with the human as in the Greek and Roman thought common in their environment was not an option for the rabbis. God was God—Unique and Perfect. Humans were humans—like God they had free will, like God they could create, like God they could reason. But unlike God, humans died, needed food, defecated, and could act unjustly and unfairly. God was a Singularity—a Perfect Immortal Just Truthful Righteous Being. Humans shared traits with God but also with the lower animals (Genesis Rabbah 1:26–28; Porton 1985: 161–8). The duality within human nature meant that humans had the potential to act justly, mercifully, honestly, and compassionately toward one another, the natural world, and the animal world. But they also had the ability to be greedy, selfish, unjust, and uncaring toward other humans, other animals, and the natural environments in which they lived. The practice of Judaism was meant to teach Jews to follow the divine, not the animal, aspects of their being.

God is Just and Truthful and the world was "very good"; but injustice, inequality, floods, earthquakes, famine, wars, and devastating illness happen throughout the world. Judaism understands human beings to have free will, which explains why they do not always interact with the other parts of the created world according to how being in the image of God suggests they should. Thus, human free will can account for much of the human misery in the world. But natural disasters, illness, the unjustified suffering of the good and the prosperity of the evil are much more difficult to understand. The rabbis explain these apparent failures of God's justice as follows.

The dual aspects of human beings—animal and divine—mean that no human is totally evil or completely good. A third-century text states: "It is as difficult for an evil person to be totally evil as it is for a good person to be totally good" (Sifré Deuteronomy 33; Porton 1985: 127), which leads the rabbis and sages to offer three explanations for why good things happen to bad people or the opposite. Because bad people also engage in good behavior, the good that they experience is their reward for their good deeds. Similarly, because good people also act incorrectly, the bad things that happen to them respond to those bad things they have done. A second explanation is that God employs illness or other "evils" to encourage people to change the course of their lives. "As a father chastises his son [to change his behavior], so God chastises human beings" says a third-century document (Sifré Deuteronomy 32; Porton 1985: 124). Bad experiences or illness may cause people to reflect on their lives and improve themselves. A third major explanation for the apparent injustice in the world is that everything will be made right only after death. The suffering the good experience in this world leads to an increased reward in the coming one, and any ease the evil experienced in this world will be balanced by correspondingly great suffering after death (Sifré Deuteronomy 32; Porton 1985: 124–6). Because Judaism argues that everyone—good or bad, Jew or non-Jew—will share equally in the Redemption at the end of time, the issue is not who will be redeemed but how the soul/or person will experience the period after death but before Redemption.

The rabbis offer another solution to the problem of evil that many of us today find unsatisfactory, as did some of the rabbis and sages themselves. Because we are not equal to God, there are things we simply cannot understand. Earthquakes, draught, famine, illness are beyond human understanding. The first eleven chapters of Genesis thus only partially explain the human condition, specifically addressing why humans do not live in the world that God first set out for them—why humans are not vegetarians, why humans don't live as long as they once did, why humans must work to survive, why women suffer in giving birth, and why humans cannot easily communicate with one another. But nothing in the Hebrew Bible adequately explains how humans can make sense of the complex world in which they live. To respond to this problem, Judaism simply says that, because humans are not God, they cannot always discern the reason behind events or actions (**biblical Book of Job**).

Why, within the framework of God's carefully planned world, did God select only one group—the Jewish people—for God's covenant? In Jewish understanding, this choice is explained by the reality that God discovered upon God's completing creation, as described in the first eleven chapters of Genesis. These chapters state that following creation, humankind consistently violated God's original plan and rules. Because of human free will, God could not force the entire world to follow God's will. God's choice of Abraham allowed God to work with one person and, through that person, to create a model of God's plan and convey it to everyone else. God responds to the reality of human freedom by choosing Abraham to make a great nation, to be blessed and a blessing to those who bless him and curse to those who curse him (Gen. 12:2–3). In Genesis 15, God promises Abraham that his descendants, the nation that follows God's will, will be as numerous as the stars (15:5) and that Abraham's descendants shall inherit "this land" (15:7).

The relationship between God and Abraham and his descendants follows the form of a covenant, a form that occurs throughout the ancient Middle East. The covenant is an agreement between a powerful ruler and his vassals. The agreement normally states that the ruler will protect the less powerful vassals if they fulfill their obligations to that ruler. While the strength of the respective parties to the covenant is radically uneven—King/vassal; God/humans—the covenant equally binds both parties to its terms. If the minor figure does what he is supposed to do, the major figure *must* fulfill his promises contained in the covenant. In our world, an apartment lease is similar; even though the property owner owns the apartment and can do with it almost anything she pleases, by signing the lease the owner cedes some power to renters, who, so long as they abide by the terms of the lease, can expect certain protections from the owner, ranging from the guarantee that all systems will be maintained in safe and working order to the promise that the owner will not even enter the property without prior permission. Similarly, while God, as creator of the world, has the power to do anything within the human realm and to humans, through the terms of the covenant, God has agreed to offer the people of Israel certain protections and to act as is appropriate to their behavior under the covenant's terms.

The Hebrew Bible used a well-known form of political agreement as the model for describing the relationship between YHWH and Abraham and, later, the entire People of Israel. In the covenant with Abraham, the terms on either side were rather straightforward. God instructed Abraham—leave your homeland—which Abraham obeyed. In response, God promised Abraham that his descendants would be as numerous as the stars, that others would receive God's blessing if they recognized Abraham as "a blessing," and that Abraham's descendants would inherit a particular parcel of land (Gen. 12, 15, 17). Much about God's side of the covenant is left ambiguous—who are Abraham's descendants, what are the land's borders, what is the meaning of blessing, when are God's obligations going to be fulfilled? Even so, the covenant makes clear that God, who is honest and just, is subject to obligations that God *must* fulfill. The terms of this covenant, along with additional rules that the Jews were to follow, were reaffirmed at Mount Sinai, following the Exodus from Egypt, under Joshua, in conjunction with the conquest of the land (Josh. 8:30–35), and again under **Nehemiah** (Neh. 7–10), when the Jews returned into the land from exile in Babylonia.

In reading the revealed text of the Torah, the rabbis find that God created the world according to a plan revealed in the Torah, and that this plan envisioned a logical and just world. In this view, Jews diverged from other ancient thinkers and writers. While some religions of late antiquity argued that all divine plans were hidden and knowledge of them either impossible or available to only a select few, the rabbis and sages after them maintained that, at Mount Sinai, God revealed the entirety of the Torah to all of the People of Israel (Exod. 20; Deut. 5).

While Judaism understands that Moses spoke all the words of God's revelation to all Israel, how people were to discern their correct meaning is another matter. Deuteronomy 1:5 states that Moses *explained* the Torah. Who was to explain it, and on what basis, after Moses's death?

Understanding the Torah/Revelation is important in Judaism after Moses, who spoke to God "face to face" (Exod. 33:31; Deut. 34:10), has died because Exodus 24:3 and 7 state that when the people heard Moses' recounting the Revelation, they all stated, "we will do and we will listen." Thus, all Israel/Jews freely accepted the covenant. The rabbis will claim that the souls of all Jews ever to be born along with the souls of all those who would convert to Judaism were included among those who accepted the covenant in Exodus 24 (**Midrash Tanhuma** Nitzavim 3), Moses seems to affirm this interpretation in Deuteronomy 29:13: "I make this covenant with its sanctions, not with you alone, but both with those who are standing here with us this day before YHWH our God and with those who are not with us here this day."

Abraham had fulfilled his obligations, so what God promised to do for Abraham could not be altered. However, the covenant at Sinai—which was continually renewed— laid out a specific set of conditions for the Jewish people. If the Jews followed the Revelation, God would allow them to live in the Land and prosper. If they chose *not to follow* the plan, God would exile them from the land and would chastise them. God would keep his promise to Abraham, eventually, but in the meantime, the fate and destiny of the Jews depended upon their living their lives according to Torah. After the Israelites enter the Land under Joshua, the rest of the story in the Hebrew Bible follows this scheme: when the Israelites observe Torah, YHWH protects them; when they violate Torah, YHWH chastises them.

Jews, like their Israelite ancestors, faced the same challenge of living their lives according to Revelation in fulfillment of their obligations under the covenant. But Jews lived throughout the known world, not within the Land's borders. God no longer spoke through prophets. Non-Jewish monarchs governed the Jews, so that in no location could Jews control their own lives. And the Temple to which Jews were obligated to bring gifts to God no longer stood. If they needed to know something about the Torah, God had appointed the priests at the Temple in Jerusalem to answer their questions; but after 70 CE the Temple did not exist. The words in the Torah were true and revealed by God. But with no Moses, Aaron, prophets or Temple priests, how would the Jews discover what the Torah meant? Who would explain the Torah's repetitions and contradictions, fill in its needed details, or explain its ambiguities?

To solve this dilemma, rabbis, a new Jewish leadership group that emerged after the destruction of the Jerusalem Temple in 70 CE, posited that, at Sinai (Exod. 24:18, 34:28), God had conveyed to Moses more than the words of the written Hebrew scriptures. The rabbis understood that in addition to the Written Torah—Genesis, Exodus, Leviticus, Numbers, Deuteronomy—which God dictated to Moses and Moses faithfully wrote down, God also transmitted an Oral Torah that contains the explanations, details and legitimate methods of interpretation that would allow the Torah's words to be implemented until God brought about the Redemption. Moses, in rabbinic understanding, passed the Oral Torah to Joshua, and eventually it was passed down to the rabbis of late antiquity, who in turn passed it down to future generations who are still passing it down to rabbis today. Thus, the words of the Torah are public and available to everyone. However, the meanings of the words and the methods for implementing them throughout time reside with the rabbis or with those who have studied with the rabbis. While God had chosen the prophets and the priests, people became rabbis by studying with rabbis, who had studied with rabbis all the way back to Moses' interacting with God "face to face." Thus, while the words of the written Torah do not change, a rabbi legitimately interprets the words and determines how they apply in the situation he or, in modern times, she confronts. In doing this, the rabbi him- or herself continues in the process of revealing the meaning of God's word to the people of Israel, as it was revealed to Moses at Mount Sinai. While the written Torah is available to everyone and is read publicly every week, only the rabbis know the Oral Torah. Thus, the rabbis are the only ones who know the totality of revelation Moses received on Mount Sinai, and they alone can make sense of it. In this way, the Torah's words are always adaptable and relevant. With the aid of legitimate expounders of the Oral Torah, Jews in any location and at any time can figure out how to fulfill their obligations to live according to the Torah.

Living one's life according to the Torah to fulfill one's covenantal obligation creates the visible and, to some, overly detailed aspects of Judaism. The rabbis understood the Torah to set out rules for virtually everything a human does every day and throughout life. The rules covered how individuals should always interact with one another. The covenant mandates rules for business; rules for paying off damages; rules for testifying before court; rules for whom one can wed; rules when and how one can divorce; rules for showing respect to the living, the dying, and the dead; rules for what one can eat; the conditions under which one can engage in sexuality; and the obligations one has toward one's spouse, children, and parents. In brief, the covenant contains rules for the "proper" way to do virtually everything a person does.

In this context, the rabbis also developed a system of prayers through which a person would recognize God's continual presence in every aspect of life. One recites a prayer after finishing a meal as well as before one eats. Each type of foodstuffs requires its own distinctive blessing. One blesses upon seeing a handsome man or beautiful woman. One even recites a blessing after going to the toilet. Tradition states that one should say at least one hundred blessings a day. The result is to live a life every aspect of which is shaped by God's plan for the world, both in one's actions and in the words that express one's perception of the presence of God in everything.

Why all these rules and what is the point of all these blessings? Judaism through these practices takes the normal everyday things that people do and that they can control—those actions that happen in their own homes, their own families, their own markets, their own places of worship, their own daily lives—and turns them into an opportunity to underscore God's existence and God's connection to the world. For Judaism, fulfilling the covenant does not take place *only* within a synagogue, or only on a special day; or only while praying, or only while performing a religious ritual; fulfilling the covenant, recognizing God's existence and singularity, happens everywhere, every time a Jew does something during the day or at night.

While some religious systems emphasize what one should believe, Judaism in this way emphasizes how one should act. Most Jews before modern times believed that

God was real and the covenantal relationship binding. Most Jews accepted that the rabbis, or at least *their own rabbi*, accurately expounded how the words of the Torah should be implemented in their daily lives. Why Jews emphasized actions over beliefs stems from many factors. One was that they had to live their daily lives according to the details of the Revelation; so, action always mattered. Furthermore, some Jewish practices and rituals require a community—Jews need properly slaughtered meat, properly prepared Passover foods, the presence of a fixed minimum number of Jews to recite certain prayers, Jews to prepare a body for burial—and the like. Within a minority that needed one another for comfort, protection, and security, one *could assume* that the Jews in one's community held similar beliefs, but *one needed to be certain* that the butcher followed the appropriate rules, that the baker prepared the unleavened bread properly, that the corpse was prepared and buried properly. Again, action mattered more than belief.

In this context, certain matters of belief, unlike questions of proper behavior and practice, were left undeveloped and abstract. The last part of God's plan, the Redemption of the world, was never worked out in Judaism in a consistent, coherent, or comprehensive manner. Jews were sure Redemption would occur, on the model of God's having redeemed the Jews from Egypt as God had promised Abraham in Genesis 15. Certain that it would happen, Jews did not worry about *when* Redemption would occur, and community leaders indeed frowned on Jewish speculation concerning this matter. Jews believed that a messiah would eventually come, but they were not sure when or how they would know.

FIGURE 1.9 *Judaism, Christianity, and Islam together in public.* Source: *RnDmS/Getty Images.*

While Jews did not claim to know how or when Redemption could occur, they were certain that the Redeemed World would be radically different from this one. But even the descriptions of that "difference" are many, contradictory, and even obscure. Judaism *is certain* that Redemption is not a personal or spiritual event. Redemption comes to all human beings as a public acknowledgment that God is the One and Only God. Everyone enjoys the final Redemption—Jews and non-Jews—and all human beings will act according to their divine nature and their animal traits will disappear.

Before the seventeenth century virtually all Jews believed in God's existence, the truthfulness of God's Revelation in the Torah, the Jewish obligation to adhere to the covenant by living the details of their daily lives according their rabbi's understanding of the meaning of Torah, and the promise of the Final Redemption of the world. The rabbis and sages had developed ways to explain the Torah's repetitions, omissions, contractions to move beyond them *without* contesting the revealed nature of the Torah or the centrality of YHWH's commandments and the covenant. There were Jewish philosophers, but we do not know any of their names before the tenth century—Saadia ben Yosef Gaon (d.942) is the first name we know. There were Jewish mystics from late antiquity, but they reached a zenith in thirteenth-century Spain with the Zohar and in sixteenth-century Safed, Israel in the person of Isaac Luria. They prosper in the modern era in some forms of Hasidism. While the philosophers and mystics offered alternatives to the ways the rabbis and sages read and interpreted the Torah, the former agreed with the latter that God existed, created the world, revealed God's will, entered into a covenant with Abraham's descendants through Jacob, and would eventually redeem the whole world.

The world after the seventeenth century became completely different, and Jews experienced those differences in many ways. It became a commonplace to accept that the Hebrew Bible was composed of a variety of sources—even if Jewish scholarship remained reluctant to accept this *about the Torah* until the twentieth century—which meant that it was not simply Moses' account of the revealed word of God. Major thinkers became convinced that human reason unaided by Revelation could explain the world, analyze its problems, and eventually solve them, so that the Bible was no longer as important as a source of truth as it had been. The world was chaotic and unjust not because of Adam and Eve, but because human beings were not acting rationally. This new perspective held that, at their core, Judaism, Christianity, and Islam were the same—they all believe in God, that God was Good, and that humans have an immortal soul.

In this setting, the Bible became less important for other reasons as well. According to this new thinking, what made Jews different from other people had nothing to do with the facts of Judaism—"the covenant"—or being a Jew "descended from Abraham"—but was, rather, the result of the Jews' exclusion from normal life, caused both by rabbinic teachings and by Christianity's pushing them to the edges of society. In this thinking, if Jews gave up their exclusive ways and Christians allowed them to participate in civil society, Jews could develop into appropriate citizens of the nations in which they live and of the new world order, and perhaps accept the truths of Christianity. Education and integration were the keys to make Jews part of the civil order. The Bible, in this view, would continue to serve as a source of moral values and ethical truths that we all share. But it no longer would determine every aspect of how Jews lived their lives.

From these and other factors, the unity that had demarcated the Jews even within much Jewish diversity was shattered. The new world allowed individuals and groups to rethink their distinctive relationship to their religious heritage. Within the Jewish community, new types of Judaism arose. Reform Judaism—arguing that a belief in God, God's goodness, and an immortal soul are the core of all religions and that religious belief, rather than practice, is all that really matters—viewed the commandments as "folk-rituals," not pertinent to modern life, which therefore could be abandoned. In response to Reform's declarations, Positive Historical Judaism—Conservative Judaism in America—argued that by studying the history of Judaism and establishing which practices and beliefs were primary or secondary, which had been corrupted and which had not, one could rationally discover the commandments that were *essential* for the continued existence of Judaism and which other ones, because of their time-limited importance, the Jewish community could "safely" disregard. Even Orthodox Judaism, championing the premodern value of observance of the entirety of the law, promoted a rationalistic, modern religious sensibility. In its new mode of traditional observance, one could employ reason, education, and science to understand what God had commanded and to participate in the modern world even as one maintained inherited practices and traditions. This meant that even a Jew committed to the commandments and to God could fully integrate into civil society, along with Christians and, today, Muslims.

Hasidism, which arose in Poland in the seventeenth century also gained in popularity, as a counter force that attempted to fight the processes of modernization that became so central in Jewish communities. It stressed the closeness of its leader (zaddik) to God and the joy and emotion of Judaism. It argued that living the commandments with joy and emotion was the main thing that God demanded of the Jew. Joy and emotion were more important than reason. Finally, in the 1920s America became the backdrop for Reconstructionism, which claims that when Jews referred to God, they meant the power within humans to create and do good. Jewish commandments are those things that the Jewish community over time has created from its collective consciousness to keep itself alive and flourishing.

In modern times, Jews have continued to think about themselves and their religion in ways familiar from past centuries. Today, Jews have also created a range of questions—theological, social, national, cultural—that are unique to the Jewish experiences today and have pushed many Jews to reevaluate what it means to be part of their 3,000-year-old, or even older, tradition.

A major factor in Jews' contemporary contemplation is the Holocaust or, as some Jews refer to it, the Shoah. Jews, religious and secular, face the trauma of the Nazis' murdering six million Jews, including one million Jewish children, an estimated 60 percent of the European Jewish population before 1939. The Shoah poses questions not only about the validity of the covenant, but also about modernity. A modern European nation—Germany, abetted by other European nations—focused its political, economic, social, and scientific forces on eradicating the Jews from the earth. How could God have allowed this to occur? What could Jews have done to deserve what the Nazis did to them? How could people who called themselves Christians and enlightened—both Europeans and Americans—have not stopped the mass murder of the Jews? How are Jews now to understand God, Torah, covenant? Some Jews have concluded that the God of the covenant is dead, while some see the founding of the State of Israel as God's, as much as people's response to the Nazis' atrocities. The very existence of two terms to denote this event—Holocaust, meaning a "sacrifice," which by definition has meaning and purpose, vs. "Shoah," a Hebrew word meaning a "calamity," which is purposeless—suggests the depth of the problem posed by the events of the Second World War. Whatever answer a Jew gives to the horrors of the Shoah, it stands as a vivid example of the failures of modernity and challenges the assumptions of the rabbis and sages—both before and after the seventeenth century.

Another unexpected event the meaning of which is difficult to discern for modern Jews was the creation in 1948 of the State of Israel. Jews had long understood that when they observed the covenant and God was pleased with them, God would allow them to reenter the Land. Now, as the result of what at least on the surface appeared to have been human initiative—the consequence of modern theories of nationalism and the desire for Jewish self-determination—Jews in the land of Israel began to exercise political, social, economic, and military power over themselves and over non-Jews. Israeli Jews, as well as non-Israeli Jews, again face questions of meaning. Does the State fulfill God's promise to Abraham? Should the State of Israel act as all other nations, or does it have an obligation to live by the Torah's mandates? How should non-Israeli Jews relate to the modern State? The State of Israel also confronts the rabbis' and the sages' assumptions as well as the promises of modernity. Some sectors of Orthodox Jews refuse to accept the State of Israel as an appropriate Jewish national enterprise; other sectors refer to it as "the beginning of the dawn of our redemption."

Jews today exist in a complex and confusing world. There is no universally accepted definition of a Jew within the Jewish community, because the Reform and Reconstructionist communities require that a Jew needs only one Jewish parent—father *or* mother. Some Jews stand out in the countries in which they live, while others live undifferentiated lives within their society. Jewish practice ranges from that of the far-right Haredi—those who "Tremble" before God—who completely reject modernity, to secular Jews who, while living a totally modern life, identify being Jewish with an ill-defined "feeling" or largely amorphous tradition. Between the two extremes lie most Jews, some of whom observe a few of the commandments, while others follow a great many of them. Yet even in what is shared among Jews who observe commandments, there is much diversity. Jews who observe most of the commandments may do so because they believe in the covenant or because they believe that being part of the Jewish community is the most important Jewish value, regardless of belief—or absence of belief—in God who actually issued commandments or cares what people eat or how they otherwise live their lives. Those who incorporate fewer of the commandments into their daily lives may do so because that is how they grew up, because they see these practices as fortifying their Jewish identity, or as spiritual practices that, without regard for their place in traditional Judaism, add meaning to their lives as modern people.

To repeat the paragraph at the outset of this chapter, determining who is a Jew today and what is Judaism is a complex endeavor.

Further Reading and Online Resources

Neusner, J. (1970), *The Way of Torah*, Belmont, CA: Dickerson Publishing Co.
Neusner, J. (1974), *The Life of Torah*, Belmont, CA: Dickerson Publishing Co.
Satlow, M. (2006), *Creating Judaism*, New York: Columbia University Press.
Seltzer, R.M. (1980), *Jewish People Jewish Thought*, New York: Macmillan.

References

Cohen, M.R. (1994), *Under the Crescent and Cross: The Jews in the Middle Ages*, Princeton, NJ: Princeton University Press.
Cohen, S.J.D. (1999), *The Beginnings of Jewishness: Boundaries, Varieties, Uncertainties*, Berkeley: University of California Press.
Dobrinsky, H.C. (1986), *A Treasury of Sephardic Laws and Customs*, Hoboken, NJ: KTAV Publishing Company.
Katz, J. (1961), *Exclusiveness and Tolerance: Jewish-Gentile Relations in Medieval and Modern Times*, New York: Schocken Books.
Porton, G.G. (1986), *Understanding Rabbinic Midrash: Text and Commentary*, Hoboken, NJ: KTAV Publishing Company.
Porton, G.G. (1988), *Goyim: Gentiles and Christians in Mishnah-Tosefta*, Atlanta, GA: Scholars Press.
Porton, G.G. (1994), *The Stranger within Your Gates: Converts and Conversion in Rabbinic Literature*, Chicago: University of Chicago Press.

Glossary Terms

Biblical Book of Job Job's life is turned upside down for reasons that seem unfair to him. At the end of the book, God tells Job that humans cannot fathom God's will or intentions.

Deuteronomy Fifth book of the Torah/ Hebrew Bible. Moses recounts Israelite history just before they enter into the Land of Canaan.

Exodus Second Book of the Torah/Hebrew Bible. It tells the story of the Israelites leaving Egypt, the revelation on Mount Sinai, and the Building of the Tent of Meeting.

Genesis The first book of the Torah/ Hebrew Bible. It records God's creating the word and the word's becoming as we know it. It also recounts the story of YHWH's working with Abraham and his descendants through Jacob.

Genesis Rabbah A collection of comments organized around the biblical book of Genesis. Some of the comments derive from the details of the Hebrew text of Genesis—exegesis. Other comments are attached to elements of the Hebrew text—eisegesis. It was probably first collected in the fifth century CE.

Joshua He became leader of the Israelites after Moses' death, and he led the Israelites into the Land of Canaan. The first book of the Hebrew Bible after the Torah carries his name, and it covers the settlement of Israelites in the Land they believed God had promised to them.

Midrash Tanhuma A collection of comments on the entire Torah, organized according to the weekly cycle, perhaps the cycle of reading the Torah in three years instead of the one year cycle most Jews follow today. It was collected over a long period of time, stretching from late antiquity to the Middle Ages.

Nehemiah A Persian Jew whom the king of Persia sent to Jerusalem in the mid-fifth century BCE to stabilize the situation in Jerusalem. In the Hebrew Bible a book carries his name, which records his deeds and Ezra's reading the "scroll of the Torah of Moses."

Sifré Devarim A collection of comments organized around the biblical book of Deuteronomy. Some of the comments derive from the Hebrew text of Deuteronomy—exegesis. Other comments are attached to elements of the Hebrew text—eisegesis. It was probably first collected at the end of the third century CE.

2

How Judaism Constructs Its History

Alan J. Avery-Peck

From the time of the Hebrew Bible until today, Jews have explained the structure of Jewish history in various ways. Jews have explicated in diverse manners the meaning of the events of history as indicators of God's engagement with the world and plan for the Jewish people. The Jews who wrote and, by the second century CE, formalized the Hebrew Bible saw history as the framework within which God's will for the Jewish people and plan for the world would be experienced. The Bible's writers and compilers thus framed the story of Israel as a historical narrative, beginning with creation and God's earliest interactions with all humanity. They detailed the election of Abraham and his descendants as the recipients of a special covenant with God, an agreement that entailed God's promises that would be fulfilled in Israel's historical experience, in the conquest of a land and establishment of a monarchy. Scripture thus narrates the historical experiences that would lead to the fulfillment of God's promise: Egyptian slavery and the Exodus, Israelite monarchical existence, exile in Babylonia, and, finally, return to the Promised Land. The Hebrew Bible presents a chronological narrative that, beginning with the life of Abraham, spans 1,500 years of the history of the Jewish people, viewed from beginning to end as a reflection of God's will for the chosen nation.

The Hebrew Bible sets the story of the people of Israel—the Jewish people—within a historical matrix. This suggests the extent to which history was consequential to the Israelites' understanding of the world and their relationship with God. While, for the Bible's authors and editors, law and ethics were clearly important—taking up substantial portions of the Pentateuch—this law was placed in the context of the broad historical narrative that extends from Genesis and through the book of Kings, recapitulated in 1 and 2 Chronicles, and in Ezra and Nehemiah developed to include the return from exile in Babylonia. There is no doubt of the centrality for early Jews of history as the context in which God's presence and actions are experienced.

But the Bible's view that history is the primary context for witnessing, and interpreting, God's actions and will is not Judaism's only or final position on the matter. In the first centuries CE, following the destruction of the Jerusalem Temple in a Jewish uprising against Roman rule, attitudes began to change. Facing a historical reality that did not reflect God's presence or expected actions in history, the **rabbis** who produced the Mishnah, Talmud, and Midrash entirely rejected chronology as an organizing principle of their writings. Nor did they focus on, let alone work at interpreting, the historical events of their day as standing in an unfolding chronology that led from the past to a new and different present, and that would, in unanticipated ways, ultimately shape a distinctive future. The rabbis, that is, moved away from the understanding of history familiar from the Bible and, it is fair to say, largely held by modern people as well. Rather than a series of unfolding events, the rabbis, to the extent that they spoke of the past at all, reflected on past events as paradigmatic occurrences. What Jews experience today reflects long-established paradigms rather than the unfolding of something new. History is lived and relived, with God's ultimate plan already fixed in the framework of established and unchanging paradigms.

The 1,500-year Jewish retreat from history responded to the world in which Jews lived from the first centuries CE and up until modernity, a period marked by Jewish subjugation under Christian and Muslim oppression. In this context, the Jewish community lost any ability to control and shape its own present or future. The rabbis of the Talmud responded by arguing that history as a category is simply not meaningful. God would do for the Jewish people what God had long before promised. In the meantime, what happened on the stage of history only repeated a paradigm of Jewish oppression, caused perhaps by sin or by some other aspect of God's inscrutable nature, but in no event subject to human control or change. In the great writings of rabbinic Judaism there was therefore no good reason or need to reflect on history. For these Jews, what happened on the stage of history did not mean what the Gentile nations said it signified: God's rejection of the people of Israel. Contrary to such a conclusion, the rabbis argued that no lesson at all could be drawn from history. What mattered, rather, was how the Jews lived within the framework of ethical and ritual behaviors set out in the Torah. This was done in the hope of encouraging God finally to bring about the advent of the promised age of messianic perfection Jews referred to as the world-to-come, a period that stands outside of and beyond history.

Since the Jewish retreat from history responded to Jewish powerlessness, it makes sense that the onset of modernity and new opportunity for Jews to control their own destiny meant a Jewish return to history. From the Enlightenment and on, Jews would act on their comprehension that their actions could shape the reality of Jewish life and the history of the world. Within this context, the almost 2,000-year consensus regarding what it means to be a Jew and how Jews should live collapsed, as Jews who underwent diverse experiences of modernity variously imagined the appropriate place for Jews in modern history. Whatever the specific approach to Judaism and Jewish identity these Jews developed, all now took for granted their own control over history, their ability themselves to shape the world in which they lived.

Certainly, many Jews in this new period chose to maintain Jewish tradition as it had long been practiced. But even these Jews recognized the changed historical context that called on them to take a place within and benefit from what the contemporary world offered. Traditionalists aside, the dominant Jewish response to modernity was to create a Judaism that abandoned many practices that once made Jews distinctive. The ritual law would now be seen as a historical artifact, valid and even necessary in the context in which it had developed but inappropriate to the totally different world in which Jews now lived. Within this thinking, Jews determined that the world-to-come, the messianic age, would arise within history itself, would be manifest in the present age of reason and acceptance. In modernity, history again became what it had been for the Bible's authors: the arena of an unfolding and changing dynamic of existence.

We see that, in thinking about how Jews construct their history, we must reflect on three distinct periods in Jewish thought, biblical, rabbinic, and modern. Let us examine each of these in turn.

The Jewish Construction of History in the Biblical Period

The Hebrew Bible takes for granted that God acts in *history*, creating an ordered and meaningful world and acting in that world in response to human actions so as providentially to lead the world in the direction God prefers. People's actions, good or bad, are their choice to make, and the world they experience, of blessing or of curse, is shaped by those actions. In this context, the world's history unfolds as a meaningful expression of the interaction between human behavior and divine response.

The importance of the category history in this setting is nowhere clearer than in scripture's story of the Israelites' experience of Egyptian bondage—the Exodus— and the events of Sinai. For scripture, these are one time (and, hence, historical) events, and they comprise the most important narrative in the Hebrew Bible. These events detail how the people of Israel evolved from a small group—the Patriarchs and their families—into a great nation that, in the covenant ceremony at Sinai, became inextricably bonded to the God who created the world. These stories reveal the Bible's understanding of how God took the Israelite people as God's own and reached an agreement with them that required God's continued devotion to and protection of the people, on the one side, and their exclusive relationship with God, marked by the observance of a detailed system of legal and theological precepts, on the other.

Central for our purposes is the role in these narratives of historical events. The Israelites do not achieve knowledge of God through their own spiritual awakening or even as a result of God's simple and direct actions in responding to the circumstance in which the people find themselves. In the Exodus story, God does not neatly and quickly rescue the tribes of Israel from Egyptian bondage. Instead, God's power in history and, thus, over nations is highlighted. To promote God's purposes and desires, God manipulates history. God hardens Pharaoh's heart to prevent him from releasing the Jews while at the same time punishing Pharaoh with increasingly harsh measures for failing to set the people free. God's actions in history force the Egyptians to recognize God's power. More important, what happens to the Israelites in history compels them to accept God's sole sovereignty over the world.

In the Bible's view, God's power is manifest in history, and this means that history itself is meaningful, the arena in which God's purposes and desires are discerned. One of the Bible's most powerful reflections of this idea appears beyond the Exodus narrative, in the prophetic literature. Contrary to the commonplace modern perception that prophets, through divine vision, predict events that will take place far in the future, Israelite prophets almost exclusively are concerned with what is happening in their own day, with history in the near-term. They take seriously the events occurring around them, and they suggest the meaning of those events for the future of the Israelite nation. The prophets are their day's historians and political analysts, who take historical events seriously and announce to the people what they mean. As the Exodus already shows, God is known and God's will is discerned through the careful analysis of what happens on the stage of earthly history.

It bears noting that, absent a conception that the people can develop faith in God apart from God's saving acts in history, the Bible sees no problem with God's hardening Pharaoh's heart and, ultimately, killing Egypt's first-born males, both those who were instrumental in the persecution and murder of Israelites and those, including children, who had no involvement at all. God's actions are justifiable because, according to the Hebrew Bible, God's nature is to use history to prove God's power and to show all nations God's control over the world, a control that can be manifested only in history. So far as scripture is concerned, whatever God does to accomplish this purpose is necessary and therefore right. And it was, moreover, effective. God acted as promised, and this alone led the people of Israel to stand at the foot of Sinai and state, "All that the Lord has spoken we shall do, and we shall be obedient" (Exod. 24:7).

The Exodus and the Bible's Construct of God and History

The Exodus narrative's sense of God's actions in history is central in the Hebrew Bible. Outside of the book of Exodus, the Exodus theme is mentioned in scripture approximately 120 times, more than any other event or theological concept. This is incontestable evidence of the Exodus' centrality in Israelite religion. Most important, as Nahum Sarna, in his 1992 *Anchor Bible Dictionary* entry on the book of Exodus, states, "from this preeminence flow certain consequential conceptions of God, of the relationship between God and Israel, of the meaning of history, and of the proper ordering of human associations." Sarna writes:

1 The Exodus negates any notion of an otiose deity and asserts the reality of
   a God who is intimately involved in the life of the world. He is the God of
   History in the sense that the coming into being of the people of Israel, their
   enslavement in Egypt, their liberation, and the events connected therewith are
   not fortuitous or the result of human endeavors, but the unfolding of the divine
   plan of history.

2 The breaking of Egyptian resistance establishes God's absolute hegemony
   over history. History is the area of divine activity and thus is endowed with
   meaning.

3 A major consequence of this is that the religion of Israel became embedded
   in a historical matrix. Its major institutions, its religious calendar, its rituals and
   observances have all been reinterpreted in terms of the Exodus and emptied
   of any theological associations with the rhythm of nature and the life of
   the soil.

(1992: 689–9)

In the biblical view, people come to know God, to recognize God's qualities, and to
understand and follow God's demands only insofar as God personally and directly
takes the initiative to reveal them in the historical events that people experience.
Everything we know about God we know because God explicitly shows or tells
us, and this means that every aspect of history is filled with meaning (as Israel's
prophets understood). Knowledge of and faith in God do not result from theological
or philosophical speculation. Such knowledge is given primarily in God's appearance
at Sinai, where God purposefully and directly dictates his will. At the same time, in
the biblical understanding, such revelation equally takes place in the events of history
more generally, for these reflect God's plans and purposes. Comparably, God's will is
revealed in his speech to prophets, through whom God explains the meanings of and
reasons for the events of history.

At the heart of scripture's view is the idea that people come to know God only
through God's own actions and speech. God makes himself known through displays
of power that force people to accept his will. It is therefore entirely appropriate that
the covenant emerges in the context of the destruction of the armies of Pharaoh and
the mixed fear and joy of the people who, having just been brought out of Egyptian
slavery, stand trembling at the foot of Sinai as Moses receives directly the word of
God. If God is in history, then what occurs in history alone can prove God's power and
the need for Israel to abide by God's will.

The Construction of History in Rabbinic Judaism

The history they experienced, and so the Jews' ability to see events of history as
reflecting some clear divine plan, changed dramatically beginning in the first century
CE. The ebb and flow of history—exile and return, destruction and rebuilding—had

until this time allowed Jews to construe history as meaningful and each event as a new expression of God's will and purpose. Now the Jews' decreased ability either to control their own history or to see God's workings in the specifics of what they experienced led to a significantly different idea. The events that led to this shift can be outlined rather starkly:

1   The new period of Judaism followed the Jewish revolt against Rome that, in 70 CE, led to the destruction of the Jerusalem Temple. The Temple had been the epicenter of Jewish worship of God and the only place in which the divinely mandated sacrifices could take place. Save for the period between the Temple's destruction by Nebuchadnezzar of Babylonia in 586 BCE and its reconstruction following Cyrus of Persia's decree of return some fifty years later, the Temple had stood and its cult operated since its construction under King Solomon, a thousand years before.

2   The failed uprising of 70 CE was followed by a devastating second Jewish revolt against Rome in 132–135 CE. This revolt was led by a man known as Bar Kokhba, whose followers declared him the Messiah, that is, the leader sent by God to fulfill the promise of a reinstated Davidic monarchy. The outcome was as many as half a million Jews dead and Jerusalem's being turned into a Roman colony, with a temple of the Roman god Jupiter Capitolinus erected on the Temple Mount.

3   The following centuries saw the firm establishment of Christianity as the official religion of the Roman world. Christians argued that their political and social dominance signified God's abandonment of the people of Israel, whom God spurned in response to their rejection of God's true Messiah, Jesus.

The destruction of the Temple, the failed **Bar Kokhba Revolt**, and the ascent of Christianity potentially meant the end of the Jews' previous perception of their historical destiny as a great and holy nation—the chosen people. As in the period of the Babylonian exile, the cult ceased operation. But that time, after fifty years, the Persian conquest of Babylonia and Cyrus's edict allowing the exiled Jews to return to their land and rebuild their Temple meant that things had returned to what they had been. Jews' experience of history proved what scripture had always claimed, that God's will for and continuing support of his people can be seen through the events of history. This time, the failure of the Bar Kokhba Revolt meant that any expectation of the rebuilding of the Temple or of a return to the way things had been was unrealistic. And the success of Christianity, with its claim to embody a new **covenant** that superseded that of God with the Jews, meant that even the notion of Israel's chosenness and unique relationship to God was subject to significant challenge. History no longer appeared to be the arena in which the Jew could witness God's presence. History no longer proved as accurate the story Jews told about their destiny and connection to God.

In this period and in response to this new reality, the rabbis constructed a program of belief and practice that allowed Jews to maintain their previous understandings of their

FIGURE 2.1 *Rubble from the Roman destruction of the Temple in the Common Era still sits on a Roman era road below the Temple Mount in Jerusalem.* Source: *Photograph courtesy of the author.*

FIGURE 2.2 *In Jerusalem, the Western Wall (sometimes referred to as the Wailing Wall) is a remnant of the Temple Mount's expansion, begun in the first century* BCE *by Herod the Great. A location of great holiness, the Wall is a site of Jewish prayer and weeping over the Temple's loss. On the Temple Mount itself now stands Islam's Dome of the Rock.* Source: *Photograph courtesy of the author.*

unique relationship with God. But this program needed to rethink Jews' attitude toward history. It needed to show that, despite what had occurred on the stage of history, the covenantal promises would ultimately be fulfilled but that the people were not well served by political leaders who insisted that history mattered and who used military means to change it. Given the disastrous results military and political aspirations had in the first centuries, the rabbis argued that Jews were better off forgetting the notion of God's acting in history. Instead they should accept foreign political domination and develop modes of piety independent of nationalistic aspirations, unconcerned, this is to say, with what was happening to them on the stage of history.

The rabbinic plan for Judaism in the aftermath of the destruction of the Temple thus grew out of conflicting interests. Under Rabbinic leadership, Judaism continued to be shaped by the model of the Temple cult and Jews continued to pray for the rebuilding of the Temple, the reestablishment of animal sacrifice, and the ingathering of the exiles and renewed Israelite sovereignty, to be achieved, to be sure, through God's personal intervention in history. But these future developments were seen now as signifiers of the advent of the messianic age, as what would happen at the end of time, not as aspects of this world, expected to occur today or tomorrow or expedited through the Jews' own military or political activities.

Beginning in the first centuries, rabbinic ideology thus refocused the people's concerns from the events of political history, which are, after all, far beyond the control of the individual, to events within the life and control of each person and family. What came to matter were the everyday details of life, the recurring actions that, day-in and day-out, define who we are and demarcate what is truly important to us. How do we relate to family and community? By what ethic do we carry out our business dealings? How do we acknowledge our debt to God not for the events of history but for the everyday things: the food we eat and the wonders of the universe, evidenced in the daily rising and setting of the sun?

By making such aspects of life the focus of Judaism, the rabbis assured that the holiness the Temple had represented would be found in the life of the Jewish family and village. Without regard for what they experienced on the stage of history, the people could live as priests, eating their common food as though it were a sacrifice on the Temple's altar, seeing in their personal daily prayers and in their deeds of loving kindness a replacement for the sacrifices no longer offered. Certainly they understood this observance of a detailed system of ritual and law as leading God to act on their behalf. But, through the rabbinic system, they were made to recognize that they neither could nor should expect any quick, spectacular response as had occurred in past Israelite history, whether in the Exodus or in the return from exile under Cyrus. A messiah would come, but only in some distant future that was beyond history. And, in light of the battles and bloodshed that were understood to come along with the messianic event, people should not even hope to live to personally witness that event.

To reconceptualize the meaning of history within the life of the Jewish people, the rabbis needed to address the seeming disparity between their own experience

FIGURE 2.3 *In Tiberias, Israel, the tomb and burial marker of Yohanan ben Zakkai, the first-century* CE *rabbi who, in the period of the destruction of the Temple, established the first rabbinic academy. He taught that acts of loving kindness, study of Torah, and prayer could replace animal sacrifice.* Source: *Photograph courtesy of the author.*

of history and the very different history detailed in scripture, the veracity of which could be neither denied nor ignored. The rabbis accomplished this in an interpretative literature known as Midrash, in which they read into scripture their own distinctive attitude toward history. Midrash has at its heart the comprehension that scripture speaks to all days and ages, that it portrays not one-time events but paradigms for how history works, such that whatever happened in scripture can be expected to repeat throughout all subsequent history. Scripture thus foretells and makes sense of the experience of later Jews, proving that what they are going through is but a prelude to the fulfillment of their covenantal destiny set out in scripture. At the core of the rabbis' interpretative enterprise thus is the evaluation of every event that the people of Israel experienced through reference to three categories of faith: Israel's election, Israel's suffering, and Israel's final redemption (Basser 1984: 6–7). The effect of the rabbis' comprehension of scripture is revealed in their belief that, "Nothing happens except that which was expected; and once experienced it proves the 'correctness' of the 'Midrashic understanding of reality'" (9). History thus is not the unfolding of unique events but the experience over and again of paradigmatic occurrences, all of which point to God's ultimate plan for the people of Israel.

In **Genesis Rabbah**, the rabbis read the book of Genesis not as a simple depiction of the history of the people of Israel but, rather, as a paradigm that accounts for all of history. The rabbis, that is, hold that what happened to and was accomplished by Israel's patriarchs and matriarchs—Abraham and Sarah, Isaac and Rebecca, Jacob, Rachel, and Leah—speaks not only or primarily of these ancestors' history and faith. Rather, the patriarchs' and matriarch's actions—the way they responded to each other and to God's demands of them—shape and foretell the future of the Israelite nation.

The book of Genesis does not simply detail events of history. Rather, even as it recounts the past, it is a statement of what Israel is experiencing now as well as of what the people of Israel will experience in the future, when God fulfills the promises made to Abraham. For Genesis Rabbah's authorship, there is no past, present, or future. There are only recurring paradigmatic truths that are experienced over and over again. This means that, for the rabbis, the category of history does not pertain to the people of Israel. What they experience is only the repetition of the paradigmatic sequence of events set out in scripture, repeated in each age of Israelite existence. There is, for the rabbis, "nothing new under the sun," and this means that history as a category does not apply to their thinking about what the Jews experience in the here and now.

This point is illustrated by the Midrash's readings of Genesis 22, the story of Abraham's binding of his son Isaac as the sacrifice that God demands as proof of Abraham's faith. In that story, on the third day of his journey with Isaac, Abraham sees the place God instructed him to perform the sacrifice. In rabbinic thinking, the third day accordingly forms a paradigm for all subsequent Israelite history, as the following passage demonstrates (Genesis Rabbah 56:1, on Gen. 22:4):

1.A. "On the third day Abraham lifted up his eyes and saw the place afar off" (Gen. 22:4):

B. "After two days he will revive us, on the third day he will raise us up, that we may live in his presence" (Hos. 16:2).

C. On the third day of the tribes: "And Joseph said to them on the third day, 'This do and live'" (Gen. 42:18).

D. On the third day of the giving of the Torah: "And it came to pass on the third day when it was morning" (Exod. 19:16).

E. On the third day of the spies: "And hide yourselves there for three days" (Josh. 2:16).

F. On the third day of Jonah: "And Jonah was in the belly of the fish three days and three nights" (Jon. 2:1).

G. On the third day of the return from the Exile: "And we abode there three days" (Ezra 8:32).

H. On the third day of the resurrection of the dead: "After two days he will revive us, on the third day he will raise us up, that we may live in his presence" (Hos. 16:2).

I. On the third day of Esther: "Now it came to pass on the third day that Esther put on her royal apparel" (Est. 5:1).

J. She put on the monarchy of the house of her fathers.

K. On account of what sort of merit?

L. Rabbis say, "On account of the third day of the giving of the Torah."

M. R. Levi said, "It is on account of the merit of the third day of Abraham: 'On the third day Abraham lifted up his eyes and saw the place afar off'" (Gen. 22:4).

The third day marks the time of fulfillment of promise, and this means that Abraham's act of obedience to God is directly related to Israel's redemption at end of time and to the eventual resurrection of the dead (B). In the rabbinic view of the cogency of God's plan for Israel, the reference to the third day at Genesis 22:2, that is, evokes the entirety of God's plan for Israel, including the certainty of Israel's redemption, seen here not as so far in the future but, rather, simply as a matter of "the third day."

In the passage that follows (Genesis Rabbah 56:2), the use of similar words in different contexts establishes a paradigm, suggesting the cogency of the entire history of Israel, seen as flowing from a series of acts of worship ("prostration").

5.A. Said R. Isaac, "And all was on account of the merit attained by the act of prostration."

B. "Abraham returned in peace from Mount Moriah only on account of the merit owing to the act of prostration: '... and we will worship [the Hebrew word refers to an act of prostration] and come [on that account] again to you'" (Gen. 22:5).

C. "The Israelites were redeemed only on account of the merit owing to the act of prostration: 'And [when told by Aaron what God had promised] the people believed, . . . then they bowed their heads and prostrated themselves'" (Exod. 4:31).

D. "The Torah was given only on account of the merit owing to the act of prostration: 'And [before giving the Torah to Moses, God instructs Aaron and the elders of Israel to] worship [prostrate themselves] afar off'" (Exod. 24:1).

E. "Hannah was remembered [with a child] only on account of the merit owing to the act of prostration: 'And [Hannah and her husband] worshipped before the Lord'" (1 Sam. 1:19).

F. "The exiles will be brought back only on account of the merit owing to the act of prostration: 'And it shall come to pass in that day that a great horn shall be blown and they shall come that were lost . . . and that were dispersed . . . and they shall worship the Lord in the holy mountain at Jerusalem'" (Isa. 27:13).

G. "The Temple was built only on account of the merit owing to the act of prostration: 'Exalt you the Lord our God and worship at his holy hill'" (Ps. 99:9).

H. "The dead will live only on account of the merit owing to the act of prostration: 'Come let us worship and bend the knee, let us kneel before the Lord our maker'" (Ps. 95:6).

Abraham's and other historical figures' acts of prostration before God earned merit from which all the generations of Israel benefited and will benefit again, in the eventual resurrection of the dead (H). At stake here for rabbinic interpreters of scripture is not simply the meaning of the passage at hand but the way in which the passage contributes to an encompassing "law of history," as Jacob Neusner has called it. While following from and expressing the rabbis' theory of history and God's justice, and while providing a hopeful message for the Israelite people in the period of the composition of Genesis Rabbah, this is, of course, beyond anything that is intrinsic to the biblical text before us, which looks at history as a sequence of independent events rather than the unfolding of a preset paradigm.

Genesis Rabbah explains the Binding of Isaac by examining its significance within and for the entire span of Jewish history.

For the Midrash's authors, each detail of the biblical story represents a paradigmatic act that epitomizes the special relationship between the people of Israel and God, and which establishes the fact of the Israelites' ultimate redemption. The Akeda in this reading elucidates the adversity the Jews face, viewed as a test God imposes on those God loves and knows can withstand whatever hardships they are made to face. The testing of Abraham thus stands for the trials of Israel in general. Israel's

FIGURE 2.4 *The Binding of Isaac (Akeda) is depicted on the mosaic floor of the sixth-century* CE *Beth Alpha synagogue, in the north of Israel. Representing the rewards of faith, the Akeda appeared next to a Zodiac, which under Greek influence was a common image in synagogues of this period.* Source: *Photograph courtesy of the author.*

being subjected to such a test marks the people as special and holy. They are the true victors in the context of God's relationships with the nations of the world and God's determination of who ultimately will experience salvation.

In many ways, this rabbinic perspective hits at the heart of the theological issues raised by the text of Genesis, concerning the meaning of faith and the nature of the relationship between humankind and God. At the same time, the rabbis' interpretations consistently read rabbinic ideology into the biblical text, rethinking the character of history to responds to and make sense of the rabbis' own experience of the world. For the rabbis, rather than a series of events shaped by the independent actions of human actors, history represents the unfolding of a predetermined system of divinely ordained paradigms, into which human intervention is impossible.

The Jewish Construction of History in Modern Times

The experience of the Jews, and so the Jewish attitude toward history, remained largely consistent throughout the medieval period. Beginning with the Enlightenment in the seventeenth century, however, modernity brought dramatic changes to Jews' sense of their place in and relationship to the communities in which they lived. Jews now began to attain citizenship and equal rights in countries in which they had lived for centuries as a separate community. Hand in hand with that new-found freedom came an expectation on the part of the non-Jewish world, matched by the Jews' own desire to adopt not only the culture but also the attitudes and outlooks of their non-Jewish

FIGURE 2.5 *Theodor Herzl (1860–1904), an assimilated, Austro-Hungarian Jewish journalist, became the father of modern political Zionism, which, by 1948, led to the creation of the State of Israel.* Source: *Carl Pietzner/public domain.*

neighbors. The goal was to fit in. It is therefore not surprising that new forms of Jewish identity and practice emerged and that these innovations in how Jews thought about themselves and their religion entailed a dramatically changed attitude toward history. Yearning to participate in the work understood to be creating a world of equality and justice, Jews reentered the sphere of history. They again saw history as the arena within which purposeful human activity could change what was and create the perfected world previously seen as possible only through God's messianic actions. History again was the sphere in which the hopes and aspirations of the Jewish people would be fulfilled. This meant that every aspect of the world, what governments did as much as how individuals behaved, reflected a meaningful reality that Jews needed to take seriously.

By the nineteenth century, this new thinking was exemplified by the emergence of political **Zionism**, promoted first by secularized Jews but subsequently taken up by religious ones as well, who saw human political action as a reflection of God's will for the Jewish people. In the Zionist perspective, it was time, and it was appropriate, for Jews to take their destiny into their own hands, to create what earlier generations had said could and should be accomplished only directly by God.

The reentry of Jews into history was actualized as they acquired a new sense of power over their future, represented in the creation of the modern State of Israel.

A second example is the development of Judaism's Reform movement, which reconceptualized Jewish religious practice and belief to closely parallel the Western, Christian norms of the communities in which Jews now lived. At the heart of this movement was the modernization of the worship service: to make it shorter, more aesthetically pleasing, focused on moral education, and by introducing prayers in the vernacular, more accessible to people who did not understand Hebrew. These reforms created a service that felt socially, culturally, and spiritually appropriate to the world Jews had taken as their own. Importantly, these changes were justified by their backers' distinctively modern understanding that Judaism, its beliefs and practices, had always been shaped by historical circumstances.

This fresh framework for understanding the impact of history was clearly expressed by the rabbis who attended a meeting of the Central Conference of American Rabbis (the Reform movement's rabbinic arm) in Pittsburgh in 1885. Dominant in the so-called "Pittsburgh Platform" is the idea that history has always been, and so must continue to be, consequential in framing Jewish thought and practice. Jews, that is, have always existed in and responded to the changing realities of their day. Rather than the fixed paradigms of history and unchanging divine revelation identified by the ancient rabbis, modern ones saw Judaism as the product of an ever changing world. Tradition was time-bound and not compulsory for contemporary Jews:

> We recognize in the Mosaic legislation a system of training the Jewish people for its mission during its national life in Palestine, and today we accept as binding only its moral laws and maintain only such ceremonials as elevate and sanctify our lives [...].

> We hold that all such Mosaic and Rabbinical laws as regulate diet, priestly purity and dress originated in ages and under the influence of ideas altogether foreign to our present mental and spiritual state […] ; their observance in our day is apt rather to obstruct than to further modern spiritual elevation.
>
> ("Declaration of Principles Adopted by a Group
> of Reform Rabbis at Pittsburgh, 1885" 1935)

Judaism has always existed within an unfolding historical framework that responded to and reflected what was new in each age. While the people of Israel once comprised a nation, today they do not. The laws that regulated diet, clothing, and the like applied during that national existence but no longer have a purpose or fulfill any need. They are obsolete, and to ignore that fact—to disregard the reality of changing history—is worse than pointless. To follow tradition rather than the reality of contemporary life prevents traditionalists from recognizing, and acting on, Judaism's religious and spiritual truths.

Most striking in the Pittsburgh statement is its authors' rethinking of the concept of messianism. Jewish messianic thinking had previously understood that, at the end of time, *God* would fulfill the promises God's covenant has set out for the Jewish people. For the reformers, a messianic *age*—not a *messiah*, that is, a savior sent by God—would be achieved by humankind's own actions in implementing universal values and acceptance. In these reformers' view, the messianic age, a human creation, manifest in history, was already emerging. It was the product of the great ideals of America and signified already in the accomplishments of the progressive society in which these rabbis lived, a "modern era of universal culture of heart and intellect":

> We recognize in the modern era of universal culture of heart and intellect the approach of the realization of Israel's great Messianic hope for the establishment of the Kingdom of truth, justice and peace among all men.
>
> ("Declaration of Principles Adopted by a Group
> of Reform Rabbis at Pittsburgh, 1885" 1935)

The messianic hope is no longer the establishment of a "kingdom of David." It is, rather, people's construction of a kingdom of truth, justice, and peace. This kingdom would be realized not at the end of time, through God's miraculous sending of the Messiah who would carry out God's will. It would be, rather, a product of human historical development and moral growth. This kingdom was already manifest in the world, represented in the progress these rabbis saw occurring around them, in their own day and age.

Human control of and action in history had yielded the ideals of freedom and equality that were fully manifested, these rabbis believed, in American social and political systems. The implication was that it was important, indeed necessary, for Jews fully to participate in the political and communal life of the world in which they lived. Through their actions they would themselves fulfill the long-time dream of a messianic age of perfection. The implication bears note: rather than subject to their own idiosyncratic culture or uniquely Jewish expectations for redemption, Jews are just like everyone else, namely, participants in, and therefore responsible for, a shared, consequential human history. Later formulations of Reform Judaism, alongside other modern modes of Jewish affiliation and observance, have thought and rethought the specifics of how Jews should practice their religion and its traditions. But the shift in thinking about history that we see here remains central to all of these ideologies. History now is viewed as consequential and shaped by human beings, who create their own destiny. This perspective has become for Jews, as for other peoples, a hallmark of modern thinking about how human beings relate to the world in which we live.

Conclusion

The evolution in Jewish thinking about history presents a challenge to those who today maintain a sense of God's authorship of history and who practice Judaism as a system of religious beliefs. How might a people that has both existed in history and strived to overcome history's sting conceptualize history as a human creation while retaining a sense—central to all religious thinking—of God's presence and power to shape the world and bring about redemption? The answer as it emerges from classical Judaism is expressed by Michael Fishbane, in his commentary (Lieber 2001: 1315–16) to the passage from the biblical prophets read in synagogues on Passover (*Pesah*). Fishbane writes:

> The linkage of [Isaiah 10–12's image of] the defeat of Sennacherib [the Assyrian king who led a military campaign against Judah] with the eve of *Pesah* [the holiday of freedom] is testimony to the Jewish tendency to relate acts of divine deliverance to great historic models. By such associations, new events in history take on the power and often the characteristics of foundational moments. History thus becomes a series of repetitive and confirming truths. For Jewish memory, God's redemptive acts constitute one such true, and the source of national hope.
>
> (Lieber 2001: 1315–16)

Judaism understands new events in history to recapitulate the truths of divinely established paradigms. Jews thus both experience history as the unfolding of humanly shaped events and see in it God's model and plan for humanity. Salvation can be both the result of human endeavor and the product of the divine plan for how history will unfold. History is both the result of human engagement and, as the rabbis of the Pittsburgh Platform put it, the "realization of Israel's great Messianic hope."

Even as the modern period has shifted toward a view of the human power to control, and hence create, our own history, the rabbinic framework for understanding history remains powerful. For those who continue to frame their lives within the mythic structure of Judaism, the classical and modern Jewish approaches coalesce.

The messianic age will emerge as a manifestation of what God has always promised and Jews have always expected; the paradigm for this is found over and over again in God's past redemptive acts. At the same time, history is entirely in our own hands and is the product of how we on Earth lead our lives. God and humanity work together in the fulfillment of the ideals and promises of God's original covenant with the people of Israel and, more broadly, with all of humanity, God's creation.

Further Reading and Online Resources

Avery-Peck, A.J. and J. Neusner (2003), *The Blackwell Companion to Judaism*, Blackwell Companions to Religion, Malden, MA: Blackwell Publishers.
Gay, P. (1995), *The Enlightenment: An Interpretation*, 2 Vols., New York: Norton.
Neusner, J. (2003), *The Idea of History in Rabbinic Judaism*, Leiden: Brill.
Yerushalmi, Y.H. (1996), *Zakhor: Jewish History and Jewish Memory*, Foreword by H. Bloom, Seattle: University of Washington Press.

References

Basser, H. (1984), *Midrashic Interpretations of the Song of Songs*, American University Studies Series VII. Theology and Religion, vol. 2, New York: Peter Lang.
"Declaration of Principles Adopted by a Group of Reform Rabbis at Pittsburgh, 1885" (1935), *The Yearbook of the Central Conference of American Rabbis*, 45: 198–200.
Lieber, D. L., ed. (2001), *Etz Hayim: Torah and Commentary*, New York: Jewish Publication Society.
Lieber, D.L. and J. Harlow (2001), *Etz Hayim: Torah and Commentary*, Philadelphia: Jewish Publication Society.
Neusner, J. (1985), *Genesis Rabbah: The Judaic Commentary to the Book of Genesis: A New American Translation*, Atlanta, GA: Scholars Press.
Sarna, N. (1992), "Exodus, Book of," in D.N. Freedman (ed.), *The Anchor Bible Dictionary*, vol. 2, 689–9, New York: Doubleday.

Glossary Terms

Bar Kokhba Revolt A Jewish uprising against Roman control of the province of Judea, led by Simeon bar Kokhba, a military figure heralded by the Judeans as the anointed leader ("Messiah") sent by God to free the Jews from Roman oppression. Fought in 132 to 136 CE, this is generally referred to as the Second Jewish Revolt, the first being the war against Rome that led to the destruction of the Jerusalem Temple in 70 CE. The dramatic failure of the revolt, which led to the loss of some 580,000 Jewish lives and Rome's banning of Jews from Jerusalem, led to a rethinking of how and when God might support Jewish military efforts such as had been led by Bar Kokhba. Under the rabbis, messianic military responses were discouraged, with Bar Kokhba himself labeled a fraud and false messiah.

Covenant The agreement God made with Abraham and his descendants, which was recapitulated at Mount Sinai, following the Exodus from Egypt, in the presence of the entire people of Israel. The covenant calls for the Jews to follow God's law, embodied in Torah. In return God promises to make of the Israelites a great nation dwelling in peace in the Promised Land. Described at Exodus 19–20 and elaborated in the legal materials of the books of Exodus, Leviticus, Numbers, and Deuteronomy, the covenant is understood also to encompass the later expansions and interpretations of scripture found within the Talmudic literature and subsequent codes of Jewish law. In light of this association with the system of Rabbinic law and learning, from the Rabbinic period and on, the term covenant has been tantamount to the concept of Torah. Covenant, this is to say, refers to the entire body of revelation that defines the agreement between God and Israel. It states the obligations Israel has accepted upon itself and sets out what the nation can expect from God in return.

Genesis Rabbah A rabbinic commentary on the book of Genesis, produced by rabbis in the land of Israel beginning as early as the mid-third century CE but, in its final redaction, dating from between the beginning of the fifth and middle of the seventh centuries. This commentary understands the events of creation and the patriarchal age to be paradigmatic of future Jewish history. In particular it holds that the merit earned through Abraham's adherence to God's will accrues to the benefit of Abraham's descendants throughout the ages.

Rabbis From the Hebrew word signifying "master" or "great," a teacher and religious thinker who emerged in the first century CE and, in the following centuries, became the leader par

excellence of the Jewish community. Rabbis held that, at Sinai, God revealed to Moses not only the written Torah, contained in the Hebrew Bible, but also a second revelation, transmitted orally through the generations until it reached the rabbis. Access to Oral Torah meant that the rabbis alone had complete knowledge of God's will. By studying and conveying the complete Torah to the people, rabbis acted on the model of Moses, referred to as "Our Rabbi," and God, also understood to embody the characteristics of the rabbi. The earliest rabbis stand behind the Talmudic and Midrashic literature, their main role having been the study of Torah so as to delineate Jewish law and practice. In the medieval and especially the modern period the rabbi become the figure more familiar today, as the skilled leader of the synagogue and officiant at Jewish worship services.

Zionism The idea that the Jews should have a homeland. While the idea that the Land of Israel (the biblical Zion) is the Jews' homeland goes back to God's promise to Abraham, modern political Zionism dates to the nineteenth century, when, under the leadership of Theodor Herzl, Jews began to work for the creation of a state in what was then known as Palestine. Between 1917 and 1947 hundreds of thousands of Jews settled in Palestine. From 1933 to 1945, the Jews in Europe, facing the threat of murder in the Nazi Holocaust, were officially prohibited from entering the region in sizable numbers. Following the Second World War, many Jews who had survived wanted to go to Palestine, and in 1947 the United Nations voted to create there Jewish and Arab states. In 1948, the Jewish state declared independence and survived a war with its Arab neighbors, fulfilling the dream of modern Zionism.

3

The Major Texts of Judaism

Paul V.M. Flesher

The people of Israel—"Jews," in today's parlance—trace their history back more than 3,500 years. During this time, Jews followed a religion that we call "Judaism." Judaism was frequently shaped and reshaped during that time. Today's Judaism differs from that just a few hundred years ago, let alone from that a thousand or two thousand years ago. A list of Judaism's Top Ten Books depends on the time and place it is created.

The main criterion for choosing Judaism's Top Ten Books is that of impact, that they inspired the behavior, actions, and beliefs of large numbers of Jews for a significant period of time. They communicated to an audience—an audience that had been created by oral and written social debate on key topics of concern. These books have an impact because they address those concerns successfully. That means that each book in the Top Ten connected to a specific movement of Jews and shaped successive generations of followers. In nearly all cases, the books on the list are symbolic because many other works were connected to them; works upon which they built, which built upon them, or with which they were in debate. On to Judaism's Top Ten!

#1 The Torah

The **Torah**, also called the Pentateuch, comprises Judaism's first sacred work. When the Jews were rebuilding Jerusalem following their return from exile in Babylonia in the sixth century BCE, the priest and scribe Ezra gathered the people together and read the Torah out loud to them and commanded them to follow its laws.

From Nehemiah 8's description of this event, the precise text that Ezra read is unclear. Most scholars—and nearly all believing Jews—think it was the five books of the Torah: Genesis, Exodus, Leviticus, Numbers, and Deuteronomy.

FIGURE 3.1 *Torah scroll open for a Sabbath reading at the Glockengasse Synagogue in Cologne, Germany, a museum.* Source: Willi Horsch.

The Torah relates the story of how the people Israel were formed and how they developed a close relationship with God. The tale is two parts, the first of which appears in Genesis and the second takes place over the remaining books. Genesis focuses on Abraham and his descendants, Isaac and Jacob. Jacob had twelve sons, who became the fathers of the twelve tribes of Israel, except for Joseph whose two sons each fathered a tribe. Abraham had a close relationship to God, which was passed down through the generations. At the end of Genesis, a famine drove this large family group to Egypt for food, where they remained for several generations. God promised Abraham two things: that he would have numerous descendants and that they would possess the land of Canaan. The first promise was fulfilled in Genesis, but achieving the second promise becomes the plot of the rest of the Torah.

Exodus opens with the Israelites enslaved in Egypt. God chose Moses to help deliver them. Their escape and journey back to Canaan is related over the next four books. Along the way, they stop at Mount Sinai, where God presents a revelation to Israel through the mediation of the prophet Moses—the Ten Commandments. In addition, the Torah also contains three law codes and instructions about how to build God's temple (called a tabernacle), ordain priests, and conduct sacrificial worship. Deuteronomy ends with the death of Moses and with the Israelites on the border of Canaan, the Promised Land.

The Torah became Judaism's central text, a position it still holds today. It became the model for Judaism's other sacred texts, the focus of study, and the basis of the weekly Sabbath liturgy (see Figure 3.1). Even when secular Zionism turned its back on Judaism's sacred texts, the Torah remained a key element of its raison d'etre.

#2 The Hebrew Bible: The Tanakh

The Torah became the foundation for the Hebrew Bible, which Judaism calls the TaNaK (usually spelled in English as **Tanakh**). This is a Hebrew acronym that stands for Torah, Neviim (Prophets), and Ketubim (Writings). The books of the Prophets were probably all chosen by the third century BCE, but the category of Writings remained unfinished until the second century CE, when its final two books (Esther and Song of Songs) were selected. All books of the Hebrew Bible are sacred, but the Torah is the "most equal of equals" because of its larger role in liturgy and study. This holy standing inspired Christianity to borrow the books of the Hebrew Bible and make them the core of its Old Testament.

The prophetic books are divided into two sections. The first is the Former Prophets and consists of Joshua, Judges, Samuel, and Kings. They present a chronological set of narratives—ranging from 1225 to 586 BCE—telling how Joshua conquered the land of Canaan, how the time of Judges lacked a central government and thus experienced many difficulties, Samuels' description of the way the Davidic dynasty of kings was established to overcome those problems, and then Kings' stories of the successes and failures of the kings. It ends with the destruction of Jerusalem by the Babylonians and the people Israel's exile to Babylon.

The books of the Latter Prophets contain oracles and prophecies given by different prophets (e.g., Isaiah, Jeremiah, and Ezekiel), along with a few narrative sections. Most oracles feature a divine view of (then) current events and how God was using them to punish or benefit the kings and people of Israel.

The Writings constitute a true miscellany of works. The book of Psalms contains hymns originally performed during Temple worship. There are three books from the Wisdom movement: Proverbs, Ecclesiastes, and Job. Three others are about historical events: Chronicles, Ezra, and Nehemiah, then there are the two books featuring female protagonists Ruth and Esther, the apocalyptic Daniel, the love poem Song of Songs, and the Lamentations for the Temple destroyed in 586.

Many of these books or parts of them feature in Jewish liturgy, either for the Sabbath or annual holy days. Different Psalms are prayed in nearly every worship service. All receive regular study. Our earliest Tanakh manuscripts come from the Dead Sea Scrolls of the second and first centuries BCE, such as the Isaiah Scroll in Figure 3.2.

FIGURE 3.2 *Two columns from the Great Isaiah Scroll, Isaiah 14–16. This is one of the oldest existing Tanakh manuscripts, dated to the second century* BCE. Source: *Wikimedia Commons.*

#3 Translations: The Greek Septuagint

Americans by and large do not notice translations; they read them as if they are identical to the original. If someone says, "I read the *Odyssey* and the *Iliad* in class last year," they mean they read them in translation, not in the original Greek. Despite this cultural invisibility of translations, we should overlook neither the role of translations in Judaism nor its invention of the religious translation. Indeed, Judaism constitutes the first religion to translate a sacred text into another language.

After Alexander the Great conquered the Middle East (334–323 BCE), Greek became a prestige language from Egypt to Iraq. Less than a century later, most Egyptian Jews had forgotten Hebrew and spoke Greek only, so they translated the Torah into Greek so they could continue to understand it. This Greek rendering became known as the **Septuagint** (Seventy) because it was supposedly composed by seventy (or seventy-two, depending on which version of the story one follows) Jewish Torah experts. This translation apparently took place during the reign of Pharaoh Ptolemy II Philadelphus (285–247 BCE).

Greek translations of the entire Hebrew Bible, as well as the Torah, became increasingly popular over the following centuries, spreading across the eastern Mediterranean, which Alexander had conquered. Controversy followed this popularity, since scholarly Jews who knew Hebrew and Greek noticed the differences between the Greek version and the original Hebrew; they pointed out that the Septuagint did not accurately reproduce the Hebrew text. To overcome these objections, several Jewish writers claimed that God himself inspired the translation.

When early Christianity borrowed Judaism's Hebrew Bible (starting in the first century CE), they took it in the form of the Septuagint, not the Hebrew original. As the Septuagint became more popular among the Christians, Jews drifted away from it.

#4 Translations: The Aramaic Targums

At the same time Greek became a linguistic feature among the land of Israel's new rulers, the previous prestige language—Aramaic—developed into a Jewish vernacular and displaced Hebrew. In the first century CE, **Targum** Onqelos translated the Torah into the Aramaic of Judea, becoming broadly accepted. Indeed, in the sixth century CE, the Babylonian **Talmud** authorized Onqelos as the only acceptable Torah translation for worship.

Targum Onqelos inspired the composition of more translations. By the third century, there were several versions of the Torah in Galilean Aramaic as well as a translation of the Prophets into Onqelos' Judean Aramaic. Most Targums of Writings books came a couple of centuries later, although an Esther Targum and an Aramaic Job translation had been composed by the first century.

While the Septuagint stood on its own in worship, the Targums were more problematic. In worship they were supposed to be accompanied by the reading of the Hebrew text, even though most people could not understand it. From the earliest descriptions of the Torah reading ritual, the reading of the Targum follows the parallel reading of the Hebrew text. This rite was practiced for centuries, and when Jews moved across the Mediterranean and into the Arab world, they composed new Targums in Arabic, Ladino (Spanish), Yiddish (German), Persian, Italian, and Turkish—to name just a few languages. Many of these continued to be used up to the modern period.

Although translations make the words of a sacred text understandable in another language, they do so by changing them—often into different meanings. Rather than declaring Targums inspired, like the Septuagint, Targum translators addressed this problem by adding words. On one level, the targumists were trying to deal with a common linguistic difficulty. Equivalencies of words in two languages are frequently inexact, conveying different connotations and nuances. A literal translation of a sentence from one language often does not produce a sentence with the same meaning in a second language. To deal with this, the Targum translators often altered the translation slightly, even adding words. On another level, sacred texts need to reflect the understanding agreed upon by centuries of religious interpretation. To transmit this meaning, targumists added even more words—sometimes phrases, sentences, or entire paragraphs—to ensure that the theological meaning came through.

Because of the ways Aramaic Targums differed from the Hebrew original, some Jews viewed them with suspicion, even as they continued to use them. Despite this, Judaism was still using Targums at the dawn of the modern age, although it had long forgotten the Septuagint.

#5 The Babylonian Talmud

After the Hebrew Bible, the Babylonian Talmud (Figure 3.3) comprises the most important book in Judaism. It is not holy in the same sense as scripture, but it is highly revered and authoritative. After its publication around 600 CE, it guided Judaism for the next 1,200 years. All other Jewish books or religious developments took place within the worldview it shaped. The New Testament can help us understand the Babylonian Talmud. Just as Christianity holds the Old Testament sacred but interprets it through the New Testament's story of Jesus and the early church, so Judaism sees the Hebrew Bible (Old Testament) as sacred but interprets it through the Babylonian Talmud. Judaism is thus as much a post-Hebrew Bible religion as Christianity is a post-Old Testament religion.

The Babylonian Talmud was not written overnight but resulted from nearly six hundred years of historical development. After Roman armies destroyed Jerusalem and its temple in 70 CE, many Jews went north to Galilee and surrounding areas. This was the start of the diaspora; the temple was never rebuilt and Jews did not return to Judea en mass until modern times.

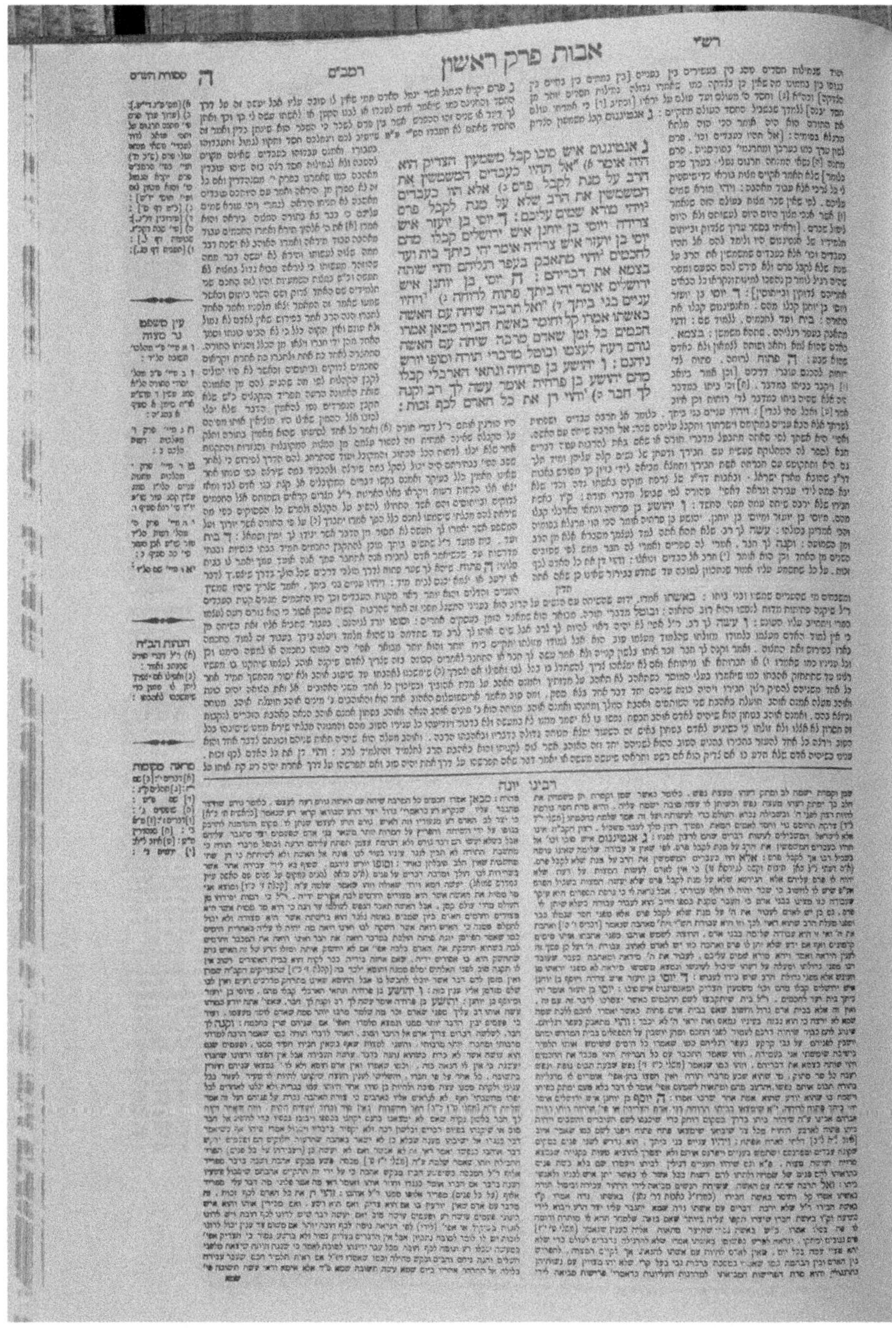

FIGURE 3.3 *A page of the Babylonian Talmud (Avot 5, to passage 1:3) with commentaries arranged in the traditional manner. The Talmud passage itself is the square of text in the upper center, with the commentary of Rashi to the right and the commentary of Maimonides to the left. At the bottom is the more recent commentary of Rabbenu Jonah. In the left margin appear various types of cross-references.* Source: *Photograph by author.*

The religion that had been centered on the Jerusalem Temple for more than one thousand years disappeared with its destruction. No longer could Jews offer sacrifices there as God commanded in the Torah. This could have been the end of Judaism, but new leaders arose called **rabbis**. They were court officials: lawyers and judges. They were neither rulers nor synagogue officials, but instead ran the law courts and the schools that trained young men for service in them. The law that they promulgated gained a new name, the "**halakha**." This word means "the walk," referring to how people should walk through, or lead, their lives. Taking the Torah as the foundation, the rabbis extended and applied it through interpretation and debate. Their rulings and judgments were not limited to civil and criminal law, but reached into areas of religious practice and moral behavior. It truly was "the way to walk" in all ways.

The Babylonian Talmud intertwined two strands of legal writing practiced by the rabbis, a legal strand and an exegetical strand. The legal strand began in 200 CE with a law code called the Mishnah. It divided law into six broad areas: the observance of religious holy days, the giving of tithes, relationships between women and men (and the children they produced), civil law, temple offerings, and religious purity. The **Mishnah** takes an unusual form for a law code; rather than giving laws directly, it features analyses and debates that work out legal details and priorities when applying laws, especially when two laws are applicable but conflict.

This approach to legal explication continues in two documents of the third and fourth century, the Tosefta and the Jerusalem Talmud. It also serves as the model for the rabbis' treatment of books of the Torah and Hebrew Bible, which they exegete from the second century onward. These interpretations are called *Midrashim* (sing. *Midrash*).

FIGURE 3.4 *The Babylonian Talmud. Since it was first published in 1520, the Babylonian Talmud has appeared in folio volumes that include traditional commentators. This has increased the size of the already large work severalfold. The pictured Talmud set appears in twenty volumes that take up a full 76-centimeter shelf.* Source: *Photograph by the author.*

The Babylonian Talmud takes these two strands of analysis and weaves them together. It takes the Mishnah as its organizing structure, explicating and debating its issues line by line. Often it will bring a passage from the Hebrew Bible for support and then continue the exegesis of that passage beyond its relevance for the immediate debate, returning only when the second one is exhausted. One point that contributed to the Babylonian Talmud's importance is that while the earlier books related the debates, they rarely gave judgments about what should be done. The Talmud often makes a point of giving a final decision.

The Babylonian Talmud and its interpretation shaped Judaism's character for the next 1,200 years. It was not until the seventeenth-century Enlightenment that the Talmud's world view received serious challenge. Many commentaries were written to explain it and, after the invention of printing in the fifteenth century, the best of these were included in its publication—many on the same page as the Talmud itself. These editions are quite large: a typical edition can appear in twenty oversize volumes taking up a 76-centimeter shelf space (Figure 3.4).

#6 Codifying the Halakha: The *Mishneh Torah* and the *Shulkhan Arukh*

The problem with the Babylonian Talmud's commentaries is that they follow the Mishnah's order. This works well if you are studying a passage and trying to understand it, but what if you seek a Talmudic decision about a religious practice and could not remember where it is? This challenge was taken up by the polymath Moses Maimonides, a twelfth-century leader of the Egyptian Jewish community who served as the physician to Sultan Saladin. He wrote philosophical treatises, medical texts, and works of theology and halakha.

In 1166 to 1168, Maimonides wrote the *Mishneh Torah*. This fourteen-volume work gathered all the important halakhic rulings in the Talmud, added to them decisions that had been made in successive centuries, and organized them in a way that placed the rulings on related matters together. Many of the topics are recognizable from Talmudic interests—religious festivals, prayer, relationships between women and men, purity, and offerings—while the areas of civil and criminal law were divided across several different books, which featured laws concerning torts, buying and selling, the exchange of money, the running of courts, and related matters.

The primary achievement of the *Mishneh Torah* was that no longer did a Jew have to be a Talmud scholar to practice the *halakha* correctly. Instead, people who spent their day working ordinary jobs could simply follow the instructions contained in this work. The simplicity of this insight and its success spurred the development of many commentaries and even new complete guides written by people who drew upon the experience of using the code to improve it. But it was not until the sixteenth century that a replacement for the Mishneh Torah came about. The halakhic expert Joseph Caro wrote a commentary on it early in his life, and then in his old age composed the *Shulkhan Arukh* (the "set table"), which finally superseded the Mishneh Torah as a guide for daily worship and religious behavior—a work that is still widely used and studied today.

#7 The Siddur: Prayer Book

From the most ancient stories in the Hebrew Bible onward, Jews have prayed. Their bond to God, both as individuals and as a people, has been sustained by prayer, along with sacrifice and other means. Temple priests led prayers that accompanied sacrifices. Group prayer, the prayers of Jews praying together, came to the fore with the rise of synagogues as worship spaces, especially after the destruction of the Jerusalem Temple in 70 CE. The Babylonian Talmud and other rabbinic literature speak of frequent public prayer in worship, prayer that took place daily, on the weekly Sabbaths, at the new moon, and during annual religious festivals.

Individuals pray with heartfelt meaning, speaking to God about the concerns closest to their heart. They often do so extemporaneously, fitting the words of the prayer to their deepest worries. Group prayer differs significantly, since the goal is to have everyone pray the same prayer, bringing the same praises, hopes, and concerns to God at the same time. This requires a prayer to have a fixed, composed text. Frequently repeated prayers can be memorized, but less common ones work best when a person reads from a written text. This is the rationale of a prayer book, which Hebrew terms a **siddur**.

Today, most Siddurs contain the daily prayers, the Sabbath rituals, and other prayers. A separate set of prayer books for the annual holy days contain their more extensive prayers—even less familiar to most Jews—and are called *mahzorim*.

Most worship services are built around the two oldest prayers: the *shema*, which derives from passages in the Torah, and the so-called Eighteen Benedictions (also known as simply "The Prayer"), which took their final form during the rabbinic period before the Talmud's publication.

The first two books that began the genre of Siddurs were written in Babylon by two Gaons—Gaon is an honorific rabbinic title—in the ninth and early tenth centuries CE: Amram Gaon and Saadia Gaon. The usefulness of these two works gave rise to numerous others, which experimented with different formats and aimed to conform to different halakhic expectations. From these developed traditional Ashkenazic and Sephardic Siddurs, as well as Yemenite ones. The three major divisions of American Judaism have each sponsored their own Siddur. Outside of Israel, most present the prayers with one page in Hebrew and the facing page in the local language.

While public prayer is often thought of as an oral activity, it is the prayer book that has enabled Jews around the world to address the same prayers to God and to do so in the same liturgical moments.

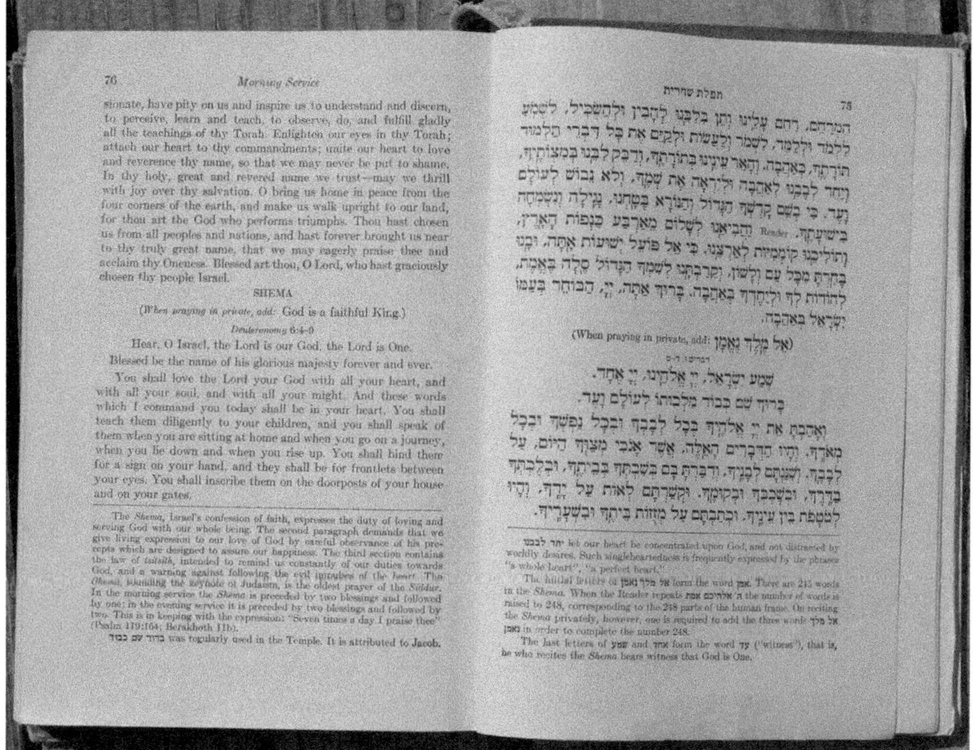

FIGURE 3.5 *A page from a well-used Siddur (prayer book). The Siddur is open to the beginning of the Shema, the oldest and perhaps most prayed prayer in Judaism. The right-hand page gives the original Hebrew text and the left-hand the English translation. This prayer book is the Birnbaum edition, the most widely used Siddur in the United States. Ha-Siddur, Ha-Shalem (Daily Prayer Book), trans. and ed. Philip Birnbaum (New York: Hebrew Publishing Co., 1949). Source: Photograph by the author.*

#8 Mysticism—the Zohar

Attentive readers of the centuries of Jewish texts occasionally catch glimpses of mysticism. Perhaps the best known are the apocalyptic works of Daniel and Enoch from the second century BCE or the rabbinic era Merkavah mysticism, which draws upon the vision of the wheeled heavenly vehicle in Ezekiel 1. But these hints were never allowed to grow or mature in the full sunlight; instead they were seen as secret and dangerous and so were kept hidden from the masses.

That began to change with the rise of **Kabbalah**, a form of mysticism that began in the thirteenth century on the border between France and Spain. When the Zohar (Splendor) was composed in the 1270s and 1280s—probably by Moses de Léon— Kabbalah had finally found a way to approach mainstream Judaism.

The Zohar tells of the second-century Rabbi Simeon bar Yochai and his son who travel around Israel meeting and talking with various rabbis. These conversations follow the standard order of the Torah's sequence of weekly readings. Embedded with this narrative are small books on other mystical topics.

The Zohar follows the general aim of Kabbalah, which is to understand God, his creation, and the purpose of humankind within it. Of course, this cannot be done directly, since looking directly at God is like looking at the sun—you will become blind. The Zohar's approach is to seek hints about God and his purpose indirectly by studying the Torah—the revelation God gave to Israel through Moses. The Torah is not seen as "just" about how God sought out Israel to make them His own people, but it also contains encoded hints and clues about the hidden secrets of God and his universe.

A brief reprise of Kabbalist theology is that when God created the world, he accidently left pieces of his divine nature in the world. These have become human souls. The kabbalist's goal then, is to return these divine pieces to God. According to the Zohar, this is done by following the standard rabbinically approved daily prayers, practicing the 613 *mitzvot*, studying Torah, and performing deeds of kindness. In other words, instead of matching its mystical theology with outlandish mystical practices, the Zohar gives new meaning to the religious practices that pious Jews already follow. By this means, the Zohar could inspire more pious activity—recognizably pious even to traditional Judaism of the time. Rather than requiring actions that would perhaps divide the Jewish community, it gave additional encouragement to following the same practices as all other pious Jews. And it was this approach that enhanced the knowledge and popularity of the Zohar within Judaism over the following centuries.

#9 Reform Judaism—the Pittsburgh Platform

The Enlightenment in Europe, which began in the 1700s and gave rise to the scientific revolution and secular culture, brought enormous changes to Judaism, as it did to Christianity and other religions. One result is that today more Jews identify with Reform Judaism and its principles than any other religious type of Judaism. In the United States alone, nearly two million Jews fall into the Reform camp, making them the largest, single Jewish "denomination" in the United States or in Israel, the two countries with the largest Jewish populations.

Reform Judaism, also known as Progressive Judaism, was born in early nineteenth-century Germany. While many Jews (and Christians) interpreted the Enlightenment and the scientific revolution it inspired as showing that God did not exist and that religions were therefore defunct, the early Reformers instead saw Judaism as a cultural movement. Like any long-lasting culture, it contained elements that were no longer relevant or viable in its present circumstances, or that were even mistakes or frauds. It needed purification, to be stripped of elements that hindered contemporary Jews in their spiritual quest to worship God.

It is easier to state this goal in principle than it is to work out the details. From the 1820s onward, in both Europe and the United States, Jewish rabbis and other leaders responded to the demands of their congregants and tried out different approaches to reforming the Judaism that came to them from centuries of Talmudic practice and thought.

The clearest and most succinct statement of these attempts is perhaps the Pittsburgh Platform, put together by a conference of American rabbis in 1885. It is only a few pages in length, but it guided Reform Judaism in America for nearly fifty years, until its revision in 1937.

The Pittsburgh Platform consists of just eight short paragraphs, each one highlighting a different principle.

Principle 1 acknowledges other religions as legitimate attempts "to grasp the Infinite" yet holds that "Judaism presents the highest conception of the God-idea."

Principle 2 holds that the Hebrew Bible presents the record of how God brought the Jewish people to be his priest, while holding that the "discoveries of scientific researches in [...] culture and history are not antagonistic to the doctrines of Judaism" even though the Bible itself does not know modern science.

Principle 3 posits that scripture's moral laws are eternally imperative.

Principle 4 indicates that ideas and rituals belonging to other ages are more likely to "obstruct" spiritual progress than help it. These include matters of diet, priestly purity and dress.

Principle 5 sees Judaism's "Messianic hope" as the "establishment of the kingdom of truth, justice and peace among all men." Jews are a religious rather than a national community, with no expectations of past rites of sacrifice or possession of territory.

Principle 6 states that Judaism is a "progressive religion," which means that it continues to purify itself in line with the "postulates of reason" as it seeks the "establishment of the reign of truth and righteousness among men."

Principle 7 holds that the human soul is immortal but that bodily resurrection, reward and punishment after death do not belong to Judaism.

Principle 8 states that Jews should work to resolve the "contrasts and evils" of modern society.

The Platform's characterization of Judaism brings it out from a religion narrowly concerned with its members and the idealization of its biblical past to a religion concerned with the breadth of humankind, pursuing concern for the well-being of others as the goal given it by God. This statement was broadly seen as an encapsulation of the beliefs reform-minded Jews had wrestled with across the nineteenth century. In hindsight, the most controversial part of the document lay in Principle 5, which rejected the notion that Jews should return to their homeland in "Palestine." This rejection of nascent Zionism was widely ignored after the Zionist Congress of 1897. While the document never became the equivalent of the Hebrew Bible or the Talmud, the principles it contained guided Reform Judaism to become the largest Jewish religious organization in the world.

The encounter between Judaism and modernity that led to Reform Judaism led also to the founding of the nondenominational Jewish Publication Society, which in 1917 published its English translation of the Hebrew Bible (*Tanakh*). This work, along with the 1985 new translation, has been the Bible version used by the vast majority of American Jews, their synagogues, and their biblical commentaries for over a century.

#10 Zionism—*The Jewish State*

After 1,200 years of Judaism based on the Babylonian Talmud, Jews were unprepared to become a nation in the realities of the nineteenth century. They continued to live scattered across the world and experience persecution—nor had the Messiah come to return them to the Promised Land. Not only did Jews need to gather together in a single location (Palestine would be preferable but it was not the only possibility that became available), Jews needed to constitute themselves as a "nation"; they needed to exhibit the features of nationhood: a shared culture, a shared language, and the shared institutions of education, governance, and law.

In Europe, the Talmudic Judaism that had united Jews for more than a millennium was losing its power as many Jews rejected it in favor of a secular education and life following the Enlightenment. Indeed, during the nineteenth century, many Jews seemed to have more in common with their non-Jewish neighbors than with their Jewish ones. Caught up in the appeal of nationalism, they wanted to be citizens of a nation, they began joining the ones in which they lived. In key ways, this is what Reform's Pittsburgh Platform aimed to help accomplish. At the same time, anti-Semitic discrimination continued to plague the relations between Jews and non-Jews.

Early Zionist writers called for a new possibility. Struggling with European anti-Semitism, they suggested that Jews gather together to regenerate a new Jewish culture. They called for an exit from Europe and the reunification of Jews in a new land. In 1896, Theodore Herzl composed a work named *The Jewish State*, calling for not just a new location for Jews to live but for the creation of a state—a nation that would enable Jews to join together to create a shared culture with other Jews rather than with non-Jews.

What made Herzl different from writers who went before him is that he matched his goals with actions. Just a year after the *Jewish State*'s publication, he convened the first Zionist Congress in 1897. This annual meeting brought together Jews from eastern and western Europe to discuss ways and means to implement a return to Palestine. Herzl used the backing he received by these congresses to pursue a diplomatic solution to finding a place, a land, a county where Jews could gather and call their own—although this approach had not succeeded by his early death in 1904 at the age of forty-four.

Herzl's *Jewish State* had two main sections. In the first, he discussed the Jewish Question and proposed Zionism as its solution, arguing that the anti-Semites would themselves help Jews move to a new Land, if only to get rid of Jews in their own. In the second section, Herzl laid out three institutions that Zionism should create to accomplish this move: a Society and a Company that would set up the mechanics of the transfer from Europe to the new Land and assist Jews in making that transition. The third element would be the local organizations, which would initially constitute groups of Jews moving from their current locations to the new Land, then taking the lead in creating settlements and building the institutions of the Jewish state.

Herzl's grand scheme was never put into place, but it inspired many Jews to become Zionists and make their way to Israel. Historical analysis of how Jews accomplished that migration and created the state shows numerous parallels to his ideas.

What does it take for a book to make the list of the Top Ten Jewish Books of all time? As we have seen: it has to have had an impact on Jews for decades or even centuries; it has to represent a movement; and it has to represent not just itself but numerous other written works. The ten works discussed above show the variety of works that have shaped Judaism from antiquity to today.

Further Reading and Online Resources

Ebeling, J., J.E. Wright, M. Elliott, and P.V.M. Flesher (2017), *The Old Testament in Archaeology and History*, Waco, TX: Baylor University Press.

Flesher, P.V.M. and B. Chilton (2011), *The Targums: A Critical Introduction*, Waco, TX: Baylor University Press.

Hertzberg, A., ed. (1997), *The Zionist Idea: A Historical Analysis and Reader*, Philadelphia: Jewish Publication Society.

Jewish Virtual Library (1998–2020), "Religion: Judaism." Available online: https://www. jewishvirtuallibrary.org/judaism (accessed November 16, 2020).

Neusner, J. (1986), *The Oral Torah: The Sacred Books of Judaism; An Introduction*, San Francisco: Harper & Row.

Neusner, J. (1994), *Fortress Introduction to American Judaism: What the Books Say, What the People Do*, Minneapolis, MN: Fortress.

Glossary Terms

Halakha The practices of Judaism. These rules or laws cover matters of worship and religion, civil law, social interaction, and relationships between the sexes. This term is a central concept of the Judaism created by the Rabbis after the Temple's destruction.

Kabbalah Jewish mysticism, commonly used to refer to mysticism from the medieval period onward.

Mishnah The first Jewish book composed after the Hebrew Bible to gain an authoritative status. Although not sacred, from the beginning of the third century CE it was seen as laying out how Judaism could be practiced and believed after the destruction of the Jewish Temple in Jerusalem in 70 CE. The first book composed by a nonbiblical group of religious authorities known as rabbis.

Rabbis The new category of religious authorities formed after the Jerusalem Temple's destruction in 70 CE. They replaced priests as Judaism's primary religious leaders.

Septuagint Translations of the Torah and the Hebrew Bible into Greek. These were first composed in the third century BCE. By the first century CE, they were widely used among Jews in the Greek-speaking eastern Mediterranean lands. Early Christianity adopted the Septuagint as its Old Testament.

Siddur The daily prayer book in Judaism.

Talmud The Babylonian Talmud forms a large elaboration of the Mishnah published about 600 CE by the Rabbis. It became the basis for Judaism for the next 1,200 years and today along with the Hebrew Bible constitutes one of Orthodox Judaism's two main religious texts.

Tanakh The Jewish acronym in Hebrew for the Hebrew Bible, essentially equivalent to the Protestant Christian Old Testament. This is Judaism's sacred scripture. The acronym stands for Torah, Neviim (Prophets), and Ketubim (Writings).

Targum Translations of the Hebrew Bible into Aramaic. These were read or recited in Sabbath and Holy Day worship during the centuries that and in the locations where Aramaic was the main language of Jews—that is, in Israel, Syria, and Mesopotamia in the first through seventh centuries CE.

Torah The first five books of the Bible, whether the Jewish Hebrew Bible (Tanakh) or the Christian's Old Testament. These are Genesis, Exodus, Leviticus, Numbers, and Deuteronomy. These were the first books Judaism identified as sacred and are read out loud consecutively in worship across the liturgical year.

4

The Jewish Library: The Hebrew Bible (TaNaKh) and Rabbinic Literature

Barry Scott Wimpfheimer

The earliest writing systems in the world were produced in Mesopotamia in the middle of the fourth millennium BCE. By the third millennium BCE there emerged two genres of ancient writing: myth and code. Pieces of the Epic of Gilgamesh, a composite poem that seems to have influenced both Homer's *Odyssey* and the biblical book of Genesis, date to the twenty-first century BCE. The epic is a work of historical fiction that narrates the literary life of Gilgamesh, who appears to have been an actual third millennium BCE king of Babylon. The poem features the bromance of Gilgamesh and the divinely created man-beast Enkidu, whose death sends Gilgamesh searching for Utnapishtim, survivor of the great flood, for the secret to eternal life. Both Enuma Elish, a Babylonian creation myth, and Atrahasis, an epic poem describing a great flood and its survival, have strong biblical parallels as well.

Seven different codes of law have survived from the Ancient Near East, most famously Hammurabi's Code. The earliest known code is one whose text doesn't survive: the code of Urukugina from 2350 BCE. The latest code in the group is a neo-Babylonian code from the seventh century BCE. The seven surviving codes have much in common with one another. Their shared style and the recurrence of certain specific and bizarre hypothetical cases cement the thesis that they reflect a shared scholastic culture, which transmitted these codes over at least a millennium and a half. Evidence indicates further that the law codes produced within this scholastic tradition were not employed as tools of practiced jurisprudence; their purpose was entirely a theoretical mapping of the cultural world.

FIGURE 4.1 *Hammurabi's Code.* Source: *Piece Yen Photography.*

The ancient Near Eastern environment was a polytheistic pagan one with writing systems commanded by scribes who were typically associated with either palace or temple. Though myths and codes proliferated, they were not productively combined. None of the mythic texts contain legal sections; though the legal codes sometimes have narrativizing prologues or epilogues, the disconnect between the style of these added materials and that of the codes themselves testifies to the unbridgeable gap between the practical casuistic law and the theoretical milieu of epic mythology.

The Hebrew Bible (also referred to as the Old Testament) is not a book but a library. This anthology consists of works that were written from the eighth century to the second century BCE. Beyond the consisting works, this library contains embedded material that is as old as much of the above referenced ancient Near Eastern material. Archaic mythic episodes embedded in the Hebrew Bible are likely from the second millennium BCE. Biblical law codes participate in the same intellectual tradition as those of the ancient Near East. Recent scholarship has asserted a direct connection between Hammurabi's code and the Covenant Code of Exodus 22.

The largest narrative of the Hebrew Bible is a story that can be gleaned from the corpus that begins with creation and continues through legendary ancestors until the birth of the nation Israel as a nation of slaves in Egypt. Miraculously departing Egypt, this group sojourns in the desert for forty years under Moses' leadership until finally entering the land of Israel under Joshua's direction. Once in Israel, the Israelites conquer and divide the promised land into tribal areas; the tribes are loosely federated. Israelite monarchy unifies all of Israel for a hundred years under the successive rules of Saul, David, and Solomon, but in 922 BCE the nation splits into a northern kingdom (Israel) and a southern one (Judea). Israel is routed by the Assyrians in 722 BCE while the Judeans survive as a kingdom until the Babylonian destruction of 587 BCE. The elite populations (royals, priests, writers, and rich) are exiled to Babylonia; a small delegation returns after the Persians conquer the Babylonians in 539 BCE. Judea is a Persian satellite until Alexander the Great conquers it in 332 BCE ushering in a long period of Greek cultural and political domination. The final work included in the library of the Hebrew Bible is Daniel, a book written around 165 BCE that talks in code using apocalyptic metaphors to describe the contemporaneous fight between the Maccabees and the Seleucid ruler Antiochus IV.

Though one can produce a narrative historiography that captures the story of the complete Hebrew Bible, the works in this library come from a variety of genres. In addition to historiography, the Bible contains a self-help genre (Wisdom Literature), law codes, a highly developed poetry collection (all of the speeches of the prophets plus the psalms and proverbs), and one work that resembles stoic philosophy (Ecclesiastes).

FIGURE 4.2 *Depiction of the Temple Mount as described by Josephus.* Source: *Getty Images.*

Even within narrative historiography, there are chronographies that simply list events and corresponding dates (1&2 Chronicles), works with linked episodic short stories (for instance the stories of Abraham in Genesis), and full-blown novellas (such as the Joseph story in Genesis). The Deuteronomistic Histories (biblical books Joshua, Judges, 1&2 Samuel, 1&2 Kings) were completed at least a century before the birth of Herodotus, the Greek historian often called "The Father of History."

Individual works of the Bible were produced by the literate elite and particularly by the professional class of scribes. As in the ancient Near East, these scribes were typically associated with temples or palaces and much of their intellectual production is tinged by these associations. The detailed instructions for offering temple sacrifices and initiating priests in the biblical book of Leviticus are an obvious case in point; the context of this work's production was certainly the temple and its intended audience was undoubtedly comprised of priests' and levites' awaiting instruction. The strong critiques leveled against the northern kingdom of Israel in 2 Kings make it likely that the Deuteronomistic Histories were produced by Judean scribes who were perhaps royally employed.

In addition to the monarchy and the priesthood, the Bible is heavily influenced by another social institution—prophecy. There is a strong historical record of prophets active from the ninth century to the fifth century BCE. These figures were poets who often produced public speeches that spoke on God's behalf to the people. Some such figures may have employed automatic speech or writing to allow God to flow through them with purported minimal agency on their parts. Some prophets associated with scribes who transcribed their words and preserved them for posterity. These scribes may also be responsible for some of the non-prophetic materials in the Bible library.

Jews traditionally divide the Hebrew Bible into three sections: Torah (literally, teaching), Nevi'im (literally, prophets), and Ketuvim (literally, writings). The Hebrew term for the bible, TaNaKh, is an acrostic composed of the first consonants (T,N,K) of the titles of these three sections. Torah is also called Pentateuch or five books of Moses; it combines the mythic origin story of Israel with a significant body of legal and ethical teachings some of which are presented in the form of an ancient Near Eastern law code. Nevi'im has two parts. The first part is the deuteronomistic histories, a royal historiography of Israel from entry into the land of Israel until the Babylonian destruction in 587 BCE. The second part are a set of prophetic speeches in three major works (Isaiah, Jeremiah, Ezekiel) and twelve minor works (the minor prophets). Ketuvim is the Bible's miscellaneous drawer with three different types of wisdom books, liturgical psalms, chronographies (1&2 Chronicles), apocalypses, and a form of historical fiction (Ruth, Esther). The finished works that populate the three respective sections (Torah, Nevi'im, and Ketuvim) appear in the Bible in rough chronological order of composition.

The diversity of the works of the Ketuvim testifies both to the flourishing of writing in the Second Temple period (c. 400 BCE–70 CE) and to coalescing notions of canonization and authority. When the Babylonian delegation returned to Judea in the late sixth century BCE it found a populace that had socially and culturally intermingled with neighboring primarily pagan populations. Jewish leaders expended energies teaching this population their culture from a book, the Torah. The import of that book and the disappearance of prophecy as a viable religious activity encouraged the ideologically minded to produce books. Some of these books survive as part of the Bible's library. Others were winnowed out of the Hebrew Bible but managed to stick in parallel libraries, such as the Egyptian Jewish Bible that became the basis of the Greek Septuagint, a translation project that began in the third century BCE, a century before some of the book of Daniel would come to be written.

The rising import of authorized works enticed authors in the Second Temple period to look for ways to establish the authority of their own works. Some authors chose to rewrite sections of the library that were already somewhat established as authoritative; we don't know if the aim was to supplant or supplement the originals with these revisions. Other authors opted to write their works under the pseudonym of a famous early biblical figure. Several books in the Hebrew Bible claim to be written by Solomon (Proverbs, Ecclesiastes, and Song of Songs). There are also books outside of the canon of the Hebrew Bible (The Wisdom of Solomon) that claim Solomon as author.

Both the rewritten bible and the pseudepigraphy are genres of literature with a clear hermeneutic relationship with earlier parts of the Bible. In addition to these two features, there is a highly developed degree of inner biblical exegesis in which one of the later books in the library (e.g., Psalms) interprets materials from some of the earlier books (e.g., Exodus). As direct lines of communication with God (i.e., prophecy) became increasingly unavailable, their function was gradually replaced first with the written production of new books (even those that claim to be older) and then with the creative interpretation of texts that have coalesced into a loose canon. Canonization is best understood in the Second Temple period as an organic process in which texts are added to the shelves of specific communities. Writers aspired to produce literature that found a space on the shelf. Readers mined those already on the shelf for relevant contemporaneous meaning.

The conflagration that stands behind the Jewish holiday of Hanukkah was an important political event that led to a degree of Jewish self-rule. It also highlights an important ideological clash. A generation after Alexander the Great's conquests of Judea and surrounding areas in 332 BCE, the Greek governance model shifted to an imperial one with regional headquarters. Judea is situated between the regional governments of the Ptolemies in Egypt and the Seleucids in Syria. Because of its central positioning, Judea occasionally found itself drawing attention from both sub-empires; it functioned as the rope in a global tug-of-war. Having lost a skirmish with the Ptolemies, Antiochus IV passed through Judea and looted its temple. Then, for reasons still not entirely understood, he rededicated the Jerusalem Temple to a pagan deity and banned certain Jewish religious practices on penalty of death. This ideological zealotry on behalf of paganism was met with an equal ideological response: individuals invented martyrdom by choosing to die rather than violate their religious principles, and the family of Mattathias known as the Maccabees engaged in guerilla warfare to pester and frustrate the stronger and better armed Seleucid army arrayed against them. The Maccabees exhausted the Seleucids and they eventually returned to Syria leaving the Maccabees in control of both the temple (the term Hanukkah refers to the rededication of the temple to the Jewish God) and (eventually) the region (Judea).

Though the Maccabees originated in an ideological battle in which they figured as anti-Hellenists, the Hasmonean dynasts who descended from the Maccabees and ruled from 165 BCE until 37 BCE manifest clear signs of Hellenization in their coins, their dress, and the education of their children. The story of the Hasmonean dynasty is a realpolitik soap opera in which individual members of the family cozied up to Seleucid leaders, rivals to the Seleucid throne and various aspirants to the Roman Empire to remain in power. Either power corrupted the ideological purity of the original Maccabees or, just as likely, their original fervor was a direct and polar response to Antiochus' attempt to suppress their way of life.

FIGURE 4.3 *A bust of Alexander the Great.* Source: *Bjørn Erik Pedersen via Wikimedia.*

While the political authorities were becoming Hellenized and increasingly Roman in their outlook, ideological zealotry reemerged with the development of new Jewish sects. These sects were active as early as the second century BCE, but almost all of our concrete information about the sects comes from the first century CE. The sects were communities of people (our evidence says almost entirely male) who adopted stringent beliefs and practices that emerged from intense investigation of their libraries of texts. Some of the adopted purities practices of these communities separated them from Jews of other sects and, especially, those of no specific sect. Disagreements between the sects about calendrical issues found the different groups celebrating shared holidays on different dates. Though there was some degree of Jewish self-rule during the Hasmonean period, the sects inherited a genre of apocalypse and its related theology, which anticipates an eventual world cataclysm and the ushering in of a post-mordial time. Increasingly, the separate existence of the different sects found them interpreting their apocalyptic days of judgment as producing a group of eventual End Time victors (the sectarians themselves) and losers (all non-members of the sect).

The Dead Sea Scrolls is an accidentally discovered library from a sect that separated itself to Qumran in the dry Dead Sea area and was decimated during the Jewish war with the Romans in 66 to 70 CE. One-third of the library is comprised of pieces of scrolls of books found in the Hebrew Bible. One-third are materials from extra-biblical work that was known to scholars before the archive's discovery. The final third of materials are remains from literary works that were unknown before their discovery. The documents are not marked differently to differentiate canonical from noncanonical books so it is possible that all of these materials were handled as sacred and authoritative materials. One of the apocalyptic writings in this collection refers to members of the Essene sect (the sect that occupied Qumran) as the "sons of light" and to other Jews as "sons of darkness." Another work, *Pesher Habaquq*, is a commentary to a biblical minor prophet Habaquq written by the leader of the Essenes, referred to as the "teacher of righteousness."

Pesher Habaquq is a commentary that turns the biblical work, written about events in the seventh century BCE, into an allegory that directly addresses world events in the first century CE. Similar allegorical turns were happening elsewhere in the Jewish interpretive world. Philo of Alexandria, a first-century Egyptian Jew who encountered his traditions in the Greek voice of the Septuagint, rails against extreme allegorizers who no longer adhere to the literal meaning of the text; Philo himself hardly sticks to the contextual meaning. Another sectarian and first-century Jew, the apostle Paul, would talk allegorically of a metaphysical circumcision of the heart in place of a physical circumcision of the body.

The Roman destruction of Jerusalem and its temple in 70 CE destroyed both the seat of Judean politics and the singular location in which religious people felt authorized to perform their cultic sacrificial worship. While royal and priestly ambitions were inseparable from Jerusalem and its temple, sectarian life could proceed somewhat along the same lines; now, though, the sects were operating in a massive cultural vacuum. The small sect that comprised early Christianity prior to the destruction of

FIGURE 4.4 *Wood engraving of the period of the Second Jerusalem Temple.* Source: *Public domain.*

the temple became a mass phenomenon after its destruction. The early church drew on Paul's messianic reinterpretations of Judaism in the direction of non-Jews to grow exponentially; in the fourth century CE Emperor Constantine converted to Christianity, which became the majority religion of the Roman Empire.

Rabbinic Judaism developed alongside and in parallel with Christianity. Like Christianity, Rabbinic Judaism can be characterized as a movement that broadened a sectarian model to include larger numbers of people. Through a scholastic movement that lasted from the first through the eighth centuries CE, the rabbis adapted their heritage, reinterpreting their traditions radically to create a portable religion no longer centrally imbricated in a single destructible site. Rabbinic Judaism employs the term Torah in a new way and produces Torah as the central cultural energy in a way that allows Torah to stand in for the missing temple. While Torah was defined above as the first section of the Hebrew Bible, for the rabbis Torah (literally, teaching) refers to the entire corpus of the Hebrew Bible as well as the traditional knowledge that was transmitted through non-written means. At times the rabbis talk of two Torahs, the written and the oral. Because of their scholastic origins, the rabbis emphasize scholarly textual study as the central religious activity; this study is simultaneously a form of knowledge production and a cultic practice. Ethics of the Fathers, one of the most historiographic of rabbinic texts, traces an uninterrupted line of Torah succession from Moses' receipt of the Ten Commandments (now referred to as "Torah") to the earliest pairs of rabbis including Hillel and Shammai who are said to have founded Rabbinic Judaism. The Rabbinic worldview that emphasized Torah led to a valuing of Torah study above all other religious activities and found the rabbis referring to themselves as heirs to the priests. During the period in which rabbinic literature was produced, the rabbis evolved from a sect to an organization aspiring to speak for all Jews; this aspiration was not yet fulfilled in reality—the rabbis did not yet have the institutional or suasive authority to speak for all of Judaism.

Rabbinic literature is produced in three genres: Midrash, Mishnah, and Talmud. Midrash, a highly creative form of biblical interpretation, can trace its genealogy back through first-century interpreters such as Josephus, Philo, and the Teacher of Righteousness, further back to rewritten biblical books, for instance Jubilees, and even further back to the practice of inner-biblical exegesis. Two exegetical innovations are the hallmarks of Midrash. The first is the habit of presuming the Bible a perfect text whose any redundancy (an extraneous word or even a letter) can be employed to produce new and contemporarily relevant meaning. The second is the practice of clarifying ambiguities in one biblical book through linkage with passages in other biblical books; this practice was employed despite the rabbis' awareness that the Bible is a library of books written in different genres at different times by different people. This second exegetical practice is the mechanism through which the rabbis established their canon of the Hebrew Bible. Their collective choice to include a work of literature within the matrix of possible linkable texts established the works that were inside and those that were outside the canon.

Because of their density of syntax, the Bible's legal texts commonly lent themselves to the search for Midrashic meaning through redundancy. In contrast, the Bible's narrative sections encouraged Midrashists to expand the narratives by exploring further plot points or the motivations of a character. Midrash was also the basis for synagogue sermons or homilies that used their tight structural requirements of connecting a passage from the Bible's writings section with the weekly reading from the Torah section that was the centerpiece of the service as a way of ritually unifying the Bible. The rabbis produced their works of Midrash orally; our earliest extant works of Midrash date from the third century CE; over thirty works of Midrash survive from the rabbinic period to modernity.

The scholastic practice of organizing life conceptually around law in the form of a code was common in the ancient Near East, reflected in some works of the Hebrew

FIGURE 4.5 *Synagogue of Beth Shearim, hometown of Rabbi Judah the Prince.* Source: *Getty Images.*

Bible and recapitulated within the Dead Sea Scrolls. In the wake of the destruction of the temple in 70 CE, individual rabbis continued this sectarian practice by producing legal rules for the religion. An individual rule or one rabbi's entire code can both be called a mishnah depending on the context. After five generations of separate rabbinic scholastic circles dotting the countryside, Rabbi Judah the Prince, a scholar politician who was the official Roman delegated patriarch of the Jewish community, arranged for the compilation of the definitive Mishnah. The Mishnah is an unusual legal code because it preserves multiple opinions that often directly contradict one another; this makes the Mishnah a difficult work to use to establish a final legal position. This unique character is best explained as a function of the decision to create a definitive Mishnah out of many earlier individual mishnahs; not wanting to decide between the positions, Rabbi Judah the Prince found it beneficial to preserve competing attributed opinions. Despite his inclusivity, the Mishnah omitted at least as many positions as it preserved. These were not immediately forgotten in the oral scholastic culture. Tosefta, a supplement to the Mishnah composed within its first generation of existence, combines these omitted positions as well as expansions and comments on statements in the Mishnah.

Both Mishnah and Tosefta are organized through a threefold organizational system consisting of orders, tractates, and chapters. There are six topical orders (Agriculture, Calendar, Family, Criminal and Civil Law, Sanctities, and Purities). Each order has as many as twelve individual tractates. For example, each holiday has a tractate in the order of the Calendar. The tractates are subdivided by thematic chapters. While Midrash is all about deriving ideas from the text of the Hebrew Bible, Mishnah articulates its ideas without justifying its positions either through logic or through reference to biblical verses.

Oral publication of the Mishnah had two profound effects on rabbinic scholasticism. First, it bifurcated the rabbinic period into two, with figures who lived before publication of the Mishnah (pl. *tannaim,* sing. *tanna*) considered more authoritative than those who lived later (pl. *amoraim,* sing. *amora*). Second, it reoriented the rabbinic curriculum. Scholars now prioritized the Mishnah as their central study texts and conducted conversations around it. Since the Mishnah does not provide justifications, these conversations often worked to unpack the basis for things found in the Mishnah. The live oral conversations around the Mishnah transpired in both rabbinic Palestine (present-day Israel) and rabbinic Babylonia (present-day Iraq). The rough minutes of these conversations were modified by later editors to become the talmuds.

The Palestinian Talmud, referred to in the Jewish tradition by the misnomer "Jerusalem Talmud," consists of four generations' worth of rabbinic conversations surrounding the Mishnah. These conversations include both Midrashic and mishnaic materials, often putting these two styles of scholarship in conversation with each other. This Talmud is much rawer than its Babylonian sibling; this lack of polish makes basic comprehension of the original meaning of the text a challenge. Compounding this problem is the fact that medieval scholars all but abandoned the project of producing a commentary on this talmud in favor of its more polished rival. Even today, basic matters of language and syntax are subject to debate.

The Babylonian Talmud consists of six generations of rabbinic conversations surrounding the Mishnah framed and annotated by a robust layer of unknown editors. While the Talmud regularly attributes individual teachings to specific rabbis by name, roughly one-third of the Babylonian Talmud is unattributed material that recent scholars have come to identify with the editorial layer of the text. This editorial layer organizes its inherited conversations into coherent sections and interprets the ambiguous part of its heritage. While the rabbis who inhabited Palestine (present-day Israel) bequeathed to the present many works of Midrash as well as the two mishnah-style works (Mishnah and Tosefta), the Babylonian Talmud is the only rabbinic document to emerge from rabbinic Babylonia. Its size and comprehensiveness dwarf its Palestinian sibling and are part of the reason it ultimately prevailed over the Palestinian Talmud.

The eighth-century Islamic conquest transformed Babylonia (present-day Baghdad) from a Zoroastrian Sassanian capital to an Islamic Abbasid one. The strong leadership of the Abbasid rulers contributed to the institutionalization of the young religion of Islam. Judaism became institutionalized alongside its Muslim sibling. The period 750–1000 CE is known in Jewish historiography as the period of the Geonim, leaders of large institutional academies in Baghdad. During rabbinic times, rabbinic learning happened informally on a local model in which individual charismatic instructors developed small and temporary followings. In the eighth century, these disciple circles grew into large and permanently structured institutions called "Yeshivot" (sing.

Yeshiva). At their height, these schools attracted as many as one thousand students from all over the Jewish world. The curriculum of the yeshivot was the Babylonian Talmud reinvented as a work of normative law. People from far flung areas would occasionally write to the Babylonian academies for religious direction and receive a reply called a *responsum* (pl. *responsa*) that would draw on the Babylonian Talmud to answer the question. For the past millennium, there has been a legacy of tension between theoretical and practical Talmud study. Some elite intellectuals have insisted on keeping the plural and unresolved nature of talmudic discourse while others, often motivated by political reasons, have continued to look to the Talmud to establish a normative vision of Judaism.

Because the Geonim were primarily interested in the Talmud for its law, an interpretive practice emerged whereby students in the academy focused on the legal materials (labeled *halakhah*) while glossing over the nonlegal materials (labeled *Aggadah*). This interpretive framework essentially divides rabbinic literature into two corpora—the legal and the nonlegal. Because the nonlegal is quite frequently narrative-related (either new stories or interpretations of biblical stories), the divide is often between law and story. Ironically, the post-rabbinic hermeneutic has returned the Jewish library to the ancient Near Eastern model of separate myth and code. One of the hallmarks of the ancient Jewish library, then, is its decision to unify and combine the legal with the mythological. This combination was originally innovated by the biblical writers and was preserved in new forms during the period of rabbinic Judaism.

Further Reading and Online Resources

Baumgarten, A.I. (2005), *The Flourishing of Jewish Sects in the Maccabean Era: An Interpretation*, Atlanta, GA: Society of Biblical Literature.
Berlin, A. and M.Z. Brettler (2004), *The Jewish Study Bible*, Oxford: Oxford University Press.
Cohen, S.J.D. (2006), *From the Maccabees to the Mishnah*, Louisville, KT: Westminster John Knox Press.
Collins, J.J. (2013), *The Dead Sea Scrolls: A Biography*, Princeton, NJ: Princeton University Press.
Hayes, C.E. (2011), *The Emergence of Judaism: Classical Traditions in Contemporary Perspective*, Minneapolis, MN: Fortress Press.
Kugel, J.L. (1997), *The Bible As It Was*, Cambridge, MA: Belknap Press of Harvard University Press.
Schiffman, L.H. (1991), *From Text to Tradition: A History of Second Temple and Rabbinic Judaism*, Hoboken, NJ: Ktav Publishing House.
Schwartz, S. (2001), *Imperialism and Jewish Society, 200 B.C.E. to 640 C.E.*, Princeton, NJ: Princeton University Press.
Wimpfheimer, B.S. (2018), *The Talmud: A Biography*, Princeton, NJ: Princeton University Press.

5

The Jewish Life Cycle

Elizabeth S. Berke

How Judaism Marks the Life Cycle

What is the function of religion but to give shape and context to life? Judaism guides Jews in relationship to food, time, and interpersonal and intimate relationships. It follows that Judaism would help in the personal cycle of one's life as well. From birth to death and occasions in between, Judaism's ritual ceremonies guide emotions, creating a pathway for celebration and mourning, and help usher Jews through the thresholds of life. Another way to think about these ceremonies is that they help formalize entrance into different life stages and purposes within the Jewish community, and at the end of life the rituals formalize our exit from the community, each moment sanctified with liturgy and communal elements.

Ritual observance in Judaism is along a continuous spectrum, which informs some of the ceremonial rites. Demarcation of these life events is also colored by one's Jewish ethnic community, which include, but are not limited to, Ashkenazi (Central and Eastern European), Sephardi (Iberian Peninsula), Eidot haMizrach (Arab), and African (Ethiopian and Ugandan). Each movement and ethnic grouping within Judaism has a unique approach to lifecycle events, but based around a common framework.

Welcoming of Babies

Judaism is a communal religion and as such, from the beginning of life, Jews have ceremonies that help the parents adjust to parenthood emotionally and spiritually, and welcome the baby into the community. These are personal events but also focus on immediate and the larger Jewish family, meaning the community in which the family lives and also the worldwide Jewish community. Historically, these ceremonies have been based on a gender binary. They are essentially naming ceremonies, but the naming for a boy also includes the physical element of ritual circumcision at eight days old (health concerns such as premature birth can delay the circumcision).

Naming of a Girl

In many Ashkenazic Jewish communities, baby girls are named as soon as possible at a service that includes the reading of the Torah (five books of Moses), which is read four times a week. In communities where women are limited in their participation in synagogue ritual, the father of the baby is honored with a blessing at the Torah, which is considered one of the highest honors. Sometimes the mother is not present at this celebration in these communities, as it may be the day after she has given birth. The father recites blessings and then a synagogue leader recites a blessing asking for a return to health for the mother and announcing the name of the baby girl.

In Sephardic communities, there are a variety of customs including *Zeved haBat* (gift of a daughter) where the father and grandfathers go to the synagogue on the first Sabbath after the birth to bless the Torah. After the final blessing, the entire congregation sings *Pizmonim* (songs) honoring the baby girl.

In Jewish communities where men and women participate equally (aka egalitarian Judaism), the naming practice for girls has changed. Most commonly the family waits until at least the eighth day, to mirror the time frame of a boy's initiation into the community, and often the family will wait until the thirtieth day or later.

Egalitarian naming ceremonies have taken many forms including both parents coming to the synagogue to bless the Torah and share stories about the name and the relative or relatives for whom the child is named, if applicable. Other families choose to have a ceremony outside of a synagogue service called a *Simchat Bat* (pronounced baht; celebration of a daughter) or *Brit Bat* (covenant of a daughter). This is a place of flexibility in the prayer texts, in contrast to the celebration of a baby boy. These celebrations may contain similar elements to the bris described below, minus any physical marking of the baby girl.

The Bris (Circumcision) Ceremony

The requirement of circumcision is based on the Torah passage from Genesis 17:9-12:

Elohim said to Avraham: And as for you, you must preserve My covenant, you and your descendants after you throughout their generations. This is My covenant which you must preserve between Me [*My Word*] and you, and your descendants after you: every male among you shall be circumcised. You shall circumcise the flesh of your foreskin. This shall be the sign of the covenant between Me [*My Word*] and you. At the age of eight days every male among you must be circumcised, throughout your generations.

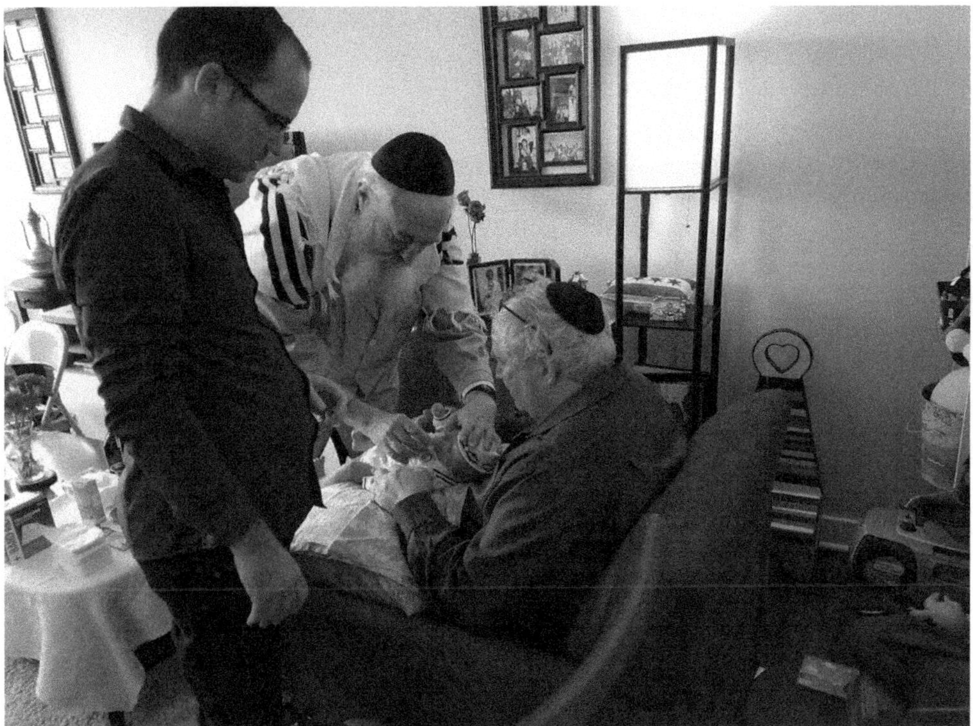

FIGURE 5.1 *The* moyel *readies a baby for circumcision on his grandfather's lap.* Source: *Photograph by author.*

In premodern Judaism, early Jews created a set ritual and liturgy for the circumcision ceremony, called a *brit*. Colloquially, the ceremony is called a Bris, which is a Yiddish/Ashkenazic pronunciation. The word brit/bris means covenant, and the performance of the circumcision enters the male child into the spiritual covenant created between God and Abraham and into the Jewish community.

There are multiple steps to a bris:

1 The community welcomes the baby stating. "blessed is the one who comes in the name of God." He is brought in by family or friends, sometimes called "godparents" but in Judaism this is not a role assigning lifelong commitment, it is an honorific for the ceremony.

2 The baby lays on a special chair called Elijah's chair. The Prophet Elijah is considered a protective presence at a bris.

3 The baby is given to the person who holds the baby during the circumcision, often a grandfather. Sometimes the ceremony takes place on a pillow on his lap, but others prefer the stability of a padded holder on a table.

4 The *mohel* (ritual circumcisor, *moyel* in Yiddish) recites a number of blessings and performs the circumcision, which is generally quick.

5   A parent holds the baby while reciting prayers over wine (a symbol of joy in Judaism), sanctifying the moment and announcing the baby's name and entrance into the covenant.

6   The parents may share the history behind the name(s), and grandparents and/or other close family and friends may play a special role in blessing the grandchild.

All of these ceremonies, for girls and boys, are followed by a special meal called a *Se'udat Mitzvah* (meal of celebration) that is intrinsic to the performance of the *mitzvah* (commandment). The Se'udat Mitzvah is a part of each joyous lifecycle event described.

Names in Judaism

Jews receive both secular and Jewish names. The secular name is in the lingua franca of the country in which the child is born, assuming it is outside of Israel (in Israel these names are one and the same since Hebrew is the spoken language). The Jewish name is in Hebrew, Yiddish, or **Ladino**. The Ashkenazi community commonly names after deceased relatives, while the Sephardi name after living relatives. Jews use these name at all lifecycle events to mark the transitional moment and address the person in front of the community in the context of their personal history. Individuals are known by their relationship to their parents. A person is referred to as: (Jewish name) son of (father's Jewish name), for example, Yitzchak ben Avraham, Isaac the son of Abraham. In egalitarian communities people add mother's names according to the preference of the individual so the name could be: Rachel bat Shalom v'Esther—Rachel the daughter of (bat) Shalom (father) and Esther (mother).

With the increasing need for nonbinary identification of gender, a person can be called by their Jewish name in this phraseology: Yael meebayt Avraham v'Sarah—Yael from the house of Abraham and Sarah, which takes gender identity out of the formula.

Pidyon HaBen *(Redemption of the First Born)*

In Exodus 13:13 the Israelites are commanded to redeem every firstborn son, and in Numbers 18: 15–16 there is clarification:

Redeem every first-born male among your sons –

Every firstling [all that open the womb] of every being which they offer before Adonoy—man or beast—shall be yours; but you must redeem the firstborn of man.. Its redemption—from a month old you should redeem them—the valuation is five silver *sela'im* of holy silver *shekalim* which is twenty *gerah*.

Families celebrate a Pidyon haBen when the first born is a son and is born vaginally. This ceremony is performed when the baby is a month old and requires the presence of someone descended from the *kohanim* (priests) that served when the Temple stood in Jerusalem. A son is redeemed from service in the Temple through a brief service that varies slightly depending on Sephardic or Ashkenazic lineage.

Sometimes the child enters the room on a silver tray that may be decorated with necklaces and other finery. The kohen asks the father if he would like to have his son or the coins, and invariably the father picks the son! In the Sephardic liturgy the mother is also asked to make sure this is her firstborn child and that she did not have a miscarriage prior to this birth. The ceremony itself is brief and ends with a blessing over wine and bread to begin the Seudat Mitzvah.

These welcoming ceremonies not only help a family make note of this special occasion but also they usher the baby into the immediate community in which the family resides and also into the larger, worldwide Jewish community. The community gathers around the new baby and parents, supporting them with meals and other assistance as necessary.

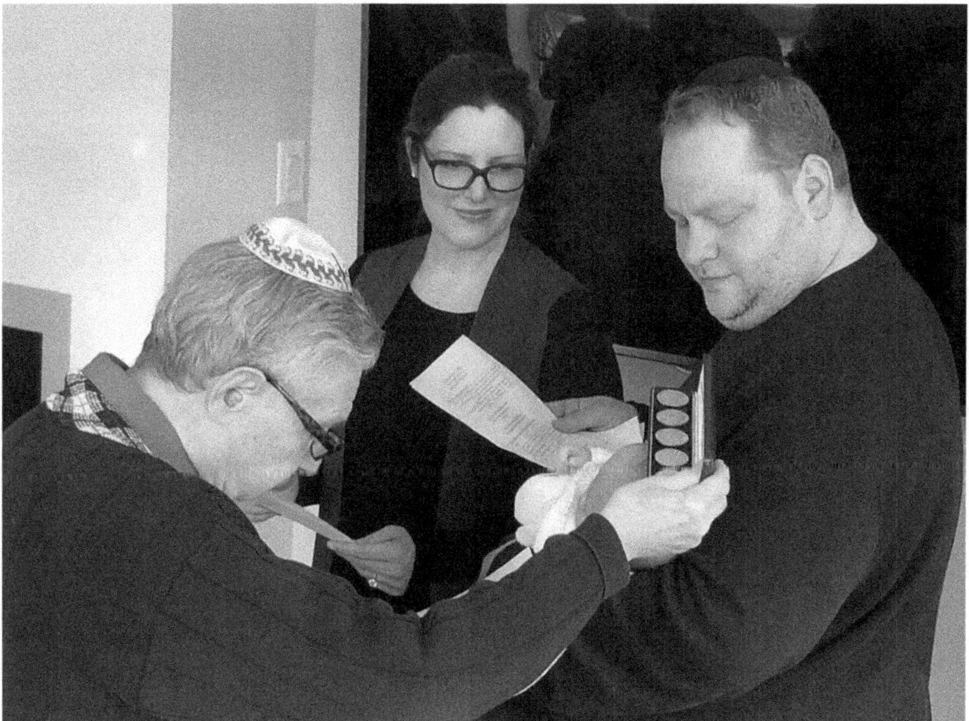

FIGURE 5.2 *A kohen holds five silver coins over the baby's head during the Pidyon HaBen ceremony.* Source: *Photograph by Aaron Zaretsky, father of the baby.*

Educational Milestones

The beginning of a child's education is momentous in the Jewish community. Historically, Jews gave children honey on their first day of school to associate sweetness with learning. There are ceremonies to mark the reception of a first *siddur* (prayer book) and other books of Jewish study. It is significant when a child learns many of the daily blessings, and Jews cherish the time when the youngest has the ability to chant the Four Questions at the Passover *seder* (ritual meal). It is also noteworthy when that individual is supplanted by a younger family member. Each of these learning accomplishments denotes a step toward full membership in the Jewish community, which is marked by becoming a Bar/Bat Mitzvah.

Coming-of-Age—Bar/Bat Mitzvah

In *Pirkei Avot* (Ethics of the Fathers 5:21), there is a teaching:

> At five years of age the study of Scripture; At ten the study of Mishnah; At thirteen subject to the commandments, etc.

Jewish communities formalized the idea that as one enters physical puberty, one is ready for spiritual connection and responsibility to the community in the religious sphere, and individual responsibility for one's actions. When a boy or girl reaches the age of thirteen or twelve, respectively, the boy is a *bar mitzvah* and a girl is a *bat mitzvah* (son or daughter of the commandments). People become a bar/bat mitzvah on the morning of their twelfth or thirteenth birthday without any ceremony necessary. It does not require pomp and circumstance and is not something that happens to you, though people do say "I was bar mitzvahed" at such and such synagogue, or such and such rabbi "bat mitzvahed me."

Through the ages, and especially in modern times, the bar/bat mitzvah ceremony and celebration have expanded. Previously, a boy would show his new role in the community by reading from the Torah scroll, reciting blessings, and giving a short lesson on the weekly Torah portion. This is the first age at which a person can be called to bless the Torah, which is a significant honor, and at its completion it is common to throw candy at the student to symbolize a sweet life ahead. This is also the first time a person can be counted in the *minyan*, the communal quorum (ten people) necessary to include particular prayers in a service. Additionally, the father or parents recite a short formula stating "Blessed is the One who has released me from the responsibility of this one." This is specifically referring to the need for making amends at *Yom Kippur* (Day of Atonement) and atoning for one's misdeeds. The bar/bat mitzvah is now responsible for the recitation of the prayers pertaining to making amends between him- or herself and God and for seeking forgiveness from those wronged.

From early on, Jewish communities have publicly celebrated a boy becoming bar mitzvah but the celebration of a girl becoming bat mitzvah, in communities that separate ritual life along gender lines, has only recently evolved into a more public celebration with teaching and possible leadership of a women's prayer service.

Current practice in egalitarian communities does not draw any distinction between the genders; the student participates in and leads many parts of the service. Outside of the service, students are involved in community projects to better the world as a way of showing their newfound responsibility to be an active participant in *Tikkun Olam* (repairing the world). Additionally, these occasions include a Seudat Mitzvah, from simple to lavish, based in family priorities and communal norms.

It is common for people to refer to a bar/bat mitzvah ceremony; however, it is a misunderstanding. The student is taking part in a service that would have all of the same elements if there were no one celebrating this event. The bar/bat mitzvah demonstrates his/her new status in the community through the performance of these rituals to show that they have reached a certain level of proficiency and can be a contributing member of the community in a ritual context. Ideally, they will regularly attend to be counted in the minyan, continue to lead services, chant Torah, and be involved with *tzedakah* (acts of righteousness).

FIGURE 5.3 *A young man chants from a Torah scroll to mark his becoming a bar mitzvah.* Source: *Susannah Gottlieb, mother of the bar mitzvah.*

FIGURE 5.4 *A young woman holds the Torah on the occasion of becoming a bat mitzvah.*
Source: *Shelli Aderman, mother of the bat mitzvah.*

Confirmation

In the mid-twentieth century Reform and some Conservative American congregations created Confirmation as a part of a teenager's experience. Sixteen or seventeen year olds have more volition in their Jewish experience, unlike the thirteen year old, who is often doing what is expected. At these ages, the students affirm their commitment to their Jewish identity since intellectually they are at a different level than when just beginning puberty. Jewish education continues in these communities post-bar/bat mitzvah, and students have a choice of classes, much like in a standard high school, but they are for a few hours one night a week or on Sunday mornings. The Confirmation ceremony may include a community project, musical performances, speeches, and worship leadership. Some communities mark the occasion with a trip to Israel.

Marriage

Depending on the community, the marriage process may start by working with a matchmaker, which is most common in traditional Jewish communities. The song "Matchmaker, Matchmaker" from *Fiddler on the Roof* is based on this aspect of Jewish life.

Upon engagement, Ashkenazi Jews may have a ceremony called a **Tenaim** (conditions), which begins the journey toward the many steps prior to the ceremony, along with the prayers and customs of the post-ceremony celebration. Couples in some Jewish communities may choose to do a portion or all of these elements. The language of this section will be based on a heterosexual couple getting married, but lesbian, gay, bisexual, transgender, queer/questioning, and other (LGBTQ+) Jews would celebrate their wedding in the same manner, adjusting the prayers to match the gender identity of the participants.

Before the wedding, an Ashkenazi couple is blessed during synagogue services with an **Aufruf**. Sephardic families celebrate after the wedding with a *Shabbat Chatan* (groom's Shabbat). Along with a blessing, the couple is showered with candy to ensure a sweet life together. Within a few days of the wedding the bride, and sometimes the groom, may visit a **mikvah** (ritual immersion pool) to mark the transition from life as an individual to life as a couple.

The day of the wedding is a day of introspection for the Ashkenazic bride and groom, and is often treated as a personal Yom Kippur with fasting and unique prayers. Some couples do choose to schedule a noon wedding if they do not want to fast all day! In contrast, in Sephardic custom the bride and groom are treated to a special meal. After the bride and groom are dressed they may each have a time to receive guests. The Ashkenazi groom has a **Tisch** (Yiddish for table, since it takes place around a table) and the bride has a room set aside to greet the female guests called **Kabbalat Panim** (literally, "receiving faces").

In Ashkenazi communities, the **ketubah** (contract) is signed prior to the ceremony while in the Sephardic world it is signed during the ceremony. Ashkenazi Jews also have a **Badeken** (literally, checking) where the groom veils the bride. After this, the couple is escorted to the ceremony by their parents, and possibly bridesmaids and groomsmen. While at the **chuppah** (wedding canopy) a groom may put on a *kittel* (white linen robe) to symbolize being in a state of purity and in a transitional moment of life. The Ashkenazi bride may circle the groom seven times before the ceremony starts, symbolically carving out the space for their life together. In egalitarian settings, the bride and groom may circle each other three times and then do a last circle around each other. Seven alludes to the creation story, since they are creating their new life together.

During the relatively brief ceremony, the couple stands under a chuppah and a clergyperson such as a rabbi and/or cantor chant blessings, read a portion or all of the ketubah, and facilitate an exchange of rings. The groom always gives a ring to the bride and it is generally an unadorned ring placed on the right index finger of the bride so it is easy for the witnesses who signed the ketubah to see the exchange. The bride does not always give a ring to the groom, but may do so. The wedding ceremony may have a brief talk in honor of the couple by the clergyperson and then they chant seven blessings which trace our history from the moment of creation to the redemptive time in Jerusalem, recognizing that with this union it is like a moment in the Garden of Eden and a glimpse into the hope of the future. The end of the ceremony is marked by the

FIGURE 5.5 *A couple signs their ketubah before their wedding ceremony.* Source: *Spencer Sanz, groom.*

FIGURE 5.6 *The rabbi speaks to a wedding couple under the chuppah.* Source: *Aaron Zaretsky, groom.*

breaking of a glass, which has many explanations, the most common being that even at times of our greatest joy we recall the sadness of the destruction of the Temples in Jerusalem. Some couples retain the shards of glass and put them in a ritual item in their home called a *mezuzah*, which goes on the doorposts of Jewish homes.

The Ashkenazi bride and groom leave the ceremony to joyous music and have some private time together called **yichud** (unity) while the guests start the Seudat Mitzvah. It is customary to entertain the bride and groom with dancing and various antics. The attendees dance the hora, a fast-paced circle dance, and may lift the bride and groom up on chairs. The meal ends with blessings, and a repetition of the seven wedding blessings recited during the ceremony. These blessings are accompanied by two cups of wine, which are mixed at the end. There is believed to be spiritual strength in this cup of wine and women hoping to get pregnant or people hoping to find a match will often take a sip.

In some communities, couples do not leave right away on a honeymoon. Instead, each night for a week they are hosted by a friend or family member for a festive meal celebrating the marriage and welcoming them into the community. The seven wedding blessings are repeated at each meal and it is customary to have guests at the meal who were not able to attend the wedding. This week is a week of transition for the couple and the community. The couple is creating its new identity as a unit, the families that are joined through the union continue to get to know each other, and the community takes time to welcome this new Jewish home into its midst.

Divorce

Should a couple decide the marriage needs to come to an end, there is also a Jewish way to divorce.

From Deuteronomy:

> If a man marries a woman and consummates with her; should she not find favor in his eyes because he found in her something lecherous, he is to write for her a document of severance and place [it] in her hand and send her from his home.
>
> (24:1)

Currently, this means that a *beit din* (court of three rabbis) is gathered along with a trained scribe to handwrite the writ of divorce. These documents are not created ahead of time like documents for baby namings or weddings, which can be fill-in-the-blank forms in anticipation of a joyous occasion. It is not assumed that there will be divorces, so each *get* (divorce document) needs to be created on the spot. Once the document is complete, it is delivered into the hands of the wife (based on the biblical text), who symbolically takes a few steps away from those gathered to mark the ending of the relationship. At the end of the movie *Hester Street*, available on YouTube, there is a scene depicting a Jewish divorce.

In some Jewish communities, you need a get to remarry, assuming both people are Jewish. The civil divorce is not sufficient to allow Jews to remarry other Jews. If a Jew was married to someone of another faith, then a get is not necessary.

Health and Healing

Praying for health is a common practice in Judaism. There is a prayer dedicated to asking for health in the daily individual prayers, recited three times a day and a prayer for healing recited when Jews read the Torah. It is common for people to send names to a synagogue to be read aloud, or for people to share the name during the service when they recite the prayer for healing.

Visiting the sick is a mitzvah. The rabbis teach that when you visit a sick person you relieve them of one-sixtieth of their illness and lift their spirits. Communities often have a committee dedicated to this mitzvah, who arrange for meals when someone is ill, and find ways to support the other family members.

Judaism informs people's choices around health care at the end of life. In general it is important to fill out advanced directives so doctors know your wishes and Jews may do so with Jewish law in mind. Jews will often consult their rabbi to determine a best course of action regarding a family member in a tenuous health situation. Sometimes prolonging medical care is only delaying death instead of increasing the chance for life, and this is an important consideration in Judaism. When death is imminent a clergyperson will come to the bedside and recite a confessional prayer along with other prayers.

Death and Mourning

Death in Judaism has three stages: taking care of the body, burial, then taking care of the mourners. Burial generally occurs as quickly as is reasonable in the Jewish community, there are no wakes or open caskets. Jews do not embalm and in some communities Jews do not cremate. The body is ritually washed by a special group of people called the *chevra kadisha* (holy society). This is thought to be the highest order of mitzvah because the person for whom you are performing the mitzvah cannot repay you. After cleansing, the body is dressed in simple white linen shrouds that mimic the clothing the high priest wore in the Temple. In death we are all as holy as one another. It is common for some earth from the land of Israel to be put in the casket, but in general, Jews are not buried with possessions except for perhaps their prayer shawl. Many opt for a simple casket, there is the concept of a "plain pine box" that is upheld in many communities, but in practice one sees more ornate and polished caskets. In Israel, the body is wrapped in shrouds and put in the ground. Until burial, in many communities, the body is not left alone. People will stay with the casket at the funeral home reciting psalms.

A Jewish funeral can take place at a funeral home, in a synagogue, or at the graveside. In Ashkenazi custom, prior to the beginning of the funeral a family gathers with clergy and performs a ritual called *k'riah* (tearing or rending). In some communities, the mourners literally tear a garment to symbolize the upheaval in their life. In other communities, a black pin with a short black ribbon is worn, which they tear. Sephardi custom is to do the tearing after the burial. The mourners wear the torn garment or the pin for up to a week after the funeral to symbolize their status as mourners. Jews rend their garment on the left side, near the heart, when a parent has died and on the right side for a sibling, spouse, or child. While we all mourn for aunts, uncles, cousins, grandparents, and other family members, Jews only follow the associated laws of mourning for their closest relatives. There are exceptions in cases where a grandparent or aunts and uncles have effectively been a parent and these moments invite consultation with a rabbi.

The funeral ceremony is very basic, consisting of a few psalms, a eulogy, and then a memorial prayer that mentions the name of the deceased. If the funeral begins away from the cemetery, Jews escort the body with pallbearers into the hearse. At the cemetery, as the coffin is brought to the grave, there is additional chanting of psalms and texts, as well as when the casket is lowered into the ground. With the words "God gives, God takes, may God's name be praised" the clergy places some earth into the grave and the family and guests participate in the burial of the casket, another mitzvah that is held in highest regard. Jews bury in a unique fashion, using the back of a shovel for the first scoop of earth to indicate that we are not in a hurry to bury our deceased. After the burial, the family stands for the first recitation of what is called the Mourner's **Kaddish** (sanctification).

The community cares for the mourners when they leave the grave by creating two lines and offer words of comfort: "may the One who gives comfort, comfort you among the mourners of Zion and Jerusalem." The guests escort the mourners back to their home for a Meal of Consolation that has been prepared by members of the community. It is customary to wash one's hands when leaving a cemetery, and there is often a pitcher of water and a washing cup placed outside the home for those who have attended the burial. Upon entering the home, they light a candle that will burn for seven days.

For the week after the burial, a period of time called *shiva* (seven), the community cares for the family of mourners. The mourners are not concerned with appearance, which means they cover mirrors, do not get haircuts, do not wear makeup, men do not shave, and the general atmosphere in the home is subdued with no music or entertainment. The mourners may sit on low chairs or stools and spouses refrain from sexual intimacy. Morning and evening services are often held in the home so the family can recite the Mourner's Kaddish, and the community provides meals for the family. The community comes to the home at specified times to offer comfort and share reminiscences, which people refer to as "going to shiva" for an individual.

On the morning of the seventh day, after the first service, the family "gets up from shiva" by taking a short walk outside of the home (in some instances, a family may only observe three days of intense mourning). It may be the first time they have left the home other than to attend the synagogue for Sabbath services (when shiva is suspended). This transition marks the end of the most intense time of mourning and people return to work and begin to integrate back into daily life as they are comfortable. This transitional time continues for twenty-three (or twenty-seven) more days, making a total of thirty days (*sh'loshim*) where the individual attends the synagogue daily to recite the Mourner's Kaddish, males refrain from shaving, and mourners do not participate in entertainment and attending joyous events, buy new clothes, or get a haircut. At the end of thirty days, Jews are done with the outward signs of mourning for a spouse, a sibling, or a child and may visit the grave. If one is mourning a parent, the mourning period continues until eleven months have passed. For all deaths, at the first anniversary of the death and all years after that on the anniversary of the death (in the Ashkenazi world this is called *yahrzeit*), Jews light a candle that burns for a day and go to synagogue to recite the Mourner's Kaddish. At the first yahrzeit, if it has not already happened, Jews have an unveiling, a short ceremony where they go to the grave and reveal the headstone. It is customary to leave a small stone at a Jewish grave to mark that someone has come to remember the person. Flowers are not a part of Jewish burial customs; keeping the memory alive is attained through donating to a cause that was important to the deceased or dedicating your own time to such an organization, and attending *yizkor* (memorial service), which happens four times a year, in addition to the annual memorial.

Conclusion

Throughout a Jew's lifespan, Judaism offers ceremonies and prayers to help individuals, families, and communities navigate life's milestones and channel the associated emotions, both expected and unexpected. These rituals and ceremonies provide grounding in what can be a chaotic world, and they provide a well-worn path so the community knows how to respond to times of sadness and joy. Through the lifecycle commemorations, Jews grow closer to their communities and the larger Jewish family, signifying their transitions from one life stage to the next. Jews become tied to the generations past, who have marked their personal journeys in the same way, and they provide a link in the chain to the future.

Further Reading and Online Resources

BimBam (2020). Available online: https://www.bimbam.com/ (accessed November 16, 2020).

Diamant, A. (2017), *The Jewish Wedding Now*, New York: Scribner.

Jewish Celebrations (1998–2020), "Home Page." Available online: http://www. jewishcelebrations.com/ (accessed November 16, 2020).

Marcus, I.G. (2004), *The Jewish Life Cycle*, Seattle: University of Washington Press.
My Jewish Heritage (2002–20). Available online: https://www.myjewishlearning.com/ (accessed November 16, 2020).
Wolfson, R. (2008), *A Time to Mourn, A Time to Comfort: A Guide to Jewish Bereavement*, Woodstock, VT: Jewish Light Publishing.

References

Correspondant, J. (1996), "Pearls, Henna and Challah: Sephardic Nuptial Customs," *The Jewish News*, November 8. Available online: https://www.jweekly.com/1996/11/08/pearls-henna-and-challah-sephardic-nuptial-customs/ (accessed August 28, 2019).
Harlow, J., ed. (1985), *Siddur Sim Shalom*, New York: The Rabbinical Assembly.
Kaufman, M. (1992), *Love, Marriage, and Family in Jewish Law and Tradition*, Northvale, NJ: Jason Aronson.
Kushner, H. (1993), *To Life: A Celebration of Jewish Being and Thinking*, Boston: Warner Books with Little, Brown and Company.
Nussbaum Cohen, D. (2018), "Historic Rituals for Welcoming Jewish Daughters," *My Jewish Learning*. Available online: https://www.myjewishlearning.com/article/welcoming-jewish-daughters/ (accessed August 21, 2019).
Pirkei Avot (2013), trans. Dr. Joshua Kulp. Available online: https://www.sefaria.org/Pirkei_Avot.5?ven=Mishnah_Yomit_by_Dr._Joshua_Kulp&lang=bi (accessed August 7, 2019).
Sefaria (n.d.), "A Living Library of Jewish Texts," with Onkelos translation. Available online: https://www.sefaria.org/?home (accessed November 16, 2020).

Glossary Terms

Aufruf (Pronounced Oof-ruf)—the couple is blessed during a synagogue service. In a community that divides ritual life along gender identification, the groom (*chatan*) is called to bless the Torah and a special blessing is said over him and his bride (*kallah*). Often candy is thrown to symbolize a sweet future together. Sometimes this is a week before the wedding, and then the bride and groom will not see each other again until just before the ceremony. In egalitarian settings, both the bride and groom bless the Torah together and receive a blessing together.

Badeken At the end of the Tisch, the groom is escorted to the bride with song and he checks to make sure he has the correct bride. This is based on the biblical story of Jacob who intended to marry Rachel, but woke up with Leah since she was the older daughter and it was customary to have the older daughter marry first. She was heavily veiled at the time of the ceremony, and it was dark in their shelter at night. He did not know he had the incorrect sister. Standard practice today is that the groom witnesses the veiling of the bride himself before the ceremony, and it is another opportunity when blessings are recited over her and the couple. This is often a time when the bride and groom sign the Ketubah themselves.

Chuppah ("ch" in Hebrew is not pronounced like "ch" in Charlie; it is pronounced in the back of the throat, as if you are trying to clear your throat) A wedding canopy that is open on four sides. The chuppah can be made of a variety of materials including flowers, a prayer shawl (*tallit*), or a quilt with squares made by family and friends. It symbolizes the home the couple will have together and how it is open to the community in the tradition of our ancestors Abraham and Sarah, who always welcomed guests.

Kaddish A piece of liturgy in Aramaic (Aramaic was the spoken language at one time) that praises God and is part of all prayer services, often multiple times. The mourners mark the end of the funeral and all daily services by reciting this text, which calls upon the congregation to bless God's name. It is an honor in Judaism to lead the congregation in prayer, and when it includes phrases that bless God it is particularly special. Mourners are given this honor to uplift their souls and the soul of their departed family member.

Ketubah A marriage document that is a contract between the couple. There are different versions, which are dictated by communal norm. It is signed by two witnesses, often before the ceremony in the presence of at least the groom, and perhaps the bride. Sephardi Jews often have the Ketubah signing during the marriage ceremony itself. In the most traditional sense, the Ketubah provides protection for the bride and assures her shelter and sustenance. There is a standard text in Aramaic that many communities use, but other communities opt for modified versions and texts that include an interpretive English translation or addendum. Many couples opt for custom-made documents with artistic renderings around the text, which they will display in their homes. These become personalized meaningful works of art that encapsulate the couple's journey to that day.

Ladino While Yiddish is a language comprised of German, Polish, and Hebrew, along with local dialects, and was spoken as a colloquial language among Ashkenazi Jews of Central and Eastern Europe, Ladino is a combination of medieval Spanish, Portuguese, and other Latin-based dialects along with Hebrew and was spoken by Sephardic Jews. Both languages are being preserved academically and in small segments of the Jewish community.

Mikvah Water is a transitional element in many religions, and Judaism is no exception. The Mikvah is a ritual pool of water into which people immerse on their own to mark transitions in life. In Judaism it is used for conversion, and some immerse before Shabbat every week, or before certain holidays or traveling to Israel. It can also be used ritually after recovery from illness, or as part of recovery from abuse or other trauma. A bride and groom immerse in a mikvah (not at the same time) to mark this momentous occasion in their lives—from life as a single person to now intertwining one's life with someone else in marriage. Couples visit the mikvah usually in the few weeks prior to the wedding, if not the week of the wedding.

Tenaim The conditions upon which the marriage is based may be formally written or verbal, and often a plate is broken by the two mothers or parents of the engaged couple to state that there is now a bond between the two families, and if anything should break, it is a simple plate. The tenaim celebration can take place well ahead of the actual wedding ceremony at an engagement party, or on the same weekend as a precursor to the ceremony.

Tisch/Kabbalat Panim In traditional communities, men gather in one room with the groom, which is the *Tisch*. The groom may try to teach a lesson of Torah, but there is often interruption by singing (and alcohol). While this is occurring, the women are gathered in another room to bestow blessings upon the bride, or receive blessings from the bride at her *Kabbalat Panim*. The bride sits on a chair that is meant to be a throne, and people approach her for blessings. A bride is believed to have great spiritual power, and if someone is hoping to find a match or start a family, a blessing from a bride is thought to help with a positive outcome. In egalitarian settings, some couples opt for these brief pre-wedding gatherings or modify them to their liking.

Yichud The time the bride and groom spend alone together, separate from the rest of the wedding celebration. In Ashkenazi custom, this happens right after the ceremony and it is an honor to be the one to guard the door of the room. In some Jewish communities, it is the first time the bride and groom are alone together and is the first opportunity for them to even hold hands, let alone kiss. It is also when they break their fast (other than the wine during the ceremony). In Sephardi custom, yichud happens after the reception.

6

The Jewish Calendar: Celebrating a Jewish Year

Alyssa A. Henning

The Jewish Calendar: An Overview

On November 28, 2013, the first day (and second night) of the eight-night Jewish holiday of Hanukkah coincided with the United States' Thanksgiving holiday. This unusual overlap, playfully dubbed "Thanksgivukkah" by some, was a coincidence of Hanukkah falling on the earliest day possible, while Thanksgiving, celebrated on the fourth Thursday of November, fell on the latest day possible (Cole 2013). Of course, according to the Jewish calendar, Hanukkah wasn't early; it was right on time: the 25th day of the month of Kislev, the same as every year.

Unlike the ubiquitous **Gregorian calendar**—a solar calendar based on the earth's orbit around the sun—the Jewish calendar is lunisolar: the Jewish year is based on the earth's orbit around the sun, while Jewish months follow the moon's cycle. A Jewish year has twelve months, each lasting 29–30 days. Adding a thirteenth "leap" month to seven out of every nineteen years ensures that Jewish holidays continue to fall during the appropriate season (Robinson 2000: 77).

Initially, the change from month to month in the Jewish calendar was based on direct observation of the new moon in Jerusalem—and Jewish communities outside of Jerusalem waited for messengers' official word that the month had changed (Robinson 2000: 79; Segal 2009: 278–9). Early rabbis added a second day to the **diaspora**'s observance of many Jewish festivals to accommodate the uncertainty of waiting for calendar news to travel from Jerusalem—a practice still observed in North American Orthodox and Conservative Jewish communities today (Robinson 2000: 79–80). But by the fifth century CE, as the center of rabbinic intellectual life shifted from Jerusalem to present-day Iraq, rabbinic authorities introduced the standardized Jewish calendar still used today (Segal 2009: 279).

Another important difference between the Jewish and Gregorian calendars is that the days of the Jewish calendar begin at sundown and end at the following sundown. This is based upon a rabbinic interpretation of the creation story found in Genesis 1:1–2:4; this story, which describes God's creation of the world over seven days, repeatedly states, "and it was evening, and it was morning" before declaring that a day had passed (Robinson 2000: 39).

This chapter provides an overview of many of the holidays that make up the Jewish liturgical year. It includes a general overview of each holiday's significance and examples of how North American Jews celebrate each holiday. This chapter describes Rosh Hashanah, Yom Kippur, Sukkot, Shemini Atzeret/Simchat Torah, Hanukkah, Tu B'Shevat, Purim, Pesach/Passover, Yom HaShoah, Shavuot, and Tisha B'Av.

Rosh Hashanah

The Jewish New Year is called Rosh Hashanah (literally, "the head of the year") and takes place on the first day of the month of Tishrei. Many North Americans celebrate Rosh Hashanah for two days, although Reform Jews usually only observe one day. In addition to marking the New Year, Rosh Hashanah marks the beginning of the Days of Awe leading up to Yom Kippur, the Jewish Day of Atonement. Common Rosh Hashanah observances include attending special services at synagogue, eating symbolically significant foods, and the ritualized blowing of the shofar made from a ram's horn; (see Figure 6.1).

Synagogue services for the first and second days of Rosh Hashanah are nearly identical, but the community reads a different portion of the Torah on each day. In most congregations, the Torah portion for the first day is Genesis 21:1–34, which describes the celebration following the birth of Abraham and Sarah's son Isaac. Isaac's birth is particularly momentous because his mother, Sarah, was infertile and because she gave birth to him when she and Abraham were already very old, suggesting God's hand in Sarah's pregnancy and Isaac's birth. The passage also details the banishment of Hagar, Sarah's servant and Abraham's concubine, and Ishmael, Abraham and Hagar's son. When Hagar and Ishmael run out of water, Ishmael nearly dies, but an angel of God reassures Hagar that Ishmael will grow to become a great nation, and a well of water miraculously appears. The Torah portion for the second day of Rosh Hashanah is Genesis 22:1–24, which is traditionally known as *Akedat Yitzhak*, or the binding of Isaac. This passage describes God's command that Abraham take his long-awaited and promised son, Isaac, to a mountaintop to offer Isaac as a sacrifice. In a dramatic moment, as Abraham pulls his arm back to slaughter his son with a knife, an angel calls out to stop Abraham from killing Isaac. When Abraham looks up, he sees a ram caught in a nearby thicket and offers that ram as a sacrifice to God instead. The ritual blowing of the shofar evokes images of the ram—and of God's reprieve.

One important Rosh Hashanah ritual is *tashlich*. During *tashlich*, Jews throw small pieces or crumbs of bread into flowing bodies of water. The bread represents sins

FIGURE 6.1 *Shofar.* Source: *Wikimedia/Creative Commons.*

committed during the previous year; throwing the bread into the water is an act of symbolically casting off those sins before the new year (Robinson 2000: 95).

Many Rosh Hashanah traditions involve eating special, symbolically significant foods. Jews eat apples dipped in honey to symbolize hopes for a sweet year ahead and round challah bread (instead of the braided challah loaves made for Shabbat). Many Jews include fish heads on their Rosh Hashanah table to symbolize the "head" (literally, "rosh") of the year and evoke Deuteronomy 28:13, in which the Israelites are told that if they follow God's commandments, God will make them "the head and not the tail." Many Jews also eat "new fruits," or fruits they have not eaten for a long time, to celebrate the new year (Jacobs n.d.).

Yom Kippur

The ten days following Rosh Hashanah are known as the "Days of Awe." These are days for reflection, during which Jews are encouraged to engage in acts of *teshuvah*—repentance—to make amends with others they have wronged during the past year. These days culminate with Yom Kippur, the Jewish Day of Atonement, on the 10th of Tishrei. Jews traditionally observe Yom Kippur by attending services in synagogues and fasting from sundown to sundown. Many not only abstain from eating and drinking, but also from wearing leather shoes, bathing, wearing makeup or perfume, or having sex on Yom Kippur (Robinson 2000: 98; Segal 2009: 288).

After eating a final pre-fast meal, many Jews begin their Yom Kippur observance by attending the Kol Nidre service at synagogue. Kol Nidre means "all vows" and refers to the opening words of the Aramaic legal formula sung at the beginning of the service (Robinson 2000: 98). This legal formula annuls all religious vows, and as Eliezer Segal explains, "during the medieval era, the ceremony was inserted at the beginning of the evening service, because of the widespread fear that divine forgiveness might be impeded by the fact that people might inadvertently have failed to fulfill all their vows" (2009: 288). The earliest liturgical versions of this formula date back to the early ninth century CE and annul all unfulfilled religious vows made in the previous year, but in the twelfth century CE, many congregations adopted a modified version of the formula that annuls all unfulfilled religious vows that may be made in the coming year (Plotkin 2012). Sephardic Jewish congregations—those who trace their traditions back to the Iberian Peninsula prior to the 1492 expulsion of Jews from Spain—typically use the original formula; Ashkenazi congregations—those who trace their traditions back to medieval eastern Europe—typically use the twelfth-century version; Sephardic and Ashkenazi congregations also recite Kol Nidre to different tunes (Phillips 2016).

Many Jews spend most of the following day at the synagogue in prayer. The Yom Kippur liturgy includes multiple recitations of a type of prayer called *vidui*, or confession. *Vidui* prayers include alphabetical lists of transgressions, with one transgression for each letter of the Hebrew alphabet. These prayers are written from a collective perspective, and they are recited communally, symbolizing the community's collective responsibility for each other's transgressions. In many Jewish communities, it is customary to gently beat one's fist over one's heart as a sign of repentance when each transgression is read aloud (Kohn n.d.).

The final Yom Kippur service, which traditionally takes place during twilight, as the holiday and its fast draw to a close, is called *Ne'ilah*. *Ne'ilah* represents Jews' final chance to offer prayers and pleas to God before the close of this holy day, and the tone of the service is often marked by a sense of urgency. In many synagogues, congregants remain standing for the entire *Ne'ilah* service. This service concludes with a final long blast from the shofar. After services, Jews break their fast with a festive meal (Robinson 2000: 100).

Sukkot

The holiday of Sukkot, the "festival of booths," begins on the 15th of Tishrei and lasts for eight days. The holiday's name is the plural form of the Hebrew word *sukkah*. *Sukkah* means "booth" or "tabernacle." To celebrate this holiday, many Jews build and decorate a *sukkah*—a booth-like, temporary structure—in their yards. The *sukkah* evokes the tradition of the temporary structures in which Jewish tradition says the Israelites dwelled as they followed Moses in the wilderness after leaving Egypt. During

Sukkot, many Jews eat their meals in a *sukkah* to fulfill the commandment to "dwell" in a *sukkah* during the festival.

A sukkah can have anywhere from two and a half to four walls, and a *sukkah's* roof, or *sh'khakh*, is made from cut tree branches and/or leaves. The *sh'khakh* must include gaps through which people in the *sukkah* can see the stars. Because Sukkot was historically associated with the fall agricultural harvest, fruits and vegetables are a common motif for *sukkah* decorations (Strassfeld, Siegel, and Stassfeld n.d.).

Hospitality is an important theme in Sukkot observance. Jews welcome family, friends, and neighbors to share meals in the *sukkah*. Additionally, many Jews observe the practice of inviting *ushpizin*, honored figures from Jewish biblical tradition, into the *sukkah* (Robinson 2000: 104). The traditional list of seven *ushpizin* consists of Abraham, Isaac, Jacob, Joseph, Moses, Aaron, and King David (104). Today, Jews modify that list in numerous ways. **Lubavitch** Jews also welcome seven **Hasidic** leaders as *ushpizin*, and others welcome prominent women from the biblical tradition, such as Sarah, Rachel, Miriam, Esther, and Ruth into the *sukkah*. More contemporary examples of historically significant *ushpizin* welcomed into the *sukkah* include astronaut Judith Resnick, US Supreme Court Justice Ruth Bader Ginsburg, and songwriter Debbie Friedman (Kogen n.d.).

Another central Sukkot ritual involves the "four species." The four species consist of an *etrog* (citron), *lulav* (date palm), *hadas* (myrtle), and *aravah* (willow); Jews also use the term *lulav* to refer to a single ritual item consisting of one date palm leaf, two willow branches, and three myrtle branches (Robinson 2000: 105). Many Jews will perform the ritual of "taking" the four species each day of Sukkot. This ritual involves saying a blessing over the *etrog* and *lulav* (see Figure 6.2), and then holding the four species together while shaking them, in outstretched arms, in six directions to symbolize God's **omnipresence**: "outward in front of them [...] to the right, over their shoulders behind them, to the left, towards the sky, and then towards the earth" (106).

Multiple interpretations of the four species' symbolic significance exist. According to one tradition, the four species represent four types of Jews:

> The *etrog*, which has both smell and taste, is the ideal Jew, one who studies Torah and performs *mitzvot*. The palm has good-tasting fruit but no fragrance; it is like a Jew who studies Torah but performs no good deeds. The myrtle has a good fragrance, but no taste; it resembles a Jew who does good deeds, but doesn't study Torah. And the willow, which has neither taste nor fragrance, is like a Jew who neither studies nor keeps the *mitzvot*. All four of these Jews are [...] an essential part of the Jewish community, even the unbelieving, nonpracticing one. When they are united, each makes up for the shortcomings of the others.
>
> (Robinson 2000: 106–7)

Another interpretation associates each of the four species with a different body part, highlighting the embodied experience of celebrating Sukkot, and the human body's

FIGURE 6.2 *A* lulav, etrog *case, and* etrog. Source: *Wikimedia/Creative Commons.*

integrated functions. According to this interpretation, the palm represents the spine, the myrtle represents the eyes, the willow represents the lips, and the *etrog* represents the heart (Siegel n.d.).

Shemini Atzeret/Simchat Torah

The eighth and final day of Sukkot is called Shemini Atzeret. In Reform congregations, Shemini Atzeret's celebration is combined with celebrating Simchat Torah, while other congregations celebrate Simchat Torah the day after Shemini Atzeret (Robinson 2000: 109). Simchat Torah literally means "the rejoicing of the Torah"; it marks both the completion of one annual Torah-reading cycle and the immediate beginning of another. When congregations gather at synagogue for Simchat Torah, members will dance with the Torah scrolls and parade them around the sanctuary in seven *hakafot*, or circuits (Segal 2009: 285). Another Simchat Torah tradition in many synagogues is to unfurl an entire Torah scroll, so that the congregation sees the entire Torah encircling the sanctuary. On Simchat Torah, the Torah-reading service includes the last portion of the book of Deuteronomy, immediately followed by the first portion of the book of Genesis, signifying the ongoing cycle of reading the Torah year after year.

Hanukkah

The eight-day festival of Hanukkah begins on the 25th day of Kislev and ends on the 2nd day of Tevet. From a religious perspective, Hanukkah is a minor holiday, historically celebrated primarily at home (rather than in synagogue). Hanukkah is also one of only two Jewish holidays discussed in this chapter that is not mentioned in the Tanakh, or Jewish Bible.

Hanukkah commemorates the military victory of the Maccabees, a band of Jewish zealots and warriors, over the Seleucid (**Hellenized** Syrian) army of Antiochus IV Epiphanes in the second century BCE. Antiochus outlawed many Jewish religious practices during his reign; during this time, his army burned Torah scrolls, forced Jews to violate kosher dietary laws and eat pork to show their loyalty to Antiochus, and forbade Jews from practicing circumcision or celebrating Shabbat (Scheindlin 1998: 37). In 167 BCE, Antiochus converted the Jewish Temple in Jerusalem into a pagan shrine and desecrated the altar by offering pork as sacrifice (Scheindlin 1998: 37). The word "Hanukkah" literally means "rededication," a reference to the Maccabees' rededication of the Temple in Jerusalem to the Jewish God in 164 BCE.

Hanukkah is celebrated by lighting candles in a nine-branch candelabra called a *chanukkiah* (see Figure 6.3). On the first night of Hanukkah, they light two candles: once candle to signify the first night of Hanukkah, and the *shamash*, or assisting candle. On each successive night, another candle is added to the *chanukkiah's* candle count, until all nine candles are lit on the final night of Hanukkah. "The candles are placed in their holders from right to left, then lit from left to right, so that the latest addition is placed last but lit first" (Robinson 2000: 114).

Traditional Hanukkah foods include fried *latkes* (potato pancakes) and *sufganiyot* (fried jelly doughnuts). Foods cooked in oil are significant because of the role oil plays in a Talmudic story about Hanukkah's significance; that same story also explains the significance of lighting Hanukkah candles. According to the story, which appears in tractate Shabbat in the Babylonian Talmud, when the Seleucids desecrated the Temple, they broke the high priest's seal on all but one of the containers of oil used to keep the Temple's lamp lit, rendering those containers impure for ritual use. When the Maccabees reclaimed the Temple, they found the single sealed bottle of oil—enough to keep the lamp lit for one day. But according to the story that single bottle of oil miraculously lasted for eight days (Rubenstein 2002: 27).

Another common Hanukkah tradition is playing with a *dreidel*, a four-sided spinning top with the Hebrew letter *nun, gimmel, hey*, or *shin* written on each side (see Figure 6.4). The letters serve as an acronym for the phrase *nes gadol haya sham* (a big miracle happened there), referring to the miracle of the long-lasting oil. The letter on each side of the *dreidel* also indicates the consequences of different *dreidel* spins. If the *dreidel* lands with the letter *nun* facing up, then "nits" (Yiddish for "nothing") happens. If the *dreidel* lands with the letter *gimmel* facing up, then the player who spun the *dreidel* collects "ganz" (Yiddish for "everything") from the gambling pool. If the *dreidel* lands with the letter *hey* facing up, the spinner collects "halb" (Yiddish for "half") of the

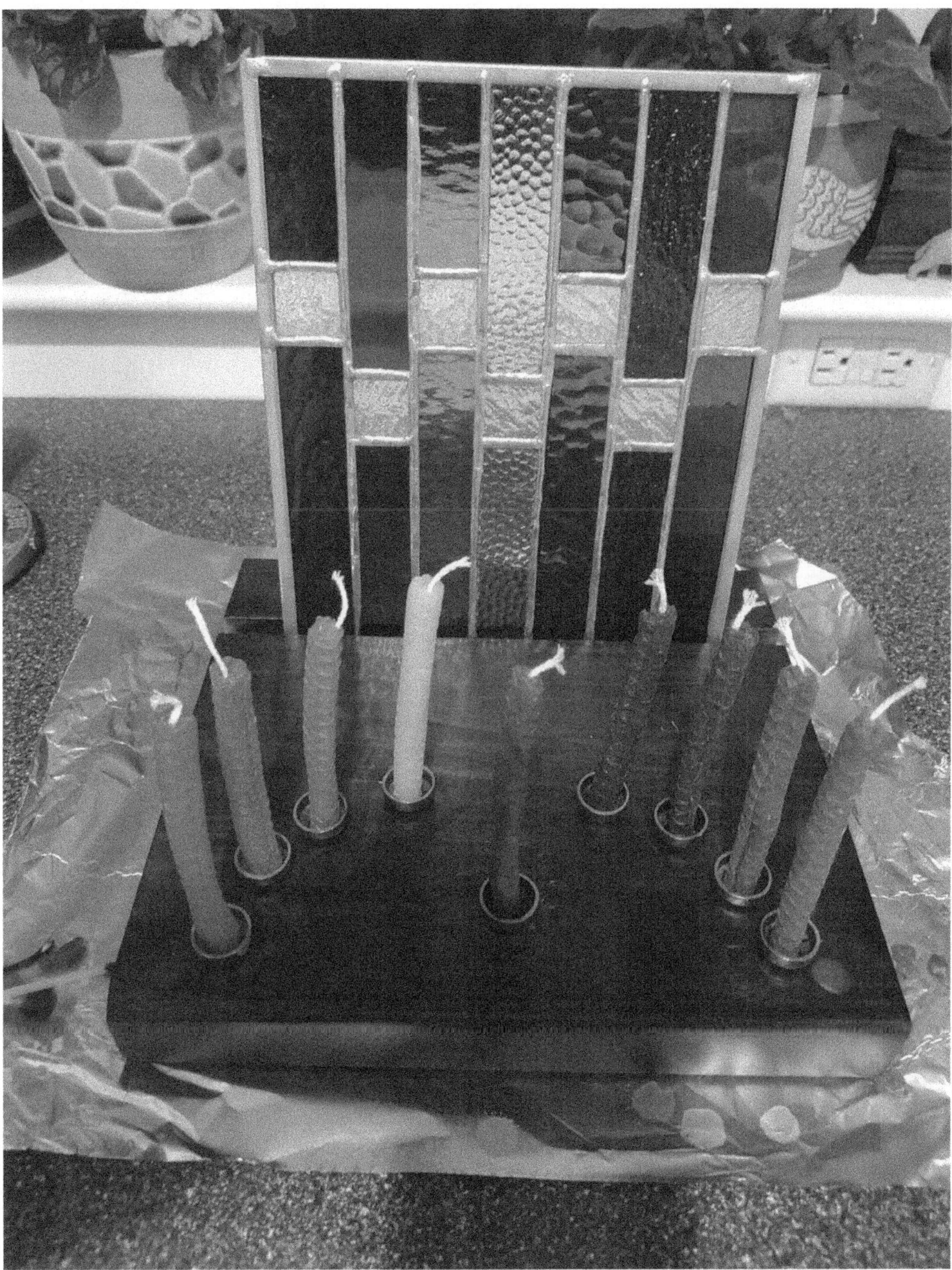

FIGURE 6.3 *A* chanukkiah *with candles ready for the final night of Hanukkah.* Source: *Author.*

gambling pool, and if the dreidel lands with the letter *shin* facing up, then the spinner is required to "shtell arein " (Yiddish for "put some in")—to pay into the gambling pool. *Dreidels* in Israel, however, have the letters *nun*, *gimmel*, *hey*, and *pey*, for "nes gadol haya po," or "a great miracle happened *here*" (Robinson 2000: 115).

Ironically, a relatively minor holiday about a resisting assimilation has itself been assimilated into the commercialized Christmas season in the contemporary United States—due in large part to Hanukkah's calendrical proximity to Christmas. Historically, Jewish children received only very small tokens of money on Hanukkah, but during the late twentieth century, Hanukkah became synonymous with gift-giving. To combat the fear that Jewish children would be wooed by the trappings of their friends' and neighbors' Christmas trees with piles of presents from Santa beneath them, a not uncommon approach—exemplified in comedian Adam Sandler's 1994 classic, "The Chanukah Song (Part I)"—emphasized that Jewish children celebrating Hanukkah get

FIGURE 6.4 *Dreidel.* Source: *Author.*

eight nights of presents, in contrast to a single day of presents for children celebrating Christmas. Another example of the commercialized Christmas season's influence over US Hanukkah celebrations is *The Mensch on a Bench*, a 2013 children's book and accompanying stuffed toy modeled on the 2005 Christmas children's book *The Elf on the Shelf*.

Tu B'Shevat

The holiday that falls on the 15th day of Shevat is called Tu B'Shevat, because the number fifteen is signified by the Hebrew letters *tet* and *vav*, pronounced together as "tu." The holiday marks the "New Year of the Trees" and in ancient Israel, the date served to help calculate tithes on orchard fruits (Robinson 2000: 115–16). Much like Hanukkah, Tu B'Shevat is a minor holiday that has gained significance in the context of the United States as a means of connecting Judaism to environmentalism. For example, many Jewish children plant trees on this day. Another, newer tradition, with roots in fifteenth century kabbalistic Tu B'Shevat practices, is to have a Tu B'Shevat *seder*. The Tu B'Shevat *seder* includes four cups of wine, representing the four seasons: one cup, symbolizing winter, contains only white wine; another cup, with a 50/50 mix of red and white wine, signifies spring; the third cup, which is 75 percent red wine and 25 percent white wine, symbolizes summer, and the final cup, which contains red wine with just a drop of white wine in it, represents autumn (Hazon 2006: 6).

Purim

The Jewish festival of Purim falls on the 14th day of the month of Adar (or the 14th day of Adar II in leap years). The holiday connected to the story told in the biblical book of Esther, which is set in the city of Shushan in the Persian Empire. According to the story, when Esther wins the favor of King Ahashveros and becomes his queen, she keeps her Jewish identity hidden (the Hebrew letters in the name "Esther" are also the root letters of the Hebrew word for "hide"). Meanwhile, her cousin and guardian, Mordecai, becomes a thorn in the side of the king's minister Haman, whose dreams of personal grandeur are repeatedly thwarted. Haman's frustration with Mordecai spills over into full-blown anti-Semitism, and Haman devises a plan to get the king to decree a day when the kingdom will massacre the Jews. The holiday's name, "Purim," is devised from Haman's casting of "lots" (literally, "purim") to select the date—the 13th of Adar—for the Jews' destruction. When Esther reveals her Jewish identity to the king, and explains that Haman's plans to massacre the Jews will also result in Esther's death, the king Ahashveros reverses his decree and executes Haman instead. The 14th of Adar becomes "the feast of Esther" to celebrate the Jews' survival. Purim is a lighthearted, revelrous holiday. Jews celebrate by dressing up in costumes; many synagogues hold

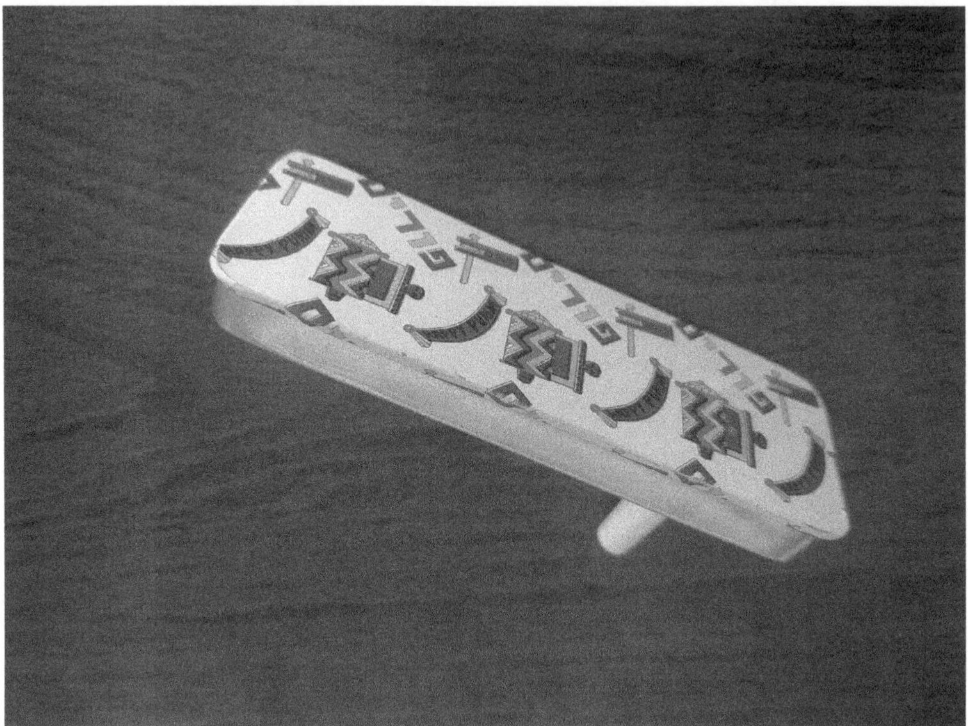

FIGURE 6.5 *Grogger.* Source: *Author.*

Purim carnivals. Public readings of Megillat Esther, the scroll (book) of Esther, involve audience participation: the congregation cheers whenever Mordecai's name is read aloud and boos and shakes noisemakers, called groggers (see Figure 6.5), whenever they hear Haman's name. Another Purim tradition is the performance of a *Purimspiel*, or Purim play, a satirical or parody theatrical performance (Robinson 2000: 117).

Perhaps the most well-known Purim food is Hamantaschen (literally, "Haman's pockets"), triangular cookies with fruit, chocolate, or poppyseed fillings (Robinson 2000: 117). A common children's song for Purim connects Hamantaschen to a triangular hat that Haman supposedly wore. Hamantaschen are often included in *mishloach manot*, gift baskets sent to friends and family in celebration of Purim.

Pesach: Passover

Pesach, or Passover, begins on the 14th day of Nissan (Segal 2009: 280). In North America, Reform Jews observe Passover for seven days, while other Jews observe the holiday for eight days. Pesach commemorates the story of the Jewish people's exodus from slavery in Egypt, and most of the rituals involved in celebrating this holiday connect symbolically to the Torah's narratives about Moses ultimately leading the Jews into freedom and the wilderness. Throughout the holiday, Jews traditionally abstain from eating leavened foods (called *chametz*), such as bread. Instead, *matzah*, an unleavened flatbread resembling a large cracker, is eaten. *Matzah* offers a symbolic connection to the exodus story, according to which the Hebrew slaves had to flee Egypt so suddenly that there was no time to wait for dough to rise; instead, they made quick-baking unleavened bread for their journey (Robinson 2000: 120).

The central Passover ritual is the *seder*, a special meal held on the first two nights of the holiday. *Seder* is Hebrew for "order," and the meal is called a *seder* because various prayers and blessings must be said, and certain foods must be eaten, in a specific order during the meal. A book called a *haggadah* contains the seder "program"; the *seder* has fourteen main steps (Robinson 2000: 121–2).

During the *seder*, Jews place a *seder* plate, which contains space for six symbolic foods, on their table. Those six foods are:

1   *charoset*, a mixture of apples, nuts, and wine symbolizing the bricks made by Hebrew slaves;

2   *maror*, a bitter herb, usually horseradish, symbolizing the bitterness of life as a slave;

3   *zeroah*, a lamb shank bone, symbolizing the lambs sacrificed the night before the Angel of Death brought the tenth and final plague upon the Egyptians;

4   *karpas*, a green leafy vegetable, such as parsley, symbolizing spring, the season of the Passover holiday;

5   *beitza*, a roasted egg, symbolizing the paschal sacrifice Jews used to offer at the Temple in Jerusalem to celebrate Passover, and the rebirth of the Hebrew slaves as free people; and

6   *chazeret*, a second bitter herb, often romaine lettuce; like *maror*, *chazeret* symbolizes the bitterness of life under slavery.

The *seder* plate has become a common site for ritual innovation. For example, some Jews replace the shank bone with a beet, for a vegetarian *seder* plate, and some also replace the egg with an avocado pit for a vegan *seder* plate (Kornfeld 2010: 52). In 2013, the Jewish organization T'ruah, in partnership with the Coalition of Immokalee Workers, encouraged Jews in the United States to place a tomato on their *seder* plates to raise awareness about and show solidarity with agricultural workers, especially in Florida, where they were subject to exploitative labor conditions and human trafficking (Coalition of Immokalee Workers 2013; Kahn-Troster 2013).

Perhaps the most widespread innovation involving the *seder* plate began in the late twentieth century. At this time, many added an orange to their *seder* plates to acknowledge women's role in the Passover story and their inclusion as full participants in Jewish life (Ochs 2007: 79) (see Figure 6.6). A common explanation for the origin of this tradition is a legend about a male rabbi who claimed that "women had as much place on the *bimah* [pulpit] as oranges do on the seder plate"

FIGURE 6.6 *A seder plate, including an orange.* Source: *Wikimedia/Creative Commons.*

(79–80). But Susannah Heschel, the Jewish feminist scholar who claims to have originated the custom of the orange, clarifies that she actually began this practice to show solidarity with lesbian, gay, bisexual, transgender, queer/questioning, and other (LGBTQ+) Jews (Heschel 2018). She relates that her inspiration came in the 1980s, after reading through a feminist *haggadah* written by Oberlin students; that *haggadah* included a tradition of placing a crust of bread on the *seder* plate in response to a story about a young woman whose rabbi told her that "there's as much room for a lesbian in Judaism as there is for a crust of bread on the seder plate" (Heschel 2003: 73–4). Heschel felt inspired by this story but sought a replacement for the bread crust because "including bread on the seder plate destroys Passover—it renders everything *chametz*. And its symbolism suggests that being a lesbian is transgressive, violating Judaism, which is not true" (74). Heschel chose an orange instead, to symbolize "the fruitfulness for all Jews when lesbians and gay men are contributing and active members of Jewish life" (74).

Yom HaShoah

In 1951, Israel first observed the 27th day of Nissan as Yom HaShoah, or Holocaust Remembrance Day, an official day to commemorate the six million Jews murdered by the Nazis during the Holocaust (Robinson 2000: 128). Throughout the United

States, many Jews mark Yom HaShoah in synagogues. Some common Yom HaShoah observance practices include reciting the Mourners' Kaddish prayer for the six million Jewish Holocaust victims and lighting six *yahrzeit* (memorial) candles to collectively memorialize them (128).

Shavuot

The Hebrew word "Shavuot" literally means "weeks," a fitting name for a holiday that comes exactly seven weeks after *Pesach*. Shavuot falls on the 6th day of Sivan, fifty days after Passover. When the Temple still stood in Jerusalem (i.e., prior to 70 CE), Shavuot was a pilgrimage holiday for which Jews brought offerings from their barley and wheat crops to the Temple. After the Temple's destruction, Shavuot's significance was reinterpreted based on rabbinic tradition that Shavuot coincided with the date when God gave the Torah at Mount Sinai (Segal 2009: 283).

Unsurprisingly, Torah study is an integral part of how Jews celebrate receiving the Torah at Mount Sinai. In many communities, Jews will stay up very late studying the Torah together on Shavuot. Reform synagogues typically hold their congregation's confirmation ceremony on Shavuot. Reform Jews may choose to pursue confirmation when they are approximately fifteen years old. Grounded partly in the idea that at twelve or thirteen years old, a child's decision to study for their bar mitzvah or bat mitzvah reflects their parents' commitment to Judaism more than their own, and partly as an effort to ensure that Reform Jewish teens' engagement with synagogue life does not end with their bar mitzvah or bat mitzvah, confirmation study is supposed to represent the teenager's conscious choice to embrace Judaism and the Torah. It is, therefore, symbolically significant to publicly recognize the culmination of teens' confirmation studies on Shavuot, when Jews celebrate the Jewish people's commitment at Sinai to follow God's Torah.

Jews usually eat foods made with dairy, such as cheesecake, blintzes, or bourekas, on Shavuot. Explanations for this tradition abound. One common explanation draws on biblical references to the land of Israel as a land flowing with milk and honey. According to another, eating dairy is a way to recreate the first meal after receiving the Torah at Mount Sinai: the newly received Torah included dietary laws, including laws about animal slaughter, and none of the meat available back at camp had been prepared according to those laws. Preparing a dairy meal took less time than slaughtering more animals and preparing a meal from that meat (Koppelman Ross n.d.).

Tisha B'Av

Tisha B'Av, the ninth day of the month of Av, is a Jewish day of mourning and fasting. The day commemorates the destruction of both the First and Second Temples in Jerusalem, by the Babylonians in 586 BCE and the Romans 70 CE, respectively (Robinson 2000: 131). The day's liturgy includes the biblical book of *Lamentations*, which is set against the backdrop of the First Temple's destruction and the Babylonian exile that followed (132). George Robinson notes, "by a hideous series of historical coincidences […] this midsummer day has seen some of the darkest moments in Jewish history" (132). Those calamities include:

- the massacre of York, England's Jews in 1190;

- a royal decree banishing all Jews from England in 1290;

- the deadline for Jews to leave Spain under royal expulsion order in 1492; and

- the beginning of Nazi transport of Warsaw's Jews to the Treblinka death camp in 1942.

Although Orthodox and some Conservative Jews in the United States have consistently observed Tisha B'Av as a Jewish fast day, many Reform Jews remain unfamiliar with the day and its religious significance. However, quite recently, some Reform and unaffiliated Jews have begun to mark Tisha B'Av through marches and vigils that connect the traditional lament for Jewish historical tragedies to contemporary atrocities, particularly in the United States. For example, in 2016, the Jews of Color Caucus of Jews for Racial and Economic Justice (JFREJ) held a Tisha B'Av rally in New York opposing systemic violence against African Americans and in solidarity with the Black Lives Matter movement; approximately three hundred people participated in that rally (Dizard 2018). In 2018 and 2019, the Jewish human rights organization T'ruah organized rallies and vigils across the United States to protest US immigration policies of separating immigrant families at the US–Mexico border. More than a dozen actions took place in 2018; in 2019, that number grew to more than fifty (T'ruah n.d.).

Further Reading and Online Resources

Is It a Jewish Holiday Today? (n.d.), Available online: http://www.isitajewishholidaytoday.com (accessed November 16, 2020).

Pogrebin, A. (2017), *My Jewish Year: 18 Holidays, One Wondering Jew*, New York: Fig Tree Books.

Strassfeld, M. (1993), *The Jewish Holidays: A Guide and Commentary*, New York: HarperCollins.

Waskow, A.O. (2012), *Seasons of Our Joy: A Modern Guide to the Jewish Holidays*, Philadelphia: Jewish Publication Society.

References

Coalition of Immokalee Workers (2013), "A Tomato on the Seder Plate …," March. Available online: https://ciw-online.org/blog/2013/03/a-tomato-on-the-seder-plate/ (accessed February 10, 2020).

Cole, D. (2013), "Thanksgivukkah Is Rare Mash-Up of Thanksgiving and Hanukkah," *National Geographic*, November 23. Available online: https://www.nationalgeographic. com/news/2013/11/131124-thanksgivukkah-thanksgiving-hanukkah-calendar-turkey-potatoes/#close (accessed February 8, 2020).

Dizard, W. (2018), "Hundreds of Jews March for 'Black Lives Matter' in New York," *Mondoweiss*, August 12. Available online: https://mondoweiss.net/2016/08/hundreds-lives-matter/ (accessed February 10, 2020).

Hazon (2006), *Tu B'Shvat: Hazon's Seder and Source Book*. Available online: http://hazon. org/wp-content/uploads/2011/06/Haggadah.pdf (accessed November 6, 2019).

Heschel, S. (2003), "Orange on the Seder Plate," in S.C. Anisfeld, T. Mohr, and C. Woodstock Spector (eds.), *The Women's Passover Companion: Women's Reflections on the Festival of Freedom*, 70–7, Woodstock, VT: Jewish Lights Publishing.

Heschel, S. (2018), "An Orange on the Seder Plate," *The New York Times*, April 2. Available online: https://www.nytimes.com/2018/04/02/opinion/orange-seder-jews.html (accessed February 10, 2020).

Jacobs, J. (n.d.), "Rosh Hashanah Customs: How to Celebrate the Jewish New Year at Home," *My Jewish Learning*. Available online: https://myjewishlearning.com/article/rosh-hashanah-customs/ (accessed February 10, 2020).

Kahn-Troster, R. (2013), "Why I'm Putting a Tomato on My Seder Plate," *New York Daily News*, March 24. Available online: https://www.nydailynews.com/opinion/tomato-seder-plate-article-1.1296337 (accessed February 10, 2020).

Kogen, L. (n.d.), "The New Ushpizot: Planting a Vineyard," *Women's League for Conservative Judaism*. Available online: http://wlcj.org/resources/resources-for-members-and-friends/seasonal-materials/the-new-ushpizot-planting-a-vineyard/ (accessed November 4, 2019).

Kohn, D. (n.d.), "A Guide to Yom Kippur Prayers," *My Jewish Learning*. Available online: https://www.myjewishlearning.com/article/prayer-services-for-yom-kippur/ (accessed February 10, 2020).

Koppelman Ross, L. (n.d.), "Why Dairy on Shavuot?" *My Jewish Learning*. Available online: https://www.myjewishlearning.com/article/why-dairy-on-shavuot/ (accessed November 5, 2019).

Kornfeld, M. (2010), "Super Seder: Mark the Start of Passover with a Delicious Vegetarian Feast," *Vegetarian Times*, March: 50–3. Available online: http://www.myrakornfeld.com/pdfs/Vegetarian_Times_Mar10_Seder.pdf (accessed November 24, 2019).

Ochs, V.L. (2007), *Inventing Jewish Ritual*, Philadelphia: Jewish Publication Society.

Phillips, L. (2016), "Kol Nidre: All Vows and One Haunting Melody," *Reform Judaism.org*, October 11. Available online: https://reformjudaism.org/blog/2016/10/11/kol-nidre-all-vows-and-one-haunting-melody (accessed February 10, 2020).

Plotkin, H. (2012), "Kol Nidre's Conundrum," *Tablet Magazine*, September 24. Available online: https://www.tabletmag.com/jewish-life-and-religion/112181/kol-nidre-conundrum (accessed February 10, 2020).

Robinson, G. (2000), *Essential Judaism: A Complete Guide to Beliefs, Customs, and Rituals*, New York: Atria.

Rubenstein, J.L. (2002), *Rabbinic Stories*, Mahwah, NJ: Paulist Press.

Scheindlin, R.P. (1998), *A Short History of the Jewish People: From Legendary Times to Modern Statehood*, New York: Oxford University Press.

Segal, E. (2009), *Introducing Judaism*, 1st edn., New York: Routledge.

Siegel, R. (n.d.), "Lulav and Etrog Symbolism," *My Jewish Learning*. Available online: https://www.myjewishlearning.com/article/lulav-and-etrog-symbolism/ (accessed February 10, 2020).

Strassfeld, M., R. Siegel, and S. Strassfeld (n.d.), "How to Build a Sukkah: Instructions for the Do-It-Yourselfer," *My Jewish Learning*. Available online: https://www.myjewishlearning.com/article/how-to-build-a-sukkah/ (accessed November 4, 2019).

T'ruah (n.d.), "Tisha B'Av: Jews Say #CloseTheCamps," *Truah.org*. Available online: https://www.truah.org/solidarity-with-immigrants-on-tisha-bav-2/ (accessed February 10, 2020).

Glossary Terms

Diaspora The term initially referred to the Judean communities living outside the territory of Judea after the Babylonian Empire exiled Judean elites from their homeland in 587 BCE. After the exile ended in 539 BCE and the exiles were allowed to return to Judea, some Judeans chose to remain outside the territory of Judea, establishing a permanent diasporic community that retained Judean traditions. Today, the term Diaspora is often used to describe Jews living outside of Israel. The term diaspora is now also used more generally to refer to any community living outside of an ancestral or traditional homeland.

Gregorian calendar The most widely used calendar today, and is likely the calendar with which readers are familiar. The calendar is named for Pope Gregory XIII, who introduced the calendar in the late sixteenth century CE. This calendar divides a 365-day year into twelve months, and adds an extra day to the month of February in leap years, which generally fall every four years.

Hasidic A form of Judaism that emerged in Ukraine and spread throughout eastern Europe in the eighteenth century CE. It was a popular movement among poorer and less educated socio-economic classes, because it emphasized the redemptive intention behind the everyday observance of Torah commandments over elite and intellectual Talmud study. Early Hasidic leaders, such as the Ba'al Shem Tov (or Besht), were charismatic rebbes, known for their storytelling and healing abilities rather than learned rabbis trained in the minutiae of Jewish law.

Hellenized Hellenization refers to the cultural influence of Ancient Greece, particularly on the territories conquered by Alexander the Great. In the context of Jewish history, Hellenization is especially relevant for understanding the stories surrounding Hanukkah's origins: Antiochus IV Epiphanes' Seleucid army was a product of Hellenization, and Antiochus tried to force the Jewish people to further Hellenize their own practices and give up Jewish rituals like kosher dietary laws, circumcision, and Torah study.

Lubavitch A subset of Hasidic Jews who trace their founding to Rebbe Shneur Zalman of Liadi, an Orthodox rabbi and charismatic figure who lived in the Russian Empire during the eighteenth century CE. Lubavitch Judaism, also called Chabad, is one of the Hasidic groups that engages most openly with the non-Hassidic, non-Orthodox, and non-Jewish worlds. Chabad teaching emphasizes outreach to encourage all Jews to observe more Torah commandments, such as lighting Shabbat candles, or attending a Passover seder. Chabad Jews live all over the world; their headquarters are in the Crown Heights neighborhood of Brooklyn, New York, and Chabad outreach is a frequent sight on college campuses in the United States.

Omnipresence The characteristic of being everywhere at once. Jewish traditions typically envision God as omnipresent.

7

How Americans View Jews

Ellie Ash

Historical Background

Early European-Americans inherited their narratives about Jews from Europe, especially England. European discourse figured Jews as outsiders to Christian society. Early modern Europeans spoke of Jews as a "nation" or a "race," similar to what we might now call an ethnic group: the Jews were the descendants of Abraham and the biblical Israelites, who in the first century had rejected Jesus and remained Jewish.

Since the early years of Christianity, church doctrine had taught that Jews as a nation bore guilt for the crucifixion of Jesus Christ. For this sin, God cursed them to be scattered throughout the world without a homeland. This was consistent with the legal status of Jews in most Christian European domains as landless and foreign. Religiously, European Christians tended to see Jews as, at best, spiritually deprived and stubbornly blind to true religion. At worst, they raged against them as "Christ killers" and suspected them of performing rituals using the blood of Christian children, an accusation called the "**blood libel**." However, Christian theologians understood Jews' continued existence as part of God's plan, an idea that later gained increased significance with the rise of evangelical Protestantism in the nineteenth century (Dinnerstein 1994; O'Donnell 1996).

At that time, messianic hopes and evangelistic fervor among Protestants added a newly sympathetic way of looking at Jews. Many understood scripture to prophesy that in the **End Times** the Jews would recognize Jesus and be restored to the Holy Land. Missions to the Jews flourished alongside missions to other non-Christian groups, and many Americans saw it as a special calling of the new United States to make possible the conversion of Jews, thereby ushering in Christ's millennium. Others, adherents of a theology called **Dispensationalism**, believed that biblical Judaism based around the Jerusalem Temple would be restored during the millennium (Ariel 2013; Whalen 1996).

European culture had associated Jews with money, in part because many European Jews in fact made a living through trade. It stereotyped Jews as moneylenders ("usurers") or merchants fixated on profit and willing to use unscrupulous, crafty means to gain it. In its worst forms, this was an image of the Jew as a parasite, financially preying on innocent Christians. Shakespeare's character Shylock is an archetype of this image: Shylock is a Jewish merchant who heartlessly insists on enforcing the terms of the contract and collecting a literal "pound of flesh" when the play's Christian hero cannot pay his debt.

Since few early Americans met a real Jew, they saw Jews largely in the mythic terms described above. Until the 1840s, Jews were never more than 0.1 percent of the American population (Sarna 2004: 37, 63). After the 1840s, Jews began to emigrate in larger numbers from Central Europe, mostly working as peddlers and shopkeepers. In the eighteenth and nineteenth centuries, negative talk about Jews and Judaism was normal. For example, American editorials sometimes used allusions to Shylock to discredit public figures, and the term "Jew" itself could be used as an insult. Sunday school children learned that Jews killed Jesus. Nonetheless, in spite of these negative tropes and a cultural image of Jews as foreign, exotic "Orientals," the United States accepted real Jews as free, white citizens. The most privileged Jews moved fairly comfortably in elite American society, often marrying Christians (Dinnerstein 1994; Sarna 1986).

From 1880 to 1924, millions of Europeans came to the United States. Among them were two million Jews, the vast majority from Eastern Europe. While the association of Jews with money and the relationship of Christianity to Judaism continued to be important, the mass migrations created a new dominant image of American Jews as poor and, later, upwardly mobile immigrants. The period from the turn of the century to the 1940s also saw rising anti-Jewish hostility, ranging from nativist prejudice of the kind directed at many immigrant groups to accusations of nefarious conspiracy.

The latter were part of a conservative ideology that proudly identified itself as "anti-Semitism," after the racial term "Semites" for Jews. Modern ideological anti-Semitism developed in Europe starting in the later nineteenth century, and its core is the idea that Jews have a hidden malignant influence on society. This idea tends to take extreme forms that imagine "the international Jew" as a single monstrous unit that aims to control society. *The Protocols of the Elders of Zion*, first printed in Russia around 1905, was a forgery appearing to be an internal document of such a Jewish conspiracy to take control of the world. Anti-Semitic conspiracy theories built on stereotypes of Jews as parasitic, money-obsessed, and anti-Christian, and added modern tropes about Jewish control of the media, finance, and international politics. Ideological anti-Semitism was never as popular or as important in the United States as it was in Europe, but it had its American proponents. One of these was the automobile manufacturer Henry Ford, who sponsored a newspaper preaching the Jewish danger in the 1920s. While political anti-Semitism remained popular into the 1940s, ordinary snobbish prejudice was probably more common, and both coexisted with positive and neutral attitudes toward Jews (Dinnerstein 1994: 80–3; Katz 1980).

FIGURE 7.1 *Satirists used the image of Shylock to criticize non-Jews as well as Jews, as in this 1897 illustration of non-Jewish politician Mark Hanna, by Frederick Burr Opper. Hanna as Shylock displays visual markers of Jewishness typical to caricature of the period: skullcap, sidelocks, and open-handed gesturing.* Source: *Cover illustration from* Puck, *July 28, 1897. Library of Congress Prints and Photographs Online Catalog, LC-DIG-ppmsca-28825.*

The Ford International Weekly

THE DEARBORN INDEPENDENT

By the Year *One Dollar*   Dearborn, Michigan, May 22, 1920   Single Copy *Five Cents*

The International Jew: The World's Problem

"*Among the distinguishing mental and moral traits of the Jews may be mentioned: distaste for hard or violent physical labor; a strong family sense and philoprogenitiveness; a marked religious instinct; the courage of the prophet and martyr rather than of the pioneer and soldier; remarkable power to survive in adverse environments, combined with great ability to retain racial solidarity; capacity for exploitation, both individual and social; shrewdness and astuteness in speculation and money matters generally; an Oriental love of display and a full appreciation of the power and pleasure of social position; a very high average of intellectual ability.*"

—*The New International Encyclopedia.*

THE Jew is again being singled out for critical attention throughout the world. His emergence in the financial, political and social spheres has been so complete and spectacular since the war, that his place, power and purpose in the world are being given a new scrutiny, much of it unfriendly. Persecution is not a new experience to the Jew, but intensive scrutiny of his nature and super-nationality is. He has suffered for more than 2,000 years from what may be called the instinctive anti-semitism of the other races, but this antagonism has never been intelligent nor has it been able to make itself intelligible. Nowadays, however, the Jew is being placed, as it were, ancient prophecies to the effect that the Jew will return to his own land and from that center rule the world, though not until he has undergone an assault by the united nations of mankind.

The single description which will include a larger percentage of Jews than members of any other race is this: he is in business. It may be only gathering rags and selling them, but he is in business. From the sale of old clothes to the control of international trade and finance, the Jew is supremely gifted for business. More than any other race he exhibits a decided aversion to industrial employment, which he balances by an equally decided adaptability to trade. The

FIGURE 7.2 The Dearborn Independent *published anti-Semitic content between 1920 and 1926. This headline is from 1920.* Source: *Dearborn Independent, May 22, 1920.*

Anti-Jewish feeling, or at least its public expression, began to decline after the Second World War. Bigotry in general became less acceptable in American public culture, and the Holocaust tarnished the respectability of ideological anti-Semitism in particular. Opinion polls show that rates of negative attitudes to Jews, particularly the "Shylock" image and complaints of excessive power, declined sharply between 1945 and the 1960s, especially among college-educated Americans. Since 1960, Americans have continued to report ever-warmer feelings toward Jews. Among other developments, Catholic and Protestant leaders came to believe that anti-Jewish attitudes in the church had been partially responsible for allowing the Holocaust, and many denominations engaged in deliberate attempts to combat religious anti-Judaism. Christian leaders began repudiating the claim that Jews are responsible for Jesus' crucifixion and affirming the spiritual value of Judaism and the continuing love of God for the Jews (Cohen 2018; Sandmel 2010; Stember 1966; Thering 1986).

In the period after the Second World War, the new generation of American Jews became overwhelmingly upper middle class and thoroughly integrated into American society. Abroad, the new Jewish State of Israel (founded in 1948) thrived and aligned itself with the Western Bloc in the Cold War. By the early twenty-first century, most Jewish people in the world lived in either Israel or North America, and Americans paying attention to Jewish issues were usually looking at one of those places.

Jews as Ethnics

When Jews began coming to the United States in large numbers in the 1880s, they were one of many European immigrant groups, along with Italians, Poles, and many others, who spoke foreign languages, practiced non-Protestant religions, and settled in urban enclaves. While Americans at the time knew that Jews were a global people with branches throughout Europe, the Middle East, and the Americas, much of the time they thought of Jews as members of the particular immigrant group that spoke Yiddish, came from Eastern Europe, and practiced the religion of Judaism. This perception of Jews as what we now call an "ethnic minority" set a paradigm that continues to inform American ways of talking about Jews into the twenty-first century.

By the 1960s, Jews had become a symbol of immigrant success in the face of prejudice. Through the 1930s to 1970s, the period in which they were transitioning to bourgeois status, some members of the established classes that Jews were joining denigrated them as up-starts: aggressively ambitious, dishonest, money-obsessed, "pushy," and crude. They also accused them of favoritism for other Jews at the expense of outsiders. Other Americans interpreted some of these same traits positively, as ethnic solidarity and the vaunted American entrepreneurship that allowed Jews to realize the American Dream. For example, many twentieth-century African American leaders, from Booker T. Washington to Malcolm X, held up Jewish strategies as a model for the African American community. In a more recent parallel, certain Hindu American leaders see the American Jewish community as a model for maintaining religious and cultural distinctiveness and group solidarity while attaining prestige and political input as Americans (Crumbley 2000; Higham 1966; Kurien 2007: 150; Moore 1986: 196–9).

Jews' economic success in America and their visibility as shopkeepers reinforced the old association of Jews with money. Survey data from 2000 shows that Americans perceive Jews to be wealthy, while entertainment media tends to give Jewish characters white-collar professions such as medicine, law, and media. On the negative side, some people use the term "to jew" to refer to haggling, a pejorative usage dating from the nineteenth century. While for some this term is likely a "dead metaphor" unconnected to actual Jews, the idea that Jews are particularly shrewd in commerce and finance remains alive (Avilucea 2019; Diamond 2015; OED Online 2019; Smith and Schapiro 2019: 133).

Another long-standing stereotype is the idea that Jewish men are physically weak and nonaggressive. Polls suggest that many Americans see Jews as less prone to violence, and media dissociates Jewish men from physical skills such as fixing cars or farming, portraying them instead as intellectual and urban. As with other stereotypes, this can be framed positively, as gentleness, or negatively, as being a "sissy." Americans may be less likely to apply this stereotype to Israeli Jews, who are often portrayed in both entertainment and news media as successful military operatives, and sometimes as excessively violent (Desser 2001; Imhoff 2017; Pearl and Pearl 1999; Smith and Schapiro 2019: 133).

It is likely that the strongest associations most Americans have with Jews are the Holocaust and the State of Israel. When they think of Jews, they first think of people who died in historical Europe or who live in Israel. Common knowledge about the Holocaust shows Jews as a European minority group, and their massacre as the ultimate example of victimization of outsiders and the dangers of racism and totalitarianism. Awareness of the Holocaust contributes to awareness and condemnation of anti-Semitism as a recurring problem. Many Americans think of Israel as an ethnic homeland for Jews that serves, above all, as a refuge from persecution.

FIGURE 7.3 *Numerous Americans learn about the Holocaust at school or through museums such as the United States Holocaust Memorial Museum. This image shows visitors at the cattle car exhibit at that museum.* Source: *Photograph by Adam Jones, Ph.D./ Flickr/ CC BY-SA.*

It seems likely that many Americans expect Jews to be attached to the Jewish state as a natural ethnic or religious sentiment. A 2003 survey suggests that a majority of Americans think American Jews are at least as loyal to Israel as they are to the United States (Hartmann, Gerteis, and Edgell 2010). While "dual-loyalty" accusations were part of earlier political anti-Semitism, it is unclear whether such a view is necessarily negative today. Many non-Jewish Americans view Israel as having a positive "special relationship" with the United States. Additionally, the rise of multiculturalism, which affirms the value of diverse ethnic and racial inheritances in American society, has made particularist loyalties of many kinds acceptable (Jacobson 2009; Mart 2004).

Jews As White

Between multicultural ideals on the political left and the valorization of a "**Judeo-Christian**" heritage on the right, Jews are currently almost unanimously accepted as true Americans, a status dating to the postwar period. In 1955 a Jewish American sociologist named Will Herberg published a book entitled *Protestant, Catholic, Jew.* Herberg argued that at that time, Americans newly respected members of all three faiths as good citizens, understanding the three to be good American religions that differ in doctrinal detail but share monotheism and the basic values of democracy. As Herberg noted, however, these good graces were extended only to *white* Protestants, Catholics, and Jews. In fact, stressing religious identity and religious tolerance rather than ethnicity allowed Jews to avoid the negative stigma of racial difference that attached to Black Americans. Today, Herberg's thesis remains relevant. Not only are most Jews considered white in the American racial system, but the language of "Judeo-Christian" values stresses their common cultural heritage with Christians. Most Americans see Jews and Judaism as Western, affecting views of both Jewish Americans and Jewish Israelis.

The idea of race is culturally relative and has changed over history. In the United States, a "color line" developed between Blacks and whites as part of the institution of slavery. For most of the United States' history, a person's race was a legal status, with certain privileges reserved for those assigned to the white side of the binary color line. European Jews in America have always been white in the eyes of the law, and nineteenth-century Americans typically considered the "Hebrew race" to be one of the white races. In the late nineteenth and the first half of the twentieth century, the binary racial system was temporarily destabilized, as some voices questioned the "whiteness" of Jews and certain other European ethnic groups, such as the Irish. This debate was informed by the then-prestigious "science" of race, which divided Europeans into multiple races. A few white nationalists continue to this day to exclude Jews from their definition of whiteness. However, since the Second World War, Americans have increasingly taken for granted the whiteness of European ethnic groups, including European Jews. Being perceived as white has allowed American Jews the social and economic benefits of a position on the white side of the color line.

FIGURE 7.4 *This illustration of Moses, his mother, and Pharaoh's daughter was published in 1984 by Christian company Sweet Publishing. It shows the ancient Israelites as phenotypically white, in contrast to the Egyptians.* Source: *BibleArtLibrary/Getty Images.*

Most Americans have probably not considered the racial status of Jews with ancestry from the Middle East or North Africa, who comprise a substantial portion of the Israeli Jewish population but probably less than 10 percent of American Jews. Instead, Americans usually think of Jews in general as being white (Belew 2018; Ducker 2006; Gerber 2012: 46; Goldstein 2006; Pew Research Center 2013: 46).

Assuming that Jews are white accompanies a tendency to see Jews as **unmarked** Americans. To say an identity is "unmarked" means that people assume that identity as the default. In the United States, whiteness is generally the unmarked race. This means, for example, that if someone mentions "a baker," or "Protestants," hearers will typically imagine a white baker and white Protestants unless another race is specified. That Jews are unmarked Americans does not mean that Jewishness itself is seen as the default, but rather that a person's Jewishness is not very important, and many people do not even notice it.

Public culture in the early twenty-first century generally treats Jewishness, like other white ethnic identities, as peripheral to one's social role. For example, few people remarked upon candidate Bernie Sanders' Jewish ethnicity in the 2016 presidential election, apparently either considering it unrelated to his political positions, or feeling that it would be inappropriate to mention. Similarly, television abounds with characters such as Ross and Monica on *Friends* (1994–2004) whose Jewishness is irrelevant to the plot (Brook 2003: 122).

Media aimed at an evangelical audience agrees with mainstream media that Jews are much like Gentiles other than in religion. In American evangelical literature, Jewish characters typically share the values of Christian characters and lack stereotypical personality traits. Judaism as a religion is often portrayed as spiritually lacking; however, Jewish characters frequently convert, often as part of a happy ending. This reinforces the status of ethnic Jews as normal people who are as capable of seeing the truth as anyone else. Frequently, these books also explicitly condemn anti-Semitism. Though evangelical leaders a generation ago sometimes got in trouble for making stereotypical statements about Jews, contemporary evangelical public discourse now talks of Jews as people with whom evangelicals and Americans can identify (Ariel 2013; Stover 2005).

For many, accepting Jews as part of the American mainstream applies to Judaism itself, with the concept that American values are based on a "Judeo-Christian" heritage. In the mid-twentieth century, liberals invoked this idea as an inclusive trope that extended American-ness beyond Protestantism, while affirming the centrality of religion in the United States, in contrast to "godless" communism. Conservatives, including the Christian Right, accepted the idea, and since the 1980s, they have tended to use the language of the "Judeo-Christian" heritage in ways that exclude secularism and Islam from American values. Judaism and Jews, however, are welcome. Both the inclusive and exclusive uses of the "Judeo-Christian" concept frame Judaism as part of Western culture, a reversal of the early modern view of Judaism as "Oriental" (Hartmann, Zhang, and Wischstadt 2005; Warne 2012).

This Western image extends to Israeli Jews as well, for both supporters and critics of Israel. Conservatives praise the state of Israel because they see it as embodying conservative "Judeo-Christian" values, and some also believe Israel and the United States face a common enemy in Islam. Many also see Israel as representing the West and democracy in the Middle East. In a mirror image, left-wing anti-Zionists criticize Israel as a settler-colonialist state that subordinates the indigenous Palestinians and enforces Western interests in the Middle East. Both the pro- and anti-Zionist views are facilitated by the disposition to think of Jews, including Israelis, as white Westerners (Durbin 2013; Jacobson 2009; Mart 2004).

As the left-wing critique of Israel shows, whiteness does not look equally good from all perspectives. Some Black scholars report learning as children in the 1960s and 1970s that Jews are not like other white people, and Blacks should sympathize with them as fellow victims of bigotry or as God's Chosen People. Another potential reason for sympathy was Jewish overrepresentation in the civil rights movement. However, starting in the late 1960s, a number of Black intellectuals (joined by some white Jewish intellectuals) pointed out that because Jews are white, they have been able to participate in and benefit from the social system that oppresses African Americans. Jewish Americans, they proposed, should not expect their civil rights record to exempt them from Black criticism or hostility toward whites. Indeed, some Black Power leaders did express animosity toward Jews as whites, and some combined that with

FIGURE 7.5 *The unexceptionability of Jewishness applies to black as well as white Jews. Rapper Drake, pictured here at a 2011 concert (foreground), has referenced his Jewish upbringing, but it is only a minor part of his image. Drake at Bun-B Concert.* Source: *thecomeupshow/CC BY.*

traditional anti-Semitic tropes. The most prominent example is the Nation of Islam's leader Louis Farrakhan (1933–), who continues today to teach that Jews have been primary instigators of white oppression of Blacks, beginning with the slave trade. Using a trope that the next section discusses further, Farrakhan also argues that Jews are not the true Chosen People of the Bible. This view contrasts sharply with that of those African American churches that encourage members to love Jews as God's Chosen (Berman 1994; Crumbley 2000; Final Call 2019; Wienberg and Stein 1970).

Jews as the Chosen People–Or Not

Biblical and religious narratives affect how many Americans conceive of Jews. The Hebrew Bible, which is part of Christian scripture, says that God chose the people Israel for a special relationship and made a covenant with them. Christian tradition, like Jewish tradition, sees contemporary Jews as the descendants of the biblical Israelites, via the Jews of Jesus' time. Different churches disagree about what the current relationship is between God and the Jews. Historically, many taught that the biblical covenant with Israel transferred to the Christian Church, and Jews who do not accept Christ are left out of it. However, many Christians today, especially after the Holocaust, affirm that God continues to hold the Jewish people as His Chosen. This is particularly stressed among evangelical Protestants.

One important attitude that incorporates the view of Jews as God's Chosen People is **Christian Zionism**, or support for the State of Israel as a Jewish nation for Christian religious reasons. These Christians emphasize that biblical prophecy promises to restore the Jews to the Holy Land in the End Times, when Christ will return. Even before Jewish Zionism got underway, there were evangelicals in the nineteenth century advocating for the return of Jews to the Holy Land. When the state of Israel was founded in 1948, and especially when it captured East Jerusalem in 1967, many evangelicals rejoiced in these events as precursors to the Second Coming of Christ. Christian Zionists also take note of a verse in Genesis in which God says to Abraham, "I will bless those who bless you" (Gen. 12:3 NRSV). They interpret this to mean that people and countries who are good to Jews will be rewarded, and they see material support for Israel and Israelis as a major way to be good to Jews. Another reason many evangelicals feel warmly toward a Jewish State of Israel is because Jesus lived there as a Jew. These religious narratives dovetail with secular views of contemporary Israel as a Western democracy and a remedy for persecution, reinforcing the political position that the United States should stand with Israel through thick and thin (Ariel 2013; Spector 2009; see also Hummel 2019).

The Christian Zionist view depends on seeing Jews as members of a people or nation, defined genealogically as the descendants of Abraham. Though not exactly the same as seeing Jews as an ethnic group, "peoplehood" is a related concept. For Christian Zionists, Israelis are the paradigmatic Jews because their membership in the Jewish people is realized in their national identity (Shapiro 2012).

If Jews are defined by genealogy, a Jew can become a Christian and remain a Jew. Many evangelicals, including Christian Zionists, do think Jews should practice Judaism; however, the Judaism they most respect is not the religion of most contemporary Jews (**Rabbinic Judaism**), but the Judaism that Jesus practiced, which they see as compatible with Christian faith. One scholar has argued that for Christian Zionists the ideal Jews are "completed Jews" who have accepted Jesus but continue to see themselves as part of the Jewish people (Shapiro 2012).

Such Jews do exist, and they call their religion "**Messianic Judaism**." Messianic congregations also attract large numbers of non-Jewish evangelicals, known as "Gentile Believers," who feel called to Hebraic-inflected worship for a variety of reasons, including the idea that they are worshipping as Jesus worshipped. Even outside such congregations, warmth toward Judaism as the religion of Jesus and the origin of Christianity motivates some evangelicals and other Christians to incorporate Judaic elements such as Passover seders into their practice (Kaell 2015; Sandmel 2010).

The chosenness of the biblical Israel is also salient in African American religious traditions. African American Protestant churches famously identify with the biblical Israel, especially the narrative of slavery, suffering, and redemption. In most cases, this identification is figurative, but some Black Americans see themselves as genealogically descended from the Israelites. This claim is not unique; other non-Jewish Americans claiming Israelite ancestry include the Mormons and the white nationalist, anti-Semitic Christian Identity Church.

This descent is central to a number of Black religious communities that describe themselves as "Israelite" or "Hebrew" and grew out of the Afro-centric ideologies of the early twentieth century. **Hebrew Israelite** communities vary greatly, but all recognize African Americans and Afro-Caribbeans as the people of Israel described in biblical prophecies. In particular, they understand the prediction in Deuteronomy 28 that Israel will unwillingly return to Egypt in ships as a reference to the Middle Passage. They teach that after being exiled from their land, the Israelites migrated to Africa, where their descendants were later captured and sent to bondage in the Americas, and only in the twentieth century rediscovered their true identity (Chireau and Deustch 1999; Goldschmidt 2006).

While there are only tiny numbers of Hebrew Israelites in the United States, similar ideas circulate in the broader African American community. Rastafarians commonly see themselves as Israelites, and it is not unheard of for Protestant preachers to teach that the ancient Israelites were Black. Hebrew Israelite ideas also show up in popular culture, as in rapper Kendrick Lamar's religiously evocative 2017 album *DAMN*. Unlike the majority American view which associates Jewishness with whiteness, these traditions associate true Jewishness with Blackness (Goldschmidt 2006; Lamar 2017).

This does not, however, usually mean seeing Ashkenazi or Sephardi Rabbinic Jews as Black. One common Hebrew Israelite interpretation is that European Jews, being white, are not descendants of the ancient Israelites at all. Some see them as usurpers, others as the children of legitimate converts. Another interpretation holds that European Jews and Black Hebrews are two branches of Israel, both part of the global community of Jews. At the other extreme are those who see Rabbinic Jews as "Edomites," the ancestral enemies of the true Israel. Outside of the Hebrew Israelite communities, most African American Christians usually assume, as other Christians do, that European Jews are the descendants of the biblical Jews. For some, this assumption combines with Black Protestant spiritual identification with the biblical Israel to lead to a sense of affinity with white Jews. In sum, Black Americans who understand themselves to be spiritually or physically the children of Israel may take any approach to white Jews from complete rejection, through indifference, to solidarity as kinsfolk and coreligionists (Crumbley 2000; Goldschmidt 2006; Wolfson 1999).

Conclusion

This chapter has described some of the ways non-Jewish Americans think about Jews. We saw that when Americans invoke stereotypes about Jewish personal characteristics, consider Israel as a Jewish homeland, or think about the history of Jewish persecution, they are thinking of Jews as an ethnic group. At the same time, American society treats Jews as racially white and accepts them into the American mainstream, in part through the notion of a "Judeo-Christian" heritage. Additionally, religious Americans committed to biblical interpretations may also understand Jewishness through the idea of God's Chosen People.

American Jews share many of the ways of seeing themselves described above, though they aim to combat the most negative ones. Many Jews are sensitive to traditional stereotypes about being unscrupulous or too good with money. Jews are especially concerned about images similar to the anti-Semitic ideas that Hitler espoused, such as claims that Jews control the media and finance or influence politics behind the scenes. With the Holocaust proving the dangers of anti-Semitism, mainstream American discourse recognizes the validity of these concerns, and claiming that a person or their ideas are anti-Semitic is a fairly severe accusation. At the time of writing, in the second decade of the twenty-first century, it is also a fairly common accusation. Democrats have called President Trump anti-Semitic for repeating stereotypes and accused him of inspiring white nationalists, who are often avowedly anti-Jewish (and sometimes violently so). Meanwhile, Republicans impute anti-Semitism to people they see as unreasonably critical of Israel or American Jews' support of Israel. Such charges raise the question of what counts as "anti-Semitism."

Many Jews are also sensitive about Christians seeing them as objects of conversion efforts. Understanding missionary efforts as a threat to the continued existence of the Jewish people, Jews are sometimes baffled by Christians who claim to love Jews and also want them to become Christian. Missions were historically a major way American Christians have related sympathetically to Jews. In response to Jewish objections, however, since the 1960s some churches have renounced such missions, while others attempt to conduct them more sensitively. Evangelism provides a good example of the interpretive difficulties in labeling something anti-Semitic. Some Jews say that wanting

Jews to convert is "anti-Semitic" because it implies a hope that Jews cease to exist as Jews, while missionaries see their work as a great expression of love for Jewish individuals in trying to bring them salvation.

While there is a place for attempting to define anti-Semitism, adjudicating all perceptions of Jews as simply either anti-Semitic or not often glosses over complexity. It is particularly difficult to judge a person (or a subculture) in this way, because most people do not have a single consistent opinion of Jews. For example, evangelical preacher Jerry Falwell (1933–2007) generally spoke warmly about Jews, as a Christian Zionist who preached that God wants the United States to protect the Jews. He was accused of anti-Semitism, however, when he joked that people do not like Jews because they are too good at making money (Hall 2007). Context affects what images are most salient at any given moment. The same person may think of Jews as the innocent victims of Nazi genocide on Holocaust Remembrance Day, as a group of rich people with suspiciously disproportionate influence in Hollywood during a conversation about movies, and in daily life relate to her Jewish coworkers as unexceptional colleagues, perhaps forgetting they are Jewish.

This chapter has tried to show the range of images of Jews that are available in American culture today. These images can be inflected and combined in ways that are accurate or inaccurate, flattering or unflattering, or neither. As with any cultural meanings, the meaning of ideas about Jews is determined by their place in the broader social context they appear in.

Further Reading and Online Resources

Brook, V. (2003), *Something Ain't Kosher Here: The Rise of the "Jewish" Sitcom*, Brunswick, NJ: Rutgers University Press.

Chireau, Y. and N. Deutsch, eds. (1999), *Black Zion: African American Religious Encounters with Judaism*, New York: Oxford University Press.

Dinnerstein, L. (1994), *Antisemitism in America*, New York: Oxford University Press.

Goldstein, E.L. (2006), *The Price of Whiteness: Jews, Race, and American Identity*, Princeton, NJ: Princeton University Press.

Kaell, H. (2014), *Walking Where Jesus Walked: American Christians and Holy Land Pilgrimage*, New York: New York University Press.

Sarna, J.D. (1986), "The 'Mythical Jew' and the 'Jew Next Door' in Nineteenth Century America," in D.A. Gerber (ed.), *Anti-Semitism in American History*, 57–78, Chicago: University of Illinois Press.

References

Ariel, Y. (2013), *An Unusual Relationship: Evangelical Christians and Jews*, New York: New York University Press.

Avilucea, I. (2019), "Trenton Mayor Demands Apology over Council President Kathy McBride's 'anti-Semitic' Remark," *The Trentonian*, September 13. Available online: https://www.trentonian.com/news/trenton-mayor-demands-apology-over-council-president-kathy-mcbride-s/article_32e03d72-d662-11e9-a820-43207c79f7a4.html.

Belew, K. (2018), *Bring the War Home: The White Power Movement and Paramilitary America*, Cambridge, MA: Harvard University Press.

Berman, P., ed. (1994), *Blacks and Jews: Alliances and Arguments*, New York: Delacorte Press.

Chireau, Y. and N. Deutsch, eds. (1999), *Black Zion: African American Religious Encounters with Judaism*, New York: Oxford University Press.

Cohen, J. (2018), "From Antisemitism to Philosemitism? Trends in American Attitudes toward Jews from 1964 to 2016," *Religions*, 9 (4): 107.

Crumbley, D.H. (2000), "Also Chosen: Jews in the Imagination and Life of a Black Sanctified Church," *Anthropology and Humanism*, 25 (1): 6–23.

Desser, D. (2001), "Jews in Space: The 'Ordeal of Masculinity' in Contemporary American Film and Television," in M. Pomerance (ed.), *Ladies and Gentlemen, Boys and Girls: Gender in Film at the End of the Twentieth Century*, 267–82, Albany: State University of New York Press.

Diamond, J. (2015), "Trump to Republican Jewish Coalition: 'I'm a Negotiator like You'," *CNN*, December 3. Available online: https://www.cnn.com/2015/12/03/politics/donald-trump-rjc-negotiator/index.html (accessed November 15, 2020).

Dinnerstein, L. (1994), *Antisemitism in America*, New York: Oxford University Press.

Ducker, C.L. (2006), "Jews, Arabs and Arab Jews: The Politics of Identity and Reproduction in Israel," *ISS Working Paper Series/General Series*, 421: 1–58.

Durbin, S. (2013), "'I Am an Israeli': Christian Zionism as American Redemption," *Culture and Religion*, 14 (3): 324–47.

Final Call (2019), "The Secret Relationship between Blacks and Jews." Available online: https://store.finalcall.com/collections/the-secret-relationship-between-blacks-and-jews (accessed August 26, 2018).

Gerber, J. (2012), "Sephardic and Syrian Immigration to America," in E. Aizenberg and M. Bejarano (eds.), *Contemporary Sephardic Identity in the Americas: An Interdisciplinary Approach*, 38–66, Syracuse, NY: Syracuse University Press.

Goldschmidt, H. (2006), *Race and Religion among the Chosen People of Crown Heights*, Brunswick, NJ: Rutgers University Press.

Goldstein, E.L. (2006), *The Price of Whiteness: Jews, Race, and American Identity*, Princeton, NJ: Princeton University Press.

Hall, L. (2007), "Falwell's Rallies Spawned Interest in Moral Majority," *Richmond Times Dispatch*, June 6.

Hartmann, D., J. Gerteis, and P. Edgell (2010), "American Mosaic Project Survey, 2003," Ann Arbor, MI: Inter-university Consortium for Political and Social Research [distributor]. https://doi.org/10.3886/ICPSR28821.v1.

Hartmann, D., X. Zhang, and W. Wischstadt (2005), "One (Multicultural) Nation under God? Changing Uses and Meanings of the Term 'Judeo-Christian' in the American Media," *Journal of Media and Religion*, 4 (4): 207–34.

Higham, J. (1966), "American Anti-Semitism Historically Reconsidered," in C.H. Stember (ed.), *Jews in the Mind of America*, 237–58, New York: Basic Books.

Hummel, D.G. (2019), *Covenant Brothers: Evangelicals, Jews, and U.S.-Israeli Relations*, Philadelphia: University of Pennsylvania Press.

Imhoff, S. (2017), *Masculinity and the Making of American Judaism*, Bloomington: Indiana University Press.

Jacobson, M.F. (2009), *Roots Too*, Cambridge, MA: Harvard University Press.

Kaell, H. (2015), "Born-Again Seeking: Explaining the Gentile Majority in Messianic Judaism," *Religion*, 45 (1): 42–65.

Katz, J. (1980), *From Prejudice to Destruction: Anti-Semitism, 1700–1933*, Cambridge, MA: Harvard University Press.

Kurien, P. (2007), *A Place at the Multicultural Table: The Development of an American Hinduism*, Brunswick, NJ: Rutgers University Press.

Lamar, K. (2017), *DAMN*, Santa Monica, CA: TDE/Aftermath/Interscope.

Mart, M. (2004), "The 'Christianization' of Israel and Jews in 1950s America," *Religion and American Culture: A Journal of Interpretation*, 14 (1): 109–47.

Moore, R.L. (1986), *Religious Outsiders and the Making of Americans*, New York: Oxford University Press.

O'Donnell, C. (1996), "Jews, the Church and The," in *Ecclesia: A Theological Encyclopedia of the Church*, 230–3, Collegeville, MN: The Liturgical Press.

OED Online (2019), s.v. "Jew | Jew, v." Oxford University Press. Available online: https://www.oed.com/ (accessed November 15, 2020).

Oliner, S.P. and J.D. Krause (2001), "Racial and Ethnic Attitudes in Rural America: Focus on Humboldt County, California," *Humboldt Journal of Social Relations*, 26 (1/2): 11–55.

Pearl, J. and J. Pearl (1999), *The Chosen Image: Television's Portrayal of Jewish Themes and Characters*, Jefferson, NC: McFarland.

Pew Research Center (2013), "A Portrait of Jewish Americans: Findings from a Pew Research Center Survey of U.S. Jews," October 1. Available online: https://www.pewforum.org/2013/10/01/jewish-american-beliefs-attitudes-culture-survey/ (accessed November 15, 2020).

Sandmel, D.F. (2010), "'Philosemitism' and 'Judaizing' in the Contemporary Church," in F.T. Harkins and J. Van Engen (eds.), *Transforming Relations: Essays on Jews and Christians Throughout History in Honor of Michael A. Signer*, 405–20, Notre Dame: Notre Dame University Press.

Sarna, J.D. (1986), "The 'Mythical Jew' and the 'Jew Next Door' in Nineteenth Century America," in D.A. Gerber (ed.), *Anti-Semitism in American History*, 57–78, Urbana: University of Illinois Press.

Sarna, J.D. (2004), *American Judaism: A History*, New Haven, CT: Yale University Press.

Shapiro, F. (2012), "Jews without Judaism: The Ambivalent Love of Christian Zionism," *Journal for the Study of Antisemitism*, 4 (2): 647–65.

Smith, T.W. and B. Schapiro (2019), "Antisemitism in Contemporary America," in A. Dashefsky and I. Sheskin (eds.), *American Jewish Year Book 2018*, 113–61, Cham: Springer.

Smith, T.W., M. Davern, J. Freese, and S.L. Morgan (2018), "General Social Surveys, 1972–2018" [Machine-Readable Data File]. Chicago: NORC at the University of Chicago [producer and distributor]. Available online: https://gssdataexplorer.norc.org/ (accessed November 15, 2020).

Spector, S. (2009), *Evangelicals and Israel: The Story of American Christian Zionism*, New York: Oxford University Press.

Stember, C.H. (1966), *Jews in the Mind of America*, New York: Basic Books.

Stover, M. (2005), "A Kinder, Gentler Teaching of Contempt?: Jews and Judaism in Contemporary Protestant Evangelical Children's Fiction," *Journal of Religion and Society*, 7: 1–16. Available online: http://moses.creighton.edu/JRS/2005/2005-1.pdf (accessed November 15, 2020).

Thering, R. (1986), *Jews, Judaism and Catholic Education*, New York: Anti-Defamation League of B'nai B'rith, American Jewish Committee; South Orange, NJ: Seton Hall University.

Warne, A. (2012), "Making a Judeo-Christian America: The Christian Right, Antisemitism, and the Politics of Religious Pluralism in the 20th Century United States," PhD diss., Evanston, IL: Northwestern University.

Weinberg, S. and A. Stein (1970), *Bittersweet Encounter: The Afro-American and the American Jew*, Westport, CT: Negro Universities Press.

Wenger, T. (2017), *Religious Freedom: The Contested History of an American Ideal*, Chapel Hill: University of North Carolina Press.

Whalen, R.K. (1996), "'Christians Love the Jews!' The Development of American Philo-Semitism, 1790–1860," *Religion and American Culture: A Journal of Interpretation*, 6 (2): 225–59.

Wolfson, B.J. (1999), "African American Jews: Dispelling Myths, Bridging the Divide," in Y. Chireau and N. Deutsch (eds.), *Black Zion: African American Religious Encounters with Judaism*, 33–54, New York: Oxford University Press.

Glossary Terms

Blood libel The accusation that Jews kidnap and murder Christian children for ritual purposes, especially using their blood for baking *matzah* for Passover. The myth originated in medieval Europe and continues to be used by modern anti-Semites.

Christian Zionism Support for the state of Israel as a Jewish nation for religious Christian reasons, especially because the national restoration of Jews in the Holy Land fulfills biblical prophecies. Not all Christian Zionists have been dispensationalist.

Dispensationalism A Protestant Christian theory of eschatology. Dispensationalists hold that history is divided into a certain number of eras, called "dispensations." The present era, the age of the church, is a "parenthesis" in the fulfillment of God's covenantal promises to the people of Israel, but when this dispensation comes to a close, those promises will be fulfilled. The Messiah, that is, Jesus Christ, will return and the Jews will be restored to the Holy Land under Jesus' kingship.

End Times In Christianity, the End Times refers to the future period of time when history will come to a close and Jesus will return to Earth. The End Times includes the periods before and after the Second Coming of Jesus, and may include the "millenium" spoken of in the Bible. Christians disagree on the specifics of the End Times.

Hebrew Israelite An umbrella term for African American and Afro-Caribbean religious groups that describe themselves as "Hebrews" or "Israelites" or similar terms, and which teach that African American and Afro-Caribbean people are descendants of the biblical Israelites, and therefore should observe the biblical commandments, such as keeping the Saturday Sabbath. Some teach faith in Christ, while others do not. The oldest and largest such groups include Ethiopian Hebrew congregations and the African Hebrew Israelite Community, which is now centered in Israel. Other communities are Israel United in Christ and the Israeli Church of Universal Practical Knowledge, along with many others.

Judeo-Christian A term describing things seen as shared between Judaism and Christianity. The term invokes the origins of Christianity in ancient Judaism and the fact that the Hebrew Bible is scripture for both religions. Many speak of the "Judeo-Christian heritage" or "Judeo-Christian tradition" as the basis for American society.

Messianic Judaism Messianic Jewish congregations bring together ethnic Jews who have come to believe that Jesus (known by his Hebrew name, Yeshua) was the Messiah, and who wish to practice a form of Judaism and retain their Jewish identity. They hold that Jews should follow Jewish law and celebrate biblical Jewish holidays even after the coming of Yeshua. Messianic congregations are part of the greater Evangelical cultural sphere, and they also attract many non-Jewish congregants, known as Gentile Believers. Jews for Jesus is an organization that also promotes the idea that Jews who become Christians are still Jewish, but they focus less on Jewish practices, and many Messianic Jews disapprove of their activities.

Rabbinic Judaism What most people mean when they say "Judaism." It refers to the Jewish tradition that follows the Rabbis of the Talmud and claims the majority of contemporary Jews. "Rabbinic Judaism" contrasts with other forms of Judaism, including ancient Judaism, Karaite Judaism (a living tradition which branched off from Rabbinic Judaism in the ninth century CE) and modern traditions such as Messianic Judaism and the African Hebrew Israelite Community.

Unmarked The concept of being "marked" or "unmarked" describes the way some words or concepts are treated as being neutral or default, while their opposites are notable, that is, marked. The best example of this is in gender. In most languages and culture, maleness is unmarked while femaleness is marked. In English, this can be seen in the older use of "man" to refer to either humans in general, or males in particular.

8

How American Jews Think about Themselves

Ellen LeVee

The Question of Jewish Identity

How do Jews view themselves? This question may have as many answers as there are Jews. After all, most people, if asked "how do you view yourself?," especially in America, would think in individualistic terms. They might choose a personality trait or an occupational category. Most Jews would do the same. However, the question, geared to Jews as a group, does not make a single answer any easier. There is an old joke among Jews: you ask two Jews a question, you'll get three different answers. While this makes for a certain contentiousness among Jews, there is no doubt that the question of Jewish identity inspires a multitude of answers. However, some general observations can be made that most Jews will probably agree with.

First, it's necessary to limit the scope of this chapter. As other chapters make clear, Jewishness comes in many different forms. Contemporary United States Jewry is this chapter's focus. American Jews constitute about 40 percent of the world's population of Jews. There's slightly over 40 percent in Israel, and the rest are scattered throughout the world. So the Jews of the United States are hardly representative of all Jews. Nevertheless, they do represent a significant group of Jews, both in numbers and in influence. Moreover, American Jews are the majority of Jews in the Jewish **diaspora**, a population dispersed from its homeland in Israel, living throughout the world. Each diaspora community is distinctive. This distinctiveness points out something else. That each diaspora community is influenced by the country it is part of. For American Jews this means that they see themselves both as Jews and as Americans.

Of course Jews are a small minority of about 2 percent in America. This small minority is precisely what makes American Jews, Americans. They hold on to being

Jewish while being profoundly affected by living in America. What does it mean to be Jewish in America? The answer involves a puzzling discrepancy. While most American Jews consider themselves Jewish by religion (70 percent), most American Jews also see Jewishness primarily as a matter of culture and ancestry (62 percent), in other words as an ethnic identity as opposed to a religious one. This suggests that Jewishness at least involves secular, that is, nonreligious, elements. If it is religious, how can it also be secular? Even if culture includes religion, how does Jewishness reconcile the religious with the secular, making them not opposites but part of a shared identity?

In addressing how Jews view themselves, this chapter answers these questions. The next section focuses on Jewishness and religion. The following section focuses on Jewishness and ethnicity. These sections also show how Jews are American. The conclusion then summarizes the discussion, showing how both religion and ethnicity come together framing American Jews' view of themselves as a distinctive blend of the religious and the secular, the Jewish and the American.

Jewishness and Religion

Perhaps the most important thing to realize about the Jewish religion is that it isn't religion in the way religion is usually understood in Christianity. For Jews, their religion is more concerned with this world than a "next" world. Traditionally Jews have believed in a world beyond this one, but living in this world is what has always mattered most. It matters because Judaism's religious goal is redeeming this world, making it a better place to live in rather than the Christian religious goal of securing personal salvation. In Judaism's emphasis on making this world a better place, physical actions took precedence over spiritual beliefs and the social took precedence over the individual. The administration of justice, care for the sick, provision for the poor and vulnerable in society, and even concern for the environment were all part of Jewish religion. Such this-worldly action as part of a social framework was realized through law. Religious law, **halakha**, created a grid of physical actions that shaped a Jewish social world. To be sure, halakha also applied to such mundane personal activities as business transactions, eating, what to wear, and making love, occasioning the accusation of empty ritualism, but not only was that frowned upon by Jewish tradition, more to the point, it obscured Judaism's concern with redemption of this world.

For most Jews, the this-worldly concern continues to predominate, forming a bridge between the religious and the secular. Both domains emphasize physical actions, although halakha has lost its authority. Some actions now fit a model of religion that looks Protestant where individualism plays a greater role. Others fit a secular ethnic model, where the social is still prominent. This split allows for a partnership between the religious, to be discussed in this section, and the ethnic, to be discussed in the next section, especially as both share concern for the physical world.

FIGURE 8.1 *Secular Jewish woman identifying as Jewish through her dress.* Source: *Photograph by Arianna Stone.*

FIGURE 8.2 *Ultra-Orthodox Jewish family.* Source: *Wojtkowski Cezary/Alamy Stock Photo.*

In focusing on the religious, the importance of physical actions is clear. The spectrum of religious actions extends from people who consider themselves Jewish but barely do anything religious to those who dress in eighteenth-century Polish garb.

Most American Jews are somewhere in-between, and they live their religious lives in America so as to conform to American ways of acting religiously. In other words, individualism has also become increasingly important. Jews see themselves mostly as Americans and choose to live their lives as most Protestant Americans do. There are synagogues instead of churches. Like Christian sectarianism, different Jewish denominations have developed, although they are concerned with the range in practices of Jewish law rather than theology, and the most popular Jewish holidays coincide with Christian holidays. Most Jews live their religion, consciously, as just one small part of their lives, and every individual sees him or herself as the ultimate authority over what he or she does.

This individual authority produces certain anomalies in religious practice. Consider the synagogue. While Judaism has become communally organized for most Jews around the synagogue, the synagogue is not a popular institution. It functions like a church: as a house of worship with educational classes, primarily for children, but most Jews do not attend worship services regularly. Less than a quarter go more than once a month (23 percent). Just about an equal percentage never go at all (22 percent); most Jews (54 percent) only go a couple of times a year.

Even more notably, Jews do not necessarily go to synagogue to pray to God. Although about three-quarters of all Jews believe in God (less than Protestants or Catholics), they do not necessarily relate to God personally. Jews who go to synagogue do it for a variety of reasons besides praying to God: connecting with tradition, being with a community, communing with one's own thoughts, or reinforcing ethical ideals. They may enjoy the religious service with its singing and/or the opportunity to see friends in a time out from the busy work week. Thus, rather than a shared and formalized belief system bringing Jews together, individual actions, holding a variety of personal meanings, coincide to bring Jews together. Through actions, the synagogue melds the American with the Jewish.

Synagogues differ by denomination. There are three major denominations. They have varying theologies, but for most Jews, the denominations reflect different actions; observance of Jewish law differs. In ascending order of observance, these denominations are: with the least concern for the authority of halakha, Reform Judaism (35 percent of American Jews), with more concern for halakha, Conservative Judaism (18 percent), and with the most concern for halakha, Orthodox Judaism (10 percent). In addition, there are several much smaller denominations: Reconstructionist, Liberal/Progressive, Humanistic, Jewish Renewal (7 percent), most falling somewhere between Reform and Conservative Jewish observance. And then there's a whopping 30 percent who don't identify denominationally and tend to care the least about Jewish law.

Historically, Reform Judaism was once the home of German Jews who had come to America in the mid-1800s. Coming from a part of Europe that distinguished differences between people within a single nation principally by religion, these Jews saw their Jewishness as a religion. They even adopted some Christian customs, such as praying in the **vernacular** rather than the traditional Hebrew, men and women sitting together, and the introduction of an organ. Coming to America, these Jews fit within the American model of religious differentiation. Their actions conformed to the Christian model.

Conservative Judaism, which in the middle of the last century was the largest denomination in American life, was home to an influx of Jews from Eastern Europe and Russia. This emigration brought ten times the number of Jews who were already in America from Western and Central Europe. Coming at the turn of the twentieth century, these Eastern European Jews emigrated from a part of the world where ethnic identity differentiated people. They were uncomfortable with German religious customs, so in adapting to American standards, these Eastern European Jews created their own synagogues that maintained more of the Jewish tradition they were familiar with. At first they also kept some of the practices that did not fit with American life, like the dietary restrictions of **kashrut**. They had their own language, **Yiddish**, which produced not only daily Yiddish newspapers but also forms of secular entertainment such as plays. As time went on Conservative Jews became more integrated into American society. They learned English—very few now understand Yiddish—and many Conservative Jews no longer keep kashrut. This has meant that Reform and Conservative Judaism have become more similar; while the Conservative assimilated more of American ways,

Reform has taken on more religious traditions. So, for example, in neither movement do men and women sit separately and now there is more Hebrew in Reform services.

The Orthodox, found among some of the Eastern Europeans who refused to give up their traditions, began to expand when Jewish refugees fled Europe after the Second World War. Many of these were Jews who had been so strongly tied to their tradition that they came only when it was clear how inhospitable Europe was for the Jews. For them the grid social model was maintained as much as possible. In subsequent decades, greater integration with American society has occurred. However, Orthodox communities have also managed to maintain their communities, reinforcing traditional actions and activities. With their large families, the Orthodox are flourishing in present-day America.

Holidays are still another area of Jewish activity paralleling Christian counterparts. The most prominent Jewish holidays in America are **Chanukah**, a relatively minor festival in traditional Judaism, and **Passover**, one of Judaism's most important holidays. Chanukah occurs around Christmas time, and Passover generally falls around Easter time. Both are seen as celebrations of freedom, coinciding with American values. Jews can celebrate when their non-Jewish neighbors celebrate, in ways that are distinctively Jewish, yet also unquestionably American.

There are also a number of other holidays that have importance in the Jewish calendar but do not coincide with the Christian calendar. These are often ignored or forgotten by American Jews, except for some among the Conservative and most of

FIGURE 8.3 *A family celebrating Chanukah.* Source: *kali9/Getty Images.*

the Orthodox. There are two exceptions: the New Year's celebration, *Rosh HaShanah*, and the holiday that is the most sacred of the Jewish year, the Day of Atonement, *Yom Kippur*. These two holidays occur in the fall, September or October, when there are no Christian holidays and the school year is just starting. If a Jew goes only a few times a year to synagogue, it is a good bet that these holidays are two of those times. They are primarily observed with communal prayer. Yom Kippur, a day devoted to soul-searching and asking God for forgiveness of sins, is also spent in fasting. Their importance in Judaism has increased the likelihood of their observance, but only slightly over 50 percent of American Jews even fast on Yom Kippur. The religious centrality of these holidays has encouraged their observance, but their odd timing in the American calendar has at the same time undermined that observance.

Yet, the holidays of Chanukah and Passover have a certain advantage over the "synagogue" holidays in that Chanukah and Passover are primarily celebrated at home. This corresponds with the individual meaningfulness observed about synagogue attendance above. The home provides a particularly individualistic setting for celebration. Personal meaningfulness can be expressed through the freedom to celebrate the holiday however desired. Additionally, these holidays spotlight the family. Chanukah and Passover are very kid-friendly. Celebrating at those times of the year that their non-Jewish neighbors do, Jewish families enjoy the occasion simply to gather together as a family. So, both Chanukah and Passover are celebrated by about 70 percent of American Jews.

In short, American Jewishness as it takes a religious form is chiefly defined by actions as they conform to American practices. As actions parallel Christian practices, the meaning of those actions is left up to individual Jews to determine. Individualism, prominent in American life, has become key to the expression of Jewish religious identity. Thus, for most American Jews, Jewishness in its religious practice has been reformulated from being a grid shaping social life to something more personal. No longer all encompassing, Judaism has become just one aspect of many in a Jew's life. To be sure, actions are still more crucial than beliefs, but most Jews are increasingly less committed to religious actions at all.

Jewishness as an Ethnicity

While for many Jews religious actions have some degree of importance, for others it holds no significance. Yet, that does not mean that these Jews do not identify as Jewish; they see themselves as ethnic Jews. Certainly, the religious and ethnic strands are not mutually exclusive; individual Jews participate in both kinds of activities. However, while religion is readily identifiable, ethnicity is a more elusive category, especially in America. The importance of religion in mainstream American life lends a helping hand to institutionalizing Jewishness as a religion. This is why so many Jews identify religiously as Jews. The ethnic form of Jewish identity has no such help. In contrast with neighbors to the north and south, Canada and Mexico, which are better structured to accommodate Jewish ethnic identification, the United States has difficulty dealing with the differentiation by the kind of ethnicity that Jewishness represents. Part of this is because Jewishness can be expressed religiously; but part of this is also because America's emphasis on individualism obscures a group identity and the minority status of ethnic identification in America is usually associated with those who have experienced oppression in America. Ethnic identity, by nature, is not individualistic, and for the most part, Jews have found America to be relatively hospitable.

At the same time, Jewishness itself fits uneasily in the category of ethnicity. Ethnicity is usually seen as something secular, so the this-worldly emphasis of Jewish religion can make ethnicity difficult to distinguish from religion. The religious and ethnic do not have clear boundaries. Not only may Jews participate in both kinds of activities but also Jewish ethnic activities are rooted in Judaism's religious foundations and religious activities may also be expressions of ethnic identity. More significantly, the most secular aspects of ethnicity, biological considerations and a singular secular culture, are not really accurate ways to define Jewishness. With respect to biology, Jewishness is not a race. Consider two different scenarios. One scenario is of a non-Jew converting to Judaism. Genetically this person is not Jewish, but he or she becomes fully Jewish upon conversion. To be sure, there are lots of arguments about what constitutes a legitimate conversion, but the point here is that biology isn't the only factor in determining Jewishness. The second scenario is the Jew, biologically

FIGURE 8.4 *Jewish boys from mixed backgrounds celebrating together.* Source: *MaestroBooks/Getty Images.*

Jewish, who converts to another religion, for instance Christianity. Most Jews—and again there are arguments here too—have difficulty considering a Jew who believes that Jesus is the Messiah to be Jewish. So being Jewish is more like a nationality. You can be born in a country and that makes you a citizen, or you can go through a process of naturalization to make yourself a citizen. If you leave a country to live elsewhere, you can lose your citizenship in the country you were born in, although you may still share many aspects of that heritage. In this framework, Jewishness as an ethnic category is a lot like citizenship, only it doesn't involve a physical country.

With regard to customs, unless religious customs are considered, the spread of Jews throughout the world means that customs differ by geographical origin. There are simply too many places Jews have lived to say that any one particular set of customs are representative of Jewish life. While it is possible to talk of subsystems of Jewish ethnicity, there are still very few customs that are shared by most American Jews aside from religious practices. So, as much as Jewishness is anomalous as a religion because of its emphasis on this-worldly action, Jewishness is also anomalous as a secular ethnic identity because it does not fit well into the usual this-worldly categories of biology and secular culture.

So what is Jewish ethnicity? While culture and biology may contribute something to Jewish ethnicity, there is also another dimension, mentioned earlier, the social. For all that Jews make individual choices about religious observance, they do not see themselves simply as totally free individual agents; they also see themselves as inextricably belonging to a group, a group that they did not choose and that is not well defined by a Protestant-style religion. This is why so many Jews see Jewishness as a matter of culture and ancestry. The citizenship metaphor, suggesting that Jews identify as a particular group, recognizes this sense of a social identity. While Jews hail from all over the world, most Jews, nonetheless, feel connected to each other by a history and heritage that dates back over three thousand years. It is as if the overflow of the social grid of Jewish life from the religious practices of American Jewry is addressed through ethnicity. In other words, while individual physical actions define the this-worldliness of religious forms of Jewishness, the social defines the this-worldliness of ethnic forms of Jewishness.

This consciousness of being a social group has often been labeled clannishness, but it is not meant to be about exclusiveness. Unlike Christianity or Islam, being Jewish is not meant to be universalized. While anyone can become a Jew, no one needs to. Given both the heavy obligations Jews were traditionally expected to maintain, along with Jews' painful history, Jewish tradition has taught that there was really no reason why anyone should become Jewish. Rather, a specifically social identity is being distinguished as an inextricable part of the self. At the same time, the differences from other groups is also acknowledged. This appears in the importance in Jewish tradition of the dichotomy between the particular, that which is internal to the Jewish social world, and the universalistic, that which applies to all humanity.

So how is this social consciousness expressed by Jews in America? At one time in America, Jewish neighborhoods insured a social experience, but now Jewish neighborhoods are rare. With their disappearance, more formalized venues have developed. Synagogues have played a major role in maintaining a sense of community. However, where religion is not important, secular organizations have performed a similar function. This has especially been the case in America. For all its individualism and inadequacy in dealing with Jewish ethnicity, the United States is structured to promote organizational life. It has a heritage of voluntary associations for any and all causes. As one astute observer of America as early as the 1840s said,

> the most democratic country in the world [America] now is that in which men have in our time carried to the highest perfection the act of pursuing in common the objects of common desires and have applied this new technique to the greatest number of purposes.
>
> (De Tocqueville 1969: 518)

Jews have easily assimilated this heritage, creating a plethora of voluntary organizations that are expressions of Jewish ethnicity.

These organizations, while secular, are informed by two key Jewish religious activities. They are learning and doing acts of kindness. Judaism has always valued the study of its sacred texts. Studying these texts, which at one time was central to traditional Jewish life, now has been replaced, secularly, with learning in nonreligious areas. Education continues to be valued, and in Jewish organizational life both religious and secular education play roles. Indeed, the multiple perspectives, noted at the beginning of this chapter, is indicative of a consideration of differing perspectives that continue the importance of the intellectual. Equally religiously central are acts of kindness and a view of charity framed as doing justly. This recalls the concern with redemption in Judaism. Acts of kindness make the world a better place to live. This religious goal can also be realized secularly. Indeed, the secular world identifies this goal with morality, distinguishing it from the religious. In the Jewish secular world, this morality has been translated into social justice programs and philanthropy to support all manner of societal needs.

The significance of both the intellect and moral activity is reflected in how Jews characterize what they think of as Jewish. Several qualities have been identified as essential to Jewish identity. Being ethical (69 percent), working for social justice/ equality (56 percent), and being intellectually curious (49 percent) are among the highest rated qualities. Of course as characterization of individual qualities, they are problematic. Such qualities are not specific to Jews. While they may be something Jews ostensibly should have, there are not only Jews who don't have such qualities, there are non-Jews who do have these qualities. Yet, the importance of intellect and moral activity are significant when it comes to a consideration of the Jewish social world. They constitute, in a variety of forms, the major content of that social world. The intellectual and the moral in combination with the particular and universal define most of Jewish organizational life.

At the most particularistic end of the spectrum are a wide variety of organizations. Some fight anti-Semitism; some organize Jewish youth activities, some support vulnerable Jews in the United States and around the world and some specialize in support for Israel. Notably there are organizations specifically concerned with Jewish communal life in America. These are called federations and most major communities of Jews have one. They collect money to support the vulnerable, provide family services such as childcare, Jewish education, and young adult activities. The various programs are not necessarily provided only to Jews, particularly those programs that serve the most vulnerable in society. In part this is because of the contribution of government funds, but it also fits with Jewish moral concern for others beyond the Jewish community. Yet, mostly these particularistic organizations serve Jews, and Jews view them as a form of moral expression in their concern for Jews and their efforts to strengthen Jewish communal life.

Another example of Jewishly particularistic organizations, but those with more distinctly universalistic aims, are the service learning programs. They have such differing goals as supporting environmental concerns, social justice, or disaster relief. Often synagogues are sponsors, but there are also independent organizations, prominently financed through private family foundations. They ground their universalistic activities

FIGURE 8.5 *Good Deed Day activity.* Source: *Photograph by Areyvut.*

in Jewish tradition through the study of classic Jewish texts. Jewish individuals concerned with specific universalistic issues come together, forming a community to address those issues. Here the social is reinforced through particularistic study and universalistic moral activity.

There are even Jewish organizations focused primarily on the universal such as Jews Against Anti-Christian Defamation or the Jewish Voice for Peace. The former, as its name suggests, works on behalf of Christians, and the later works on behalf of Palestinians. For such organizations, the traditional Jewish concern for making the world a better place informs their activities. Note that in the latter's case, the universalist concerns are so strong that they trump support for what might seem to be a quintessentially Jewish social secular concern, the State of Israel. While ties between Jews may define Jewish ethnicity, here what is perceived by some Jews as moral takes precedence, yet these Jews still feel the necessity to form a Jewish organization to accomplish their goals.

Indeed, the social is so important that Jews may seek to claim it even individualistically. While some part of the social dimension occurs simply through friendships, it also can rely on the support of the larger community. A personal expression of association, manifesting the individualism that is part of American life, can depend upon multiple venues allowing anyone with an interest in things Jewish to explore those interests, be they Jews or non-Jews. They often center around educational concerns and include film festivals, podcasts, websites, and museums. On the more particularistic end of the spectrum are film festivals, podcasts, and websites. These may create temporary or virtual communities, but they are directed toward individual participation, a matter of choice that does not require commitment. Jewish themes, both secular and religious, can be subjects of focus, and sometimes even non-Jewish themes are explored. For some Jews, these options, providing a kind of Jewish community, are a significant way to identify Jewishly without being religious. Here a secular, particularistic format provides individuals with a way to identify with the Jewish social world.

Somewhat more universalistic are museums. They tend to frame their Jewish content as representative of a shared human experience. So, historical museums tell Jewish stories, universalistically. Colonial synagogues, besides being religious, serve as models of how a group can maintain its identity and integrate into a pluralistic society. Museums dedicated to the history of local Jewish communities are concerned with how their stories mirror the stories of other immigrants to the United States, and **Holocaust** museums, while telling the story of the Jewish experience in Europe during the Second World War, include exhibits of other peoples' experiences of genocide. Art museums, picking up on universalistic themes, may focus on Jewish artists whose art need not be concerned with particularly Jewish concerns. Indeed, several Jewish art museums do not restrict themselves to Jewish artists. They call for exhibits on themes derived from Jewish tradition or experience, but not specific to it. These include the environment and even something as broad as "beginnings." Here the universal includes multiple, differing voices. In these secular Jewish venues, the particularistic Jewish ethnic is promoted through universalistic concerns, providing multiple ways for individual Jews to connect to their heritage.

Thus, Jewish ethnicity takes a complex form in America. As a secular manifestation of Jewish identity, Jewish ethnicity is deeply informed by its religious heritage, where Jewish ethnicity is part of the overflow from the once religious grid that does not fit well with a model of Judaism that is practiced in its Protestant form. This residual part of the Jewish heritage highlights the existence of a Jewish social world and runs through a range of concerns from the particular to the universal, highlighting traditional Jewish values of education and morality. So, Jewish ethnicity, not easily defined, has in fact been well accommodated by America's heritage of voluntary associations. Yet, America is also home to individualism. Such individualism increasingly undermines the formation and maintenance of voluntary associations in America, both for Jews and non-Jews. Just as America is becoming increasingly individualistic, so too have Jews.

Jewishness as American

In this brief excursus on how Jews view themselves, religion and ethnicity have been key identities. Yet, Judaism, traditionally, was neither what is commonly thought of as religious because of its this-worldly social grid nor what is commonly thought to be ethnic because it lacks a purely biological base and/or a single secular cultural form. Jewishness is, quite simply, an anomalous identity. This distinctiveness is not just a matter of discreet details of content, like different holidays or a particular history, but is constitutive of Jewish culture, allowing for what is usually thought of as secular and religious to overlap. Thus, for Judaism, the importance of the intellect, as the prominence of study suggests, and the appreciation of the physical, as the centrality of actions establishes, have provided means to accommodate Judaism to secular American life. However, this should not obscure this unique cultural constellation, which applies both ethnically and religiously.

So, too, an emphasis on a social morality reinforces Jewish distinctiveness, although here there is a tension with American values. Rather than prizing the lone hero who pulls him (or her) self up by the bootstraps, Jewish culture deems communal support part of morality. America's history of voluntary associations has its own tensions with the celebration of individualism, but distinctions are to be made between American and Jewish forms. The diverse goals of Christianity and Judaism make problems of individualism arising out of conceptions of personal salvation, somewhat different from problems arising out of the Jewish concern with redemption. Suffice it to say that Judaism, in placing crucial importance on the social world, in particular and universal forms, shapes a perception of morality that is shared by both secular ethnicity and Jewish religious tradition, in another example of Judaism's distinctive cultural constellation.

Nonetheless, Jews have also viewed themselves as American. They see themselves as part of the mosaic of diversity that characterizes America. As different as they are, they have integrated into American society in ways that allow their Jewishness to fit

FIGURE 8.6 *Jewish and American.* Source: *Ira L. Black—Corbis/Getty Images.*

within the structures of American life. For many Jews, Judaism has been reshaped to conform to American standards of religious practice with many of its other aspects expressed as part of an ethnic identity through secular voluntary associations. At the same time, even Jews who wish to retain the religious social grid of tradition have also found a place. Thus, Jews have thrived in America. Jews have made a success of their lives both because America has welcomed them, structurally and with relatively little anti-Semitism, and because of resources within Judaism nourishing its success, its empowering of this-worldliness and its own strong support structures. The multiple ways in which Jewish life has flourished in America confirms the view of American Jews that they are both distinctively Jewish, religiously and ethnically, while also thoroughly American.

Further Reading and Online Resources

Kaplan, D.E. (2009), *Contemporary American Judaism: Transformation and Renewal*, New York: Columbia University Press.
Lederhendler, E., ed. (2011), *Ethnicity and Beyond: Theories and Dilemmas of Jewish Group Demarcation*, Oxford: Oxford University Press.
Maccabeats (2016), "Maccabeats and Naturally 7 – Shed a Little Light – MLK Jr. Day – (James Taylor Cover)," *YouTube*, January 11. Available online: https://www.youtube.com/

watch?v=crKDDS5D_os (accessed November 15, 2020). [This video shows Orthodox Jews from Yeshiva University singing a capella with an a capella African American group. It sums up the article by showing how Jews can hold on to their particularist religious and ethnic traditions, also expressing universalistic concerns, in a very American way.]
Pew Research Center (2013), "A Portrait of Jewish Americans," October 1. Available online: http://www.pewforum.org/2013/10/01/jewish-american-beliefs-attitudes-culture-survey/ (accessed August 18, 2019).

References

Boman, T. (1970), *Hebrew Thought Compared with Greek*, trans. J.L. Moreau, New York: W.W. Norton and Co.

BTW Consultants (2008), *Jewish Service Learning: What Is and What Could Be*. Available online: https://www.bjpa.org/content/upload/bjpa/jewi/Jewish-Service-Learning-Summary-Document.pdf (accessed November 15, 2020).

Cohen, S.M. and A. Eisen (2000), *The Jew within: Self, Family, and Community in America*, Bloomington: Indiana University Press.

De Tocqueville, A. (1969), *Democracy in America*, ed. J.P. Mayer, Garden City, NY: Doubleday and Company.

Geertz, C. (1973), "Religion as Cultural System," in *The Interpretation of Cultures*, 87–125, New York: Basic Books.

Graizbord, D.L. (2019), "Men and Women of the Nation," *Tablet*, August 20. Available online: https://www.tabletmag.com/jewish-arts-and-culture/289739/men-and-women-of-the-nation (accessed November 15, 2020).

Jewish Film Festivals (2020), [Blog]. Available online: https://jewishfilmfestivals.org/ (accessed November 15, 2020).

Kaplan, D.E. (2009), *Contemporary American Judaism: Transformation and Renewal*, New York: Columbia University Press.

Lederhendler, E., ed. (2011), *Ethnicity and beyond: Theories and Dilemmas of Jewish Group Demarcation*, Oxford: Oxford University Press.

LeVee, E. (2018), "Contemporary Jewish Demography, Society, and Culture: Secularization and Its Discontents," in D. Bell (ed.), *The Routledge Companion to Jewish History and Historiography*, 182–94, London: Routledge.

Pew Research Center (2013), "A Portrait of Jewish Americans," October 1. Available online: http://www.pewforum.org/2013/10/01/jewish-american-beliefs-attitudes-culture-survey/ (accessed November 15, 2020).

Pirke Avot, 1:2 (1945), trans. J.H. Hertz, New York: Behrman House.

Putnam, R. (2000), *Bowling Alone*, New York: Simon and Schuster.

Sarna, J.D. (2004), *American Judaism: A History*, New Haven, CT: Yale University Press.

Sklare, M. and J. Greenblum (1979), *Jewish Identity on the Suburban Frontier: A Study of Group Survival in the Open Society*, Chicago: University of Chicago Press.

Wertheimer, J. (2018), *The New American Judaism: How Jews Practice Their Religion Today*, Princeton, NJ: Princeton University Press.

Wikipedia (2013), "Jewish Museums in the United States," last modified July 28. Available online: https://en.wikipedia.org/wiki/Category:Jewish_museums_in_the_United_States (accessed November 15, 2020).

Woocher, J. (1986), *Sacred Survival: The Civil Religion of American Jews*, Bloomington: Indiana University Press.

Glossary Terms

Chanukah This is a holiday commemorating the rededication (Chanukah means dedication) of the Second Temple in Jerusalem after the defeat of the Greek Seleucids (Greeks ruling in Syria) by the Jewish Maccabees in 165 BCE.

Diaspora With the destruction of the First Temple in 586 BCE, Jews were dispersed eastward into Babylonia. Although Jews did return to Palestine, a significant community remained in Babylonia. With the destruction of the Second Temple in 70 CE, some Jews fled eastward and some Jews were taken westward. All communities that did not remain in Palestine are considered part of the Jewish diaspora.

Halakha This refers to the collective body of Jewish religious laws derived from the written laws found in the Pentateuch (first five books of the Bible) and oral laws that have been passed down through Jewish tradition. The word derives from the root that means to behave (or go).

Holocaust This refers to the extermination of six million Jews by the Nazis during the Second World War.

Kashrut This refers to what may be eaten according to Jewish law. Animals have to be killed in a prescribed manner. Pork and shellfish are forbidden. Milk and meat may not be eaten together, and there are even separate pots, pans, and dishware for each.

Passover This holiday in the spring celebrates the freeing of Hebrew slaves from Egyptian slavery. Traditionally the holiday begins with a special festive meal and continues for seven or eight days.

Vernacular This refers to the language commonly spoken in a particular region.

Yiddish This refers to the language of Eastern European Jews. It involves a combination of German and Hebrew and there are many dialects, depending on geographical region.

9

Jewish Diversity

Lewis R. Gordon

Asticky issue with discussing any human community is that to study its people requires not only determining what makes them distinct from other human communities, but also recognizing their humanity, which involves understanding what makes them distinct from each other. This is a problem faced not only by those who study various groups from without but also by those who do so from within. To make matters worse, as Jewish people are linked to Judaism—one of the twelve "world religions"—it is rare to meet someone who has never heard of Jews and lacks an opinion of Jewish people. As the latter goes, many opinions are based on literacy at best, ignorance often, and bigotry at worst. In some cases, the opinions are not based on ignorance of Jewish people or even hatred of Jewish people but, instead, on an ordinary tendency of many people, including Jews: every community considers their Jews to be *the Jews*.

The following discussion will outline some of the difficulties of talking about Jewish people in general, followed by a very short history of Jewish people, and then a summary of some recent debates about Jewish diversity.

Preliminary Problems

In addition to the problem of most people considering their Jews to be *the Jews*, there is also the impact of popular portrayals of Jewish people in literature, cinema, and historical propaganda. These images are also misinformed by faulty historiography and general problems of the relationship of history to what could be called theological history. Added to all this is the problem of tendencies to ignore the highly politically charged situation of almost any discussion of Jews pretty much since the existence of Jewish people.

The popular images of Jews depend on the societies in which they are produced. Remember, the presumption of each society is that their Jews exemplify all Jewish people. Thus, even if their portrayals were accurate about the Jews they know—including those Jews' portrayal of themselves—the presumption of their applicability to Jewish people elsewhere would be at times an over generalization. What makes many popular cultural images problematic, however, is that they are often infused with stereotypes about Jews, which makes the dominant images more a projection of anti-Jewish sentiments than the lived reality of Jewish peoples. Dominant images of Jews in many people's imagination, including many Jews', are those from Hollywood blockbusters such as Cecil B. DeMille movies and millions of biblical portraits of a past in which Jews are, simply put, white.

The problematic historiography that supports a white Jewish past is premised on many problematic views not only of Jewish people but also of any diasporic people. The presumption is that a people could spread out across the globe but remain homogeneous and endogamic without incest. That would mean that the Jews one meets are exactly—in appearance and genetic makeup—like the Jews from the moment Jewish people came into being. Additionally, problematic historiography ignores social and political forces such as colonization, attempted genocide, anti-miscegenation, and litanies of laws that stimulate migration and, in some cases, force forms of endogamy in some places and exogamy in others. As we will see, looking at Jewish history through the lens of colonialism and the impact of that on what it means to be "modern" offers a different picture of Jewish people than neat, linear narratives of an insular and homogenous people throughout history.

Finally, though not exhaustively, there is the reality of anti-Semitism or anti-Jewish racism. "Racism" is a tricky word to use here because of debates over the religious identity of Jews versus that of nationhood or race. Jewish identity as a *religious* identity shifts back and forth throughout history. The movement from a people to a religion took place during the ancient Roman Empire, but the domination of a people returned in the Holy Roman Empire, and then there was, after the rise of Islam and the various Caliphates since the seventh century, a form of medieval Christian hatred in which both Jews and at least Afro-Muslims were organized under the concept **raza**, from which the term "race" was born. The Jewish "race" then underwent changes as Jewish people spread through the colonies of the various Euromodern Christian empires since the fifteenth century.

With regard to anti-Jewish hatred, most anti-Semites know nothing about Judaism. In fact, in the cases of Christians and Muslims, those with some knowledge regard Jewish religion as foundational to their own. There are those among them who hate Jewish people, not Judaism, despite the latter entailing the existence of the former. Regarding hatred of Jewish people, much depends on whatever stereotypes and fears are at work in the given society's stereotypes of Jews. The result is often a form of demonization in which whatever ills are at work in the society have some kind of Jewish malevolence behind them.

Anti-Jewish hatred, from this perspective, is the demonization of Jewish people. I prefer to use "anti-Jewish hatred" instead of "anti-Semitism" at this point because of the loaded historical evolution of the latter. The adjective "Semitic" was coined by the German historian August Ludwig von Schlözer, who devised it to refer to groups of Northeast African and West Asian languages such as Amharic, Arabic, Aramaic, Hebrew, and Tigrinya. Although not intended as a racialized term, racism was tagged specifically to the term as a reference to Jewish people, which led to the Austrian Jewish scholar Moritz Steinschneider's referring to that form of hatred as "anti-Semitism." Today, the nation-state of Israel uses the term officially—although there are members of Israeli society who reject this—as any critical stand against it. Expanding the debates about this issue would take us too far afield, so we will proceed with using the terms "anti-Jewish hatred" and where I mention "anti-Semitism" it will be referring to that interpretation.

How demonized Jewish people are imagined depends on what that local understanding of Jewish people is. In Europe, it is of European Jews; and so is the case in each continent except for the fact that the historical Jews on many continents have been displaced by whichever Jewish people become hegemonic because of being located at the center of the extant empires from which they come or in which they reside. Today, because of US hegemony and the after-effects of recent European empires ranging from the British to the French, that means various historic Jewish populations being replaced by European Jews as the authentic image of Jewish people.

A Very Short History of Jewish People

Understood from the perspective of religion, identifying a Jewish person is simple. Whoever practices Judaism—the Jewish religion—is Jewish. This simple formula is made complicated by several factors. The first is that Judaism has many denominations and not all of them recognize the other as authentic. To make matters worse, nearly all of these denominations come out of the European Jewish experience. Before those changes in the eighteenth century, there were simply people who identified themselves as Abrahamic, Hebrew, Israelite, Jewish, and a variety of other local names in various countries. The Reform movement in nineteenth-century Germany was an effort to "modernize" Judaism. I place "modern" in quotation marks because this amounted to becoming, for the most part, almost indistinguishable from any other European. It is a cultural understanding of what it means to be modern, although the term, from the Latin "modo," simply means to belong to the present. The formation of Reform Judaism was posed against "Orthodox" Judaism. I added quotation to "Orthodox" since before that there was no reason to identify any kind of Judaism in such terms. Objecting to the Orthodox movement, the Conservative movement was formed in the late nineteenth century. Objecting to that movement, the Reconstructionist movement was formed in the first quarter of the twentieth century. Objecting to all of these, "ultra" Orthodox Judaism followed. These are all primarily European-descended forms of Judaism. Beyond them were the other families of Hebrew, Israelite, or Jewish practices ranging from Sephardic and **Mizrahi** (which most European Jews consider "Orthodox") across Europe, parts of Africa, and West Asia, to the many others to which we will shortly turn, which, because of Eurocentrism, are considered either "crypto" or "non-traditional" or, worse, not Jewish at all. "Sephardic" refers primarily to historically Iberian and North African Judaism. "Mizrahi" refers to West Asian or Middle Eastern Judaism. The problems with these designations should be evident, since they are clearly older than the European forms since Jerusalem, the holiest location of Judaism, is located in West Asia/East Africa/the Middle East depending on how one interprets that area of the world culturally and geographically.

These various denominations and groups affect the question of who is Jewish because some don't recognize the others as properly practicing Judaism. Much of this is connected to Jewish religious law—**Halakha**—through which being Kosher (satisfying the requirements of Jewish law often properly referring to diet) is determined. Although it is generally presumed that all recognize the Ultra-Orthodox, this is not entirely the case. There are Jews who argue that over-adherence to the written law, which in Judaism amounts not only to **Torah** (simultaneously "the Law," "Teachings," "Instructions," sometimes referred to as the books of Moses or the first five books of the "Hebrew Bible") but also the **Talmud** ("Instruction," "Learning"), which consists of the Mishnah (the written Rabbinic oral history) and the Gemara (elucidations of the Mishna and related texts). Jewish critics argue that sometimes the ethical dimension of Judaism is lost to fetishization of a set of texts, many of which are actually rich with exceptions on ethical grounds. To this I should add that arguing is a vital part of Judaism, which leads to endless jokes in the form of two Jews conversing equaling at least three opinions. On the matter of textual authority, there are Karaite and Samaritan Judaism, which go further and argue for strict adherence to Torah alone. But what complicates this matter is also the debate about what it means to be born Jewish.

In most denominations of Judaism, one is born Jewish through being the child of a Jewish woman. The Ultra-Orthodox require an Ultra-Orthodox Jewish woman; the Orthodox, at least an Orthodox mother; the Conservative, at least a mother from Conservative Judaism or the Orthodox or Ultra-Orthodox groups; and so on among the European-based forms of Judaism. In Reform and Reconstructionist Judaism, one could also be Jewish through one's father being Jewish under the criteria of those denominations, so long as one is raised Jewish. Alongside all these is "Conservadoxy," practices among Jews who identify as Hebrew-Israelites, which is a mixture of Orthodox, Conservative, and unique African American Jewish elements (to be discussed), wherein membership varies according to various groups. What complicates all this are traditions outside of the European ones in which authentic Jewish membership depends on fathers. These groups are sometimes referred to as practicing First Temple Judaism or Priestly Judaism, which was patrilineal. The tradition of matrilineal membership is a feature of the Rabbinic tradition (hegemonic Judaism in Europe and parts of West Asia since the sixth century CE), which grew out of a response to the fall of the Second Temple, although patrilineality was practiced in the Judea of the times in which the Second Temple was built.

There are many more permutations and debates that would make this discussion go too far afield and cannot be addressed because of the limits of space. The interested reader could consult some of the works in the further reading and reference lists at the end of this chapter.

Beyond Judaism—the religion—there is of course the complicated history of the people who practice the religion and members of that community who don't. The latter are called "cultural" and "secular" Jews. For many among the religious, if they are born Jews, they are still Jews, although not in their view very good ones. And for others, they can be very good Jews if even not practicing Judaism so long as they exemplify Jewish ethical life, albeit in a limited way. This is especially so in the important concept of *bachar*, which is often translated as to be chosen or elected. The concept is actually one that occasions the fear and trembling of taking responsibility for ethical life, including, radically understood, for responsibility at all; it is a responsibility for responsibility. An additional complication is the history of Jewish people beyond accounts in religious texts. This is where history and theological history collide. Worse, both at times fall prey to narratives that ignore basic facts of the worlds they study. For instance, there was no reason for ancient peoples to have defined themselves in terms of future geopolitical boundaries and territories. Ancient African peoples couldn't imagine their world stopped at what would be the future Suez Canal or the Sahara Desert. Another one is that prejudices could be such that it would be unthinkable to consider elements such as African origins of many ancient practices that have become known as Jewish.

Here, a remark about creolization is needed. Creolization is where cultural encounters may lead to fusions despite one group being politically subordinate to another. This mixture could take on meaning in a group where it becomes a living feature of their identity. The adoption of a practice could transform it into what is meaningful for that group. Thus, circumcision, although originating in ancient East Africa, could be transformed among some East African and West Asian peoples into a mark of their identification through an innovation such as occurring within eight days of the male child's birth instead of at the age of puberty. Another could be the rejection of circumcising female offspring. Stepping on the glass at a wedding—an old Persian ritual—could be transformed through attaching a Jewish meaning to it.

The historical evidence is that the ancient country of Kmt (ancient Egypt) reached as far south as Nubia (present-day Sudan) and as far north as the Balkans at various periods of its history, as far west as today's Libya (and perhaps farther) and as far east as Canaan or present-day Israel. It was in ancient Kmt that a monotheistic movement of emanation from an invisible deity emerged under the leadership of Akhenaten and Nefertiti three and a half millennia ago. A few centuries before this period was also the one-century rule of the Hyksos kings (reputed to have been from the West Asian area of the Levant). The ancient Jewish historian Flavius Josephus referred to them to support the narrative of Jewish people as originating from West Asia (e.g., Abraham being from Ur in ancient Mesopotamia) and then moving into Egypt. What is clear is that eventually a group of Northeast African and West Asian peoples came about in the Levant in what was known as Canaan, in which many small kingdoms, some large ones, followed through which there was Israel to the north and Judah to the south, whose center was Jerusalem. These kingdoms suffered many invasions, among which was the one by the Akkadian king Nebuchadnezzar II in 587 BCE during which the Temple of Solomon or the First Temple was destroyed. The Temple was the holy center of the constellation of clans and peoples known today as Hebrews or Israelites. The Second Temple was built in approximately 516 BCE. It lasted through a variety of invasions, periods of colonization, and, with the aid of the Roman Empire, the ascent of the short-lived Hasmonean Dynasty (*c.* 140–*c.* 116 BCE). Judah eventually became Judea, a colony of the Roman Empire in the first century BCE through to the second century CE, during which, under Herod I, reconstruction and renovations continued to achieve its renowned splendor. As all this was happening under colonization, rebellion persisted until the Emperor Titus destroyed the Temple in 70 CE. The Romans, under the Emperor Hadrian, destroyed Judea, renamed the entire set of former kingdoms Palestine in 135 CE, the Roman name for Philistia, and built the city of Aelia Capitolina on top of Jerusalem in 136. That non-Jewish city remained until 324.

Among Roman conventions was the concept of "religion" (in some etymologies from *religere*—to reread; in others from *religare*—to bind fast or be bound). The Romans, recognizing polytheism, permitted multiple religions so long as their adherents followed Roman law. The ancient people of Judea did not regard their practices as compatible with polytheism and the supremacy of Roman law. There wasn't a clear separation of the cultural and the sacred, as found in many societies where ethnic identity and sacred practices were inseparable. This raised many questions in the midst of colonization. Think, for example, of what the Akan of Ghana or the Wolof of Senegal faced under British and French colonialism. Debates on whether to follow the colonizers' laws or the traditional laws of their people were plentiful. Some regarded the colonizers' laws as "modern"—that is, of the present and thus foundations of the future. Others saw them as polluting and degrading and sought to return to precolonial times. And others argued for a fusion of both. Among Jews, this is a heavily contested area. For our purposes, Judeans were patrilineal; matrilineality is notably evident after the fall of the Second Temple and peculiarly so among Jews within the Roman worlds—ancient and medieval—from which Rabbinic Judaism eventually emerged. On the issue of conversion, it was clear that the earlier people of Judah and then Judeans focused more on females converting into the community. After the fall of the Second Temple, however, there was a period of massive conversion alongside the growth of Messianic Judeanism, which became Christianity. The Roman concept of religion worked well for this proselytizing period in which this now religious group of people, since great numbers were not born Judean, became known as Jews. The numbers, as with nearly everything regarding Jewish people, receive much debate, but estimates are that Roman census suggest anything from 150,000 (though some critics claim four million) Judeans before the fall of the Second Tempe and approximately eight million by the fourth century CE.

For our purposes, the point isn't the total numbers—which would put us in a quagmire of disputes over homelands and imagined histories—but the location of the people. As Judea was located in a place where Africa, Asia, and Europe met, the idea of a morphologically homogenous group of people all without diverse views of themselves is absurd. Add the many invasions and trade, and it is highly unlikely that the people were not, in contemporary terms, multiracial. Similarly, the ancient Roman Empire reached as far north as Britannica or what is the present-day UK, as far South as upper Egypt (Southern Egypt), as far west as present-day Spain, and as far east as the borders of present-day Iran. The Jewish people across that range could not help but be diverse. Because of colonization, enslavement, trade, politics, and even curiosity, earlier peoples of Judah were already found in Asia and across East Africa as far south as Ethiopia. By the time of the Roman Empire, present-day Western Europe came into their history. In the fourth century, much changed when the emperor Constantine converted to Christianity. Along with Christianity achieving the status of a state religion, Jewish proselytizing was outlawed. Jews under the jurisdiction of the Holy Roman Empire faced outlawed exogamy—since for Jews who expected to remain Jews meant converting the spouse who was not born Jewish—in Christendom punishable by death.

Although Islam came about later in the seventh century and spread throughout Northern through Central Africa, much of South Asia, and into Europe as far as southern France, Christendom continued its aspirations of "conquest" through which groups such as Jews and the Afro-Muslims in control of much of Southern Europe were placed under *raza* as people to be placed under its yoke through the Crusades. By the fifteenth century, these efforts took a decisive turn when the Moors were defeated in Grenada; the Inquisition inaugurated forced conversions and challenges to the already converted, and the conflict took to the Atlantic Ocean with Christopher Columbus landing in the Bahamas. The age of Euromodern colonialism began and so, too, a new chapter in the transformation of Jewish people.

There are many elements to consider before the events of the fifteenth century. As with the Holy Roman Empire or Christendom, there were Jews throughout the various Caliphates. For instance, Moses ben Maimon (Maimonides, known among Jews also as RaMBaM)—the greatest rabbi and Jewish scholar of the medieval period, lived throughout Caliphates from Córdoba to Morocco to Egypt where he died in 1204. In the variety of other Muslim kingdoms and rising groups, including the Ottoman Caliphates (now known as the Ottoman Empire), Jewish people were present. Although understood as a distinct minority people, Jewish people were clearly mixing in, culturally and through miscegenation, with the various groups in those Caliphates and kingdoms. In cases where Jews were in places where restrictions on conversion were relaxed, there were converts through exogamy and whose descendants were then interpreted as endogamous. The situation of Jews meeting Jews wherever they traveled was a source of Jewish diversity. To this should also be added the importance of gender. From antiquity through to this period of expanded kingdoms and Caliphates, there was the everyday fact of enslavement to which girls and women were particularly vulnerable. For this reason, Jewish traders were predominantly males, which meant, through the formation of minyans (a quorum of ten Jewish men required for Jewish public worship), the founding of new Jewish communities invariably involved converted local females. It is no accident today that Jewish genetic "tracing" focuses on Y-chromosomal markers or male genes. It is also one of the reasons why, despite the criterion of matrilineality, Jewish genealogists throughout Africa, Asia, the Caribbean, and Latin America tend to focus on patrilineal ancestors until more recent times when the dangers of females traveling have declined (although have not been eliminated).

There were already the makings of many Jewish or at least Jewish-descended peoples across Africa, Asia, and Europe by the fifteenth century. The variety of factors from colonialism, enslavement, politics, and trade led to Jews in Cochin, in Kerala, India; there were Jews in Kaifeng, in the Henan Province of China; there were Jews migrating from Yemen along the coasts of Africa whose descendants became the Lemba people of Zimbabwe and South Africa; there were Jews across North Africa whose descendants are Berber and Arab Jews; others along the Sudan became Kushite Jews; others followed trade routes across the Sahara into the Congo and along the coasts to what are today countries such as Ghana, Nigeria, and Senegal. Many of these groups were unaware of the changes occurring in the fifteenth century when Christendom took its conflicts with all non-Christian peoples to the world's oceans and other shores.

Since the fifteenth century, European Jewish life changed in a variety of ways. First, there were now Christian colonies with new kinds of people for Christians to colonize. Second, the Peace of Westphalia (1648) transformed the wars of religion over Catholicism, Protestantism, and various Christian dominions into Euromodern nation-states. This meant that what these new Europeans sought in the colonies was extractions of wealth under European control with a reduced interest in the salvation of souls. This created a demand for Europeans, which, for European Jews, offered possibilities similar to what the Caliphates offered in parts of Africa and Asia. At this point an old rule came to the fore. Different Jews took center stage according to which country dominated the rest. Thus, Jewish presence in the early European colonies of the Caribbean, Central, and South America were predominantly those from the Spanish and Portuguese empires. Those were **Sephardim**. As the Inquisition continued in those countries, there were also Sephardic Jews who fled to countries such as The Netherlands and those of Scandinavia. Thus, when the Dutch Empire spread through North America and as far as the South Pacific, the Jews who were in tow were Sephardic. As other European countries got in on the action, their Jews were also involved. Added to all this was the early sixteenth-century shift from focusing on the enslavement of the Indigenous peoples of those colonies—primarily because of impending genocide—to the kidnapping of Africans. The process of *raza* moving from a theological mode of differentiation shifted to a secular naturalistic form of differentiation. The European, in short, became white as the rest of the world came under the orbit of nonwhites. For European Jews, this posed an unusual situation since they were, as a "race," not accepted as properly European (which was presumed Christian), but in the colonies their European origins placed them closer to the Christian colonizers than to the Indigenous peoples and kidnapped and enslaved Africans. Opportunities, once barred in Europe, were available for European Jews in the colonies. A problem, however, is that at times there were Jews among the kidnapped and the colonized.

Although also Jews, those people were not *European* Jews. The **Ashkenazi** Jews' European identity increased along with these empires, and as these empires achieved global domination, their Jews became the main face of Jewish people in their epoch.

Europeanness and whiteness became one. The question for European Jews was, then, whether they were white. Here the concepts of integration and assimilation come into play. Integration involves placing a people under the jurisdiction of a particular system. In this case, there is at first the European empires. Eventually, as the ruling elites in the colonies rebelled, it became their understanding of national identity. In the United States, this national identity was not only racial but also Anglo-Saxon Protestant. Although racial concepts were loose—where Anglo-Saxons, Celts, and Germans were referred to as "races"—there was an eventual understanding that authentic whiteness was to be European and culturally Anglo-Saxon Protestant. Thus, as white Anglo-Saxon Protestants asserted control over all the peoples within the borders of the United States (and eventually the hemisphere), they at the same time denied full citizenship to anyone who was not white and discriminated against those who were not culturally Anglo-Saxon Protestant. This meant that being European afforded many rights, but assimilation into Anglo-Saxon cultural practices afforded more. This was solidified in the addition of religious freedom in the Bill of Rights in the US Constitution. This afforded a powerful opportunity for European Jews. Focus on Judaism offered a case for religious protection. Focusing on European ancestry afforded racial membership. Put differently, the elimination of a religious identity enabled the possibility of a racial one alone, and that one was white. Jews who could not make such a claim were pushed to the wayside and began to disappear.

There are three additional concerns of Jewish diversity into the present that should be borne in mind. One is from *Halakha*. There are restrictions in Jewish law about enslavement. Jewish law basically requires the eventual manumission of an enslaved non-Jew who serves in a Kosher home. At manumission, that individual is fully a Jew. In other words, there is, through enslavement, conversion to Judaism. Jews who participated in the institution of slavery faced this law. This is not to say that they adhered to it, but it was there, and there were Jewish slave owners who obeyed it. There were also those who found ways around it. In Curaçao and Surinam, for instance, there were Jewish slave masters who summoned Catholic priests to baptize their slaves. In some cases, the baptized was a child born from enslaved women and masters who were their fathers. There were also instances in which subterfuge did not occur, and the Jewish families manumitted the enslaved. The difficulty is that manumitted individuals were living in a world of racialized enslavement and segregation. Those freedwomen and freedmen responded by founding their own Jewish communities in the United States. Limitations on how they could register as religious communities often led to many of them being misrepresented as Christians when they were in fact *halakhic*. Those people today are among sets of distinctively African American communities under the titles Hebrews, Israelites, and Jews, although there are also Christian groups who identify with similar titles or in some cases are explicitly Christian such as the Seven Day Adventists.

As well, there were nonwhite populations of people who came to Judaism through mass conversion. A notable example is the **Abayudaya** people of Uganda. They were Indigenous Ugandans who rejected Christian missionary conversion and opted for the Old Testament in the early twentieth century, which in effect made them at first more like Karaites. They eventually went through conversions under Conservative Judaism, and some among them under other forms of Judaism.

Another concern is, of course, the catastrophic events of the first half of the twentieth century in Europe. The total number of Jews in the world before the Second World War in Germany depends much on how Jews are defined. Many demographers estimate the total number of Jews before the Second World War to be about nineteen million. Six million were slaughtered in the *Shoah*, the preferred Jewish term, which means (roughly) calamity or destruction. The rest of the world denotes it as the Holocaust. The collective trauma of those events impacted Jewish identity in a way that brought into focus three considerations through which European Jewish experience eclipsed and practically erased the rest of the Jewish world. The first is imperial: Jews at the center of global hegemonic empires, such as the British and the American, the political

FIGURE 9.1 *Abayudaya women carrying Torah.* Source: *Courtesy of Be'chol Lashon.*

and economic location through which to articulate Jewish experience. The second is traumatic: European Jewish experience was marked by anti-Jewish racism or anti-Semitism and genocide. The combination led to the third: Zionist efforts, began in the nineteenth century, found the perfect opportunity to found the Jewish nation-state. As the Zionists were predominantly Ashkenazi, their understanding of Jewish people took center stage.

Thus, despite the de facto diversity of Jewish peoples, the hegemonic understanding of Jewish people ignored and, in some cases, erased that understanding for the singularity of what eventually became a white Jewish identity. By the last quarter of the twentieth century, challenges to this view came about through Ethiopian Jewish migration to Israel. Before that, there were varieties of Jews fighting against their invisibility. There were Ethiopian, African American, and Afro-Caribbean Jews in varieties of Black Liberation movements such as Marcus Garvey's Universal Negro Improvement Association (UNIA) and African Communities League (ACL). As the Rastafari movement came out of the Garvey movements, their brand of Zionism is not coincidental.

FIGURE 9.2 *100th anniversary celebration of Abayudaya with members of Be'chol Lashon.*
Source: *Courtesy of Be'chol Lashon.*

Jews of Color

At this point, it should be clear that, despite the prejudices external and internal to Jewish communities, the diversity of Jewish people is a fact. It is also a fact that the Euromodern age, which reaches into the twenty-first century, is one of white hegemony. Given the lure of whiteness, this posed a problem for Jewish communities. Certain Jewish communities invested in whiteness and segregated themselves from nonwhites. It was this process that created "white Jews." This identity wouldn't be a problem if it weren't for its consequence of white Jewish normativity—namely, the presumption of Jews being white. To say "Jews" today pretty much refers to white Jews, or worse: the notion that "real Jews" are white.

In the late 1980s through early 1990s in the United States, the expression "people of color" became an umbrella term for all nonwhite peoples. During this period, the formulation "Jews of color" came about from Jews linked to communities who, beyond their Jewishness, do not identify with being white. Those Jews acknowledged white Jews' white identification and thus decided to affirm nonwhite Jewish identification across nonwhite identities. Although Black and Indigenous Jewish people are included in that umbrella, their histories were different. This is because although Black Jews have been designated as "negro," "black," "Black," "Afro-," and varieties of designations from "African American," "Afro-Canadian," "Afro-Caribbean," or "Afro-European," many lived their Jewish identities as Hebrew, Israelite, or simply Jewish. This was similar for Jews who were of Indigenous descent. The racial adjectives were often imposed upon them from white Jews who "discovered" them. These "discoveries" were often in bad faith since it was rarely the case that religious Black and Indigenous Jews did not reach out to Jewish institutions. Additionally, as we saw with Jewish migration, miscegenation was always a possibility. This increased where—contrary to stereotypes—Jewish migrants were poor. They often lived among poor people of many kinds, and since Black and brown peoples have large numbers of poor people in often ghettoized conditions (as European Jews faced in Eastern Europe), they invariably met

FIGURE 9.3 *Camp Be'chol Lashon.* Source: *Courtesy of Be'chol Lashon.*

each other under challenging material conditions through which also desire and love followed. Additionally, there is the long history of Jewish activism that brought Jews together with historically non-Jewish people in causes of liberation and justice. There are many famous people of color who are also Jewish from parents who met through such struggles. The self-reference as Black Jews came about during periods of Black nationalism since the 1960s. The idea there is to fight against assimilation models of cultural whiteness in favor of cultural Blackness in which the East African foundations of Judaism took center stage.

These considerations of inclusivity and distinctness were also responses to problematic attitudes from Jews who insisted on white Jewish normativity. For such Jews, a nonwhite Jew raised the question of the legitimacy of their origins. The prevailing questions were: How were they Jewish? How did they become Jewish? The first involves suspicion over their authenticity; the second presumes they were not born Jewish.

The obvious answer to the first question is: the same way any other Jew is Jewish. Behind the question is the presumption, already stated, that the dominant Jews in a

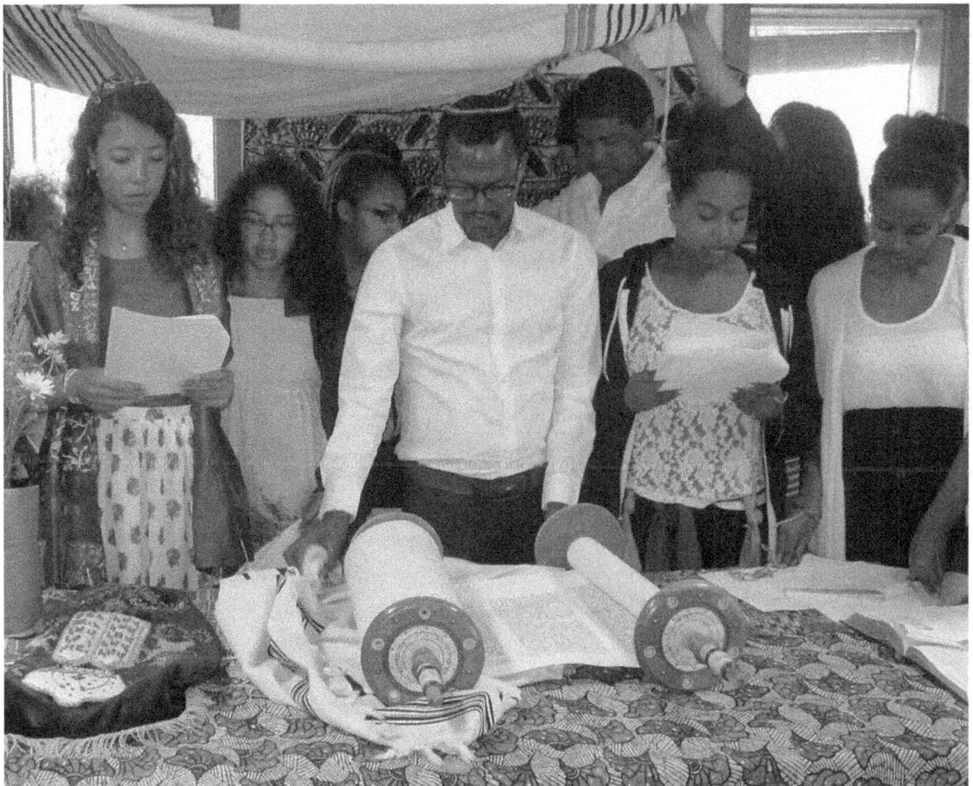

FIGURE 9.4 *Camp Be'chol Lashon.* Source: *Courtesy of Be'chol Lashon.*

particular country are *the Jews*. Thus, in North America, white Jewishness is normative. What those Jews don't know is that there are countries in which there are Jews for whom the idea of a white Jew is alien. I have witnessed Jews, whose sole image of Jewish people is not normatively white, question the authenticity of pale-skinned, blond Jews.

The second question presumes that nonwhite peoples, especially those from the African diaspora, enter the Euromodern world through Christianity. Their Jewishness must, then, be from a process of conversion. If the Jew of color states having been born Jewish, interrogation often continues through deferring the same question to the mother of the questioned. Now, where the mother turns out to be a European Jew, normative Jewish whiteness isn't threatened. Where maternal origins are entirely of African descent, Indigenous, or another nonwhite background, a search for evidence of conversion down the line often follows. The need for a Jewish past that was white persists, despite a Jewish mother's possible origins in any of the diverse nonwhite communities of Jews in Africa and Asia being evident. Where the case is different is among indigenous peoples of the Americas and South Pacific. There was no Jewish past among those peoples before the advent of Euromodern colonialism. But even there, the presumption of its introduction coming from a European Jew is problematic. As Africans, West Asians, and East Asians also came along with Euromodern colonialism, their Jews could also be the ancestor through whom Indigenous non-converts are *halakhic*.

Conclusion

The outline of Jewish diversity offered here is but a portrait on which to build some understanding of Jewish people in general. What should be clear is that much nuance is brought to the study of Jewish people if insightful questions are asked. What is clear is that Jewish people, despite our minority status, are persistently creative and dynamic, despite efforts to erase those attributes. Jewish people in each age are simultaneously different but connected to past Jewish peoples. A similar consideration pertains to the present and future. There may be technological developments and new kinds of additional identities that would challenge and expand what it means to be *halakhic*. Additionally, discussions are already underway on the status of being Jewish through a mother who is a transwoman. What happens to one's status if one's Jewish mother becomes a transman? Given these considerations, and the humility of our not being able to predict other considerations to come, what may connect Jews of today to those of tomorrow may be barely recognizable to the former while, as with many of us looking to our past, coherent to the latter.

FIGURE 9.5 *Queer Jews.* Source: *Courtesy of Be'chol Lashon.*

Further Reading and Online Resources

Abrahams, I. (1919), *Jewish Life in the Middle Ages*, New York: MacMillan.

Be'chol Lashon (2000–2020). Available online: https://globaljews.org/ (accessed November 16, 2020).

ben-Jochannan, Y. (1996), *We the Black Jews: Witness to the "White Jewish Race" Myth*, 2 Vols., Baltimore: Black Classics Press.

Brodkin, K. (1988), *How Jews Became White Folks and What That Says About Race in America*, New Brunswick, NJ: Rutgers University Press.

Cohen, S.J.D. (1999), *The Beginning of Jewishness: Boundaries, Varieties, Uncertainties*, Berkeley: University of California Press.

Fernandes, E. (2015), *The Last Jews of Kerala: The 2,000-Year History of India's Forgotten Jewish Community*, New York: Skyhorse Publishers.

Finch, III, C.S. (1991), *Echoes of the Old Darkland: Themes from the African Eden Decatur*, Atlanta, GA: Khenti.

Goldstein, E. (2007), *The Price of Whiteness: Jews, Race, and American Identity*, Princeton, NJ: Princeton University Press.

Gordon, J.A. (2015), "What Should Blacks Think When Jews Choose Whiteness?: An Ode to James Baldwin," *Critical Philosophy of Race*, 3 (2): 227–58.

Gordon, L.R. (2018), "Afro-Jewish Ethics?" in C. Hutt, B.D. Lerrner, and J. Schwartzmann (eds.), *Explorations in Jewish Religious and Philosophical Ethics*, 213–27, London: Routledge.

Isaac, W. (2006), "Locating Afro-American Judaism: A Critique of White Normativity," in L.R. Gordon and J.A. Gordon (eds.), *A Companion to African-American Studies*, 512–42, Malden, MA: Blackwell Publishers.

Jewish Multiracial Network (n.d.). Available online: https://www.jewishmultiracialnetwork. org/ (accessed December 12, 2020).

Jews for Racial and Economic Justice (2020), "Our Campaigns." Available online: https:// www.jfrej.org/ (accessed November 16, 2020).

Kaye/Kantrowitz, M., ed. (2007), *The Colors of Jews: Racial Politics and Radical Diasporism*, Bloomington: Indiana University Press.

Nirenberg, D. (2007), "Race and the Middle Ages: The Case of Spain and Its Jews," in M.R. Greer, W.D. Mignolo, and M. Quilligan (eds.), *Rereading the Black Legend: The Discourses of Religious and Racial Difference in the Renaissance Empires*, 71–87, Chicago: University of Chicago Press.

Roden, C. (1998), *The Book of Jewish Food: An Odyssey from Samarkand to New York*, New York: Knopf.

Solomin, R.M. (2002–20), "Sephardic, Ashkenazic, Mizrahi and Ethiopian Jews," *My Jewish Learning*. Available online: https://www.myjewishlearning.com/article/sephardic-ashkenazic-mizrahi-jews-jewish-ethnic-diversity/ (accessed November 16, 2020).

Tobin, D.K., G.A. Tobin, and S. Rubin (2005), *In Every Tongue: The Racial & Ethnic Diversity of the Jewish People*, San Francisco: Institute for Jewish & Community Research.

References

Fishbande, M.A. (1988), *Judaism*, San Francisco: Harper.

Gordon, L.R. (2016), "Rarely Kosher: Studying Jews of Color in North America," *American Jewish History*, 100 (1): 105–16.

Isaac, W. (2006), "Locating Afro-American Judaism: A Critique of White Normativity," in L.R. Gordon and J.A. Gordon (eds.), *A Companion to African-American Studies*, 512–42, Malden, MA: Blackwell.

Johnson, P. (1987), *A History of the Jews*, New York: Harper & Row.

Key, A. (2011), "What's My Name?: An Autoethnography of the Problem of Ethnic Suffering and Moral Evil in Black Judaism," PhD diss., Philadelphia: Temple University.

Tapper, A.J.H. (2016), *Judaisms: A Twenty-First-Century Introduction to Jews and Jewish Identities*, Berkeley: University of California Press.

Glossary Terms

Abayudaya Lugandan for "People of Judah." This is the name of the Ugandan Jews.

Ashkenazim Primarily European Jews. There are Jews in or from Europe who are not properly Ashkanazi. Origins of the term are unclear. Speculation includes Hebrew Ashkenazzim, plural of Ashkenaz, eldest son of Gomer (Gen. x.3), also the name of a biblical nation (Jer. li.27).

Halakha In Hebrew, "the way," refers to the collective body of Jewish religious laws derived from the written and oral Torah. The term is also spelled *Halakhah, Halakah,* or *Halachah.*

Mizrahim Also *Mizrachi.* Hebrew for "East," and often translated as "Oriental." The term refers to North African and West Asian/Middle Eastern Jews.

Raza A term from Andalusian Spain referring to breeds of horses, dogs; Jews and Moors (Afro-Muslims). It is connected to the Arabic words *ra* and *ras,* which in turn are linked to the Amharic word *ras,* the Hebrew word *rosh,* and the Mdw Ntr (ancient Egyptian) word *ra,* each of which means "head" and "beginning."

Sephardim Jews from Iberia. The term is plural for *Sephardi,* from Modern Hebrew *Sepharaddim* ("Spaniards, Jews of Spain").

Talmud From late Hebrew, meaning "instruction." The central text of Rabbinic Judaism, it is the body of Jewish civil and ceremonial law and legends. There are two versions: the Babylonian Talmud (from approximately the fifth century CE) and the earlier Palestinian or Jerusalem Talmud, Talmuda de-Eretz Yisrael (from approximately the second century CE) based on the Mishna ("study by repetition") or the Jewish oral tradition.

Tanakh Also called *Miqra,* the canonical collection of Hebrew scripture. The "a"s and "h" are added. It is originally TNK, an acronym of the first Hebrew letter of each of the Masoretic (Hebrew Aramaic) text's three traditional divisions of the twenty-four scriptures: Torah ("Teaching," also known as the five books of Moses), Nevi'im (prophets), and Ketuvim (writings). Most ancient formal writings didn't use vowels, which means it was up to the reader, often through familiarity with conventions, to surmise the vowels or missing sounds. Thus, TNK becomes TaNaKh.

Torah In Hebrew, "instruction, law, teaching," from the verbal noun *horah,* "he taught, he showed." The law of *G-d* as revealed to Moses and recorded in the first five books of the *Tanakh.* This is commonly known as the "Written Torah." It can also mean the continued narrative from all the twenty-four books, from the book of Genesis to the end of the *Tanakh.*

10

Shifting Identities: The Rise of Jewish GenZ

William Scott Green and Ronen Dar Pink

Judaism is not a religion of solitude. To the contrary, nearly every Judaic activity and expectation presupposes connection to community. Judaism values marriage and family over celibacy and isolation. It holds to shared destiny over individual salvation. It requires a quorum for the central parts of the liturgy and the recitation of God's word in the Torah. The community has the responsibility to care for the deceased. The study of Torah is best done in pairs or groups. The resistance of highly observant communities to the social distancing required for Covid-19 graphically illustrates Judaism's conviction about the importance of collectivity.

Judaism's covenantal structure provides two paths for establishing that connection. The covenant God makes with Abraham, Isaac, and Jacob is familial. One inherits membership in the covenanted community at birth. The later covenant at Sinai supplements this conception by creating a framework for voluntary association. By accepting and observing God's commandments, one can join the Jewish family by adoption and then transmit the covenantal relationship to one's offspring at birth. The two halakhic paths to membership—descent from a Jewish mother or acceptance of the principles and practices of Judaism through conversion—reflect the two aspects of the covenant. For centuries, they have been the two primary ways individuals became part of the Jewish People.

According to *halakhah* (Judaic religious practice), in principle, membership in the Jewish People, whether by birth or conversion, is indelible, not conditional. Jewish denominations disagree about the validity of one another's conversion process. Orthodox Judaism, for instance, does not recognize Reform conversion. Despite such differences, within each denomination the principle of indelible membership appears to hold. God addresses the heirs of Abraham, Isaac, and Jacob—however each denomination may define them—and calls them to a life of sanctity and substance through the commandments. But failure to fulfill the commandments does not nullify covenantal heritage. In general, and in principle, even if one is expelled from a particular Jewish community or converts to another religion, one remains part of the Jewish People. The two paths to Jewish peoplehood produce the same result: the primacy of inherited covenantal membership. Whatever engagement Jews have had—or not had—with the practices of Jewish religion, historically they have known they are Jews primarily by knowing who their parents are.

The dramatic events of modernity and the cultural shifts of postmodernity have made the idea of inherited membership in the Jewish People complex, complicated, and, according to some, perhaps even outmoded. For instance, in an explicit departure from *halakhah*, the State of Israel's Law of Return defines as Jewish and accepts for automatic Israeli citizenship people with one Jewish grandparent (male or female), but it denies automatic citizenship to born Jews who practice another religion. The Reform and Reconstructing movements accept patrilineal descent in addition to matrilineal descent.

Recent scholarship contends that the openness and diversity of contemporary US culture may justify and legitimate new forms of community connection and Jewish self-understanding. Shaul Magid makes the basic argument:

> It is my contention that the ethnic anchor of Jewish identity has been irreparably torn in post ethnic America. The inclusion of non-Jews in Jewish communities resulting from intermarriage, and the ways in which postethnicity has contributed to Jews defining their Jewishness by constructing/performing their Judaism outside any normative framework—including free and open expressions of religious syncretism and borrowing—has moved Judaism to what I have been calling a "post" state.
>
> (Magid 2013: 4)

He elaborates:

> Jews in America today do not need Judaism in order to identify as "Jewish," and they do not need to identify as "Jewish" or to identify with a Jewish collective (nor do they need to convert to some other religion) in order to live fully engaged lives in twenty-first century America. Yet increasingly many Jews in America want to identify as Jews—even many who are married to non-Jews or who have one non-Jewish parent—and they want Judaism in some form to serve that identity. But they want it on their terms in part because the myth of tradition no longer operates for them as authoritative. Moreover, being ethnically Jewish (Jewishness sans religion) is no longer sufficient when a growing minority—and soon the majority—of American Jews are multiethnic. For many of them, being Jewish is one part of a more complex narrative of identity.
>
> (Magid 2013: 11)

Robert Mnookin raises similar points with his proposal for a "Big Tent" American Jewish community, in which "the standard should be public self-identification. Are you willing to identify yourself publicly as a member of the Jewish people?" He suggests that "the Big-Tent standard minimizes the importance of descent and makes membership in the American Jewish community a matter of individual choice" (Mnookin 2018: loc. 2130). Mnookin proposes a focus of Jewish connectivity on five groups in particular who might otherwise be overlooked or excluded: 1) children of intermarriage; 2) non-Jewish spouses raising Jewish children and participating in a Jewish community; 3) people with no Jewish parent but a Jewish grandparent; 4) people with remote Jewish ancestry; 5) "adults who are Jews by birth and consider themselves ethnically Jewish but also have ties to another religion" (loc. 2134–202).

A Pew Research Center report entitled *The Religious Typology: A New Way to Categorize Americans by Religion* (2018) devised cross-denominational categories that classify "Americans into seven groups based on the religious and spiritual beliefs they share, how actively they practice their faith, the value they place on their religion, and other sources of meaning and fulfillment in their lives." The report divided the responses into three categories with subgroups: the "highly religious" category (with three subgroups) comprised 39 percent of the respondents; the "somewhat religious" category (with two subgroups) 32 percent; and the "non-religious" category (with two subgroups) 29 percent. The report included American Jews "who identify their religion as Judaism" and not those who self-identify as Jewish "culturally or ethnically." A comparison of the percentage of different religions in the three major categories showed that "Jewish Americans are the only religious group with substantial contingents at each end of the typology." The report showed that only 20 percent of the Jewish respondents were in the "somewhat religious" subgroups. By contrast, 35 percent classified themselves in the three "highly religious" subgroups, while 45 percent placed themselves in the two "non-religious" subgroups. These statistics indicate the divergence in American Jews' sense of connection to Judaism's religious heritage.

In pioneering work on the issue of Jewish identity in American Jewish education, Tel Zelkowicz outlines some of the key challenges to established modes of connectivity:

> Determined to live in two worlds at once, to be both American and Jewish, requires complex identity work that features an array of boundary navigations. Jews of all kinds regularly face dilemmas of differentiation (when, how, and to what extent to be apart from mainstream American society) and synthesis (when, how, and to what extent to be a part of it). They need to find strategies for deciding when and how to be selective and permeable, integrating American culture under some conditions, while filtering it out under others. This is tricky, and proves especially frustrating without the cultural tools and strategies to navigate the situation productively.
>
> (Levisohn and Kelman 2019: loc 3956)

Jon A. Levisohn makes the same point in a somewhat different way:

Thus, we can ask contemporary Jews: What is the Judaism or Jewishness that they affirm when they identify as Jews? (The use of the sociological term "Jewishness" instead of the more religious term "Judaism" may help disrupt that assumption that Jewish practice is synonymous with traditional Jewish religious practice.) What are the practices associated with those ideals? (The plural "practices" instead of the singular "practice" may also help to disrupt the assumption that Jewish practice is synonymous with the practice of the ritual aspects of halakha.)

(Levisohn and Kelman 2019: loc 5648)

All of this scholarship suggests that the American realities of increased intermarriage, multiethnic heritages, and a progressively personalist worldview may have created new contexts of Jewish connectivity and self-understanding. As Magid puts it, "biological descent increasingly yields to consent, where Jewishness is, for many, a choice rather than fate" (Magid 2013: 5).

The emergence of new forms of Jewish engagement and connectivity is particularly relevant to Generation Z, those born between 1995 and 2012. In 2018, *The New York Times* solicited names for this generation. Although Generation Z (signifying the last generation of the prior millennium) took the prize, perhaps GenZ's most revealing sense of themselves is captured in the comments that received the second most affirmative votes: "Don't call us anything. The whole notion of cohesive generations is nonsense" (Engel Bromwich 2018).

GenZ are the first to be coextensive with the internet. A report by McKinsey and Company describes them as "digital natives," whose early exposure to the internet, social networks, and mobile systems has yielded "a hypercognitive generation" that easily collects and cross-references many sources of information and integrates virtual and actual (i.e., face-to-face) experiences. GenZ live both online and in place. Because GenZ have unprecedented informational and experiential options, their individual interests translate into multiple connections to websites and social networks (Francis and Hoefel n.d.). Those under age twenty-four, for instance, average 8.7 social media accounts on varied platforms, and young people between age sixteen and twenty-four devote one-third of their time to social media (Seemiller and Grace 2019: 46). Other data show that 44 percent of Generation Z check their social media sites hourly (Jenkins n.d.), and some even more frequently. Platforms such as Snapchat, Instagram, and Twitter platforms allow them to craft an image and shape an audience, and 71 percent of GenZ use Snapchat more than six times a day (Seemiller and Grace 2019: 46; Jenkins n.d.). GenZ personify fluid, evolving, constructed individual identity, what recent researchers have called "hyper-customization."

There are meaningful differences between GenZ and millennials (born 1981–96). Millennials were born into a relatively secure and prosperous world, which was shattered by 9/11 and the economic crash of 2008. GenZ never knew a world without chaos. Their world was marred by terrorist attacks, school shootings, and the Great Recession. Millennials were raised by the confident and lenient generation of baby boomers (1946–64), but GenZ were raised by a more cautious and skeptical

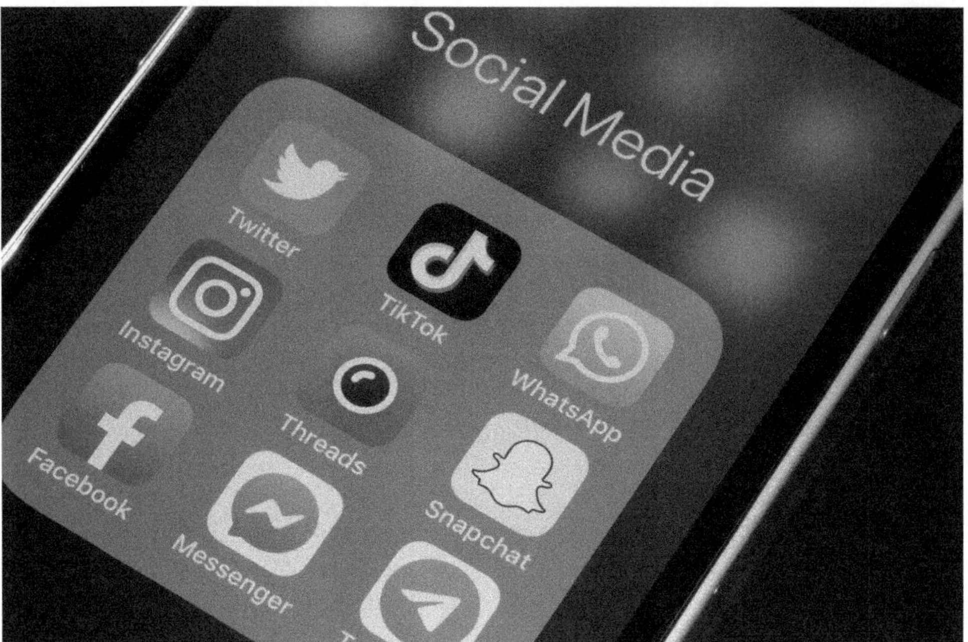

FIGURE 10.1 *Social media options.* Source: *Chesnot/Getty Images.*

Generation X (1965–80). Millennials were the first generation to learn social media, and their fascination about and excitement with the new technology resulted in limitless posting with little understanding of the issues of privacy. By contrast, because they are "digital natives," GenZ avoid unconstrained sharing, protect their personal data, and are hyperaware of their "personal brands" ("Generation Z News" 2020).

US Census data show a 50 percent increase in multiracial youth born between 2000 and 2017. Generation Z is the most diverse in US history, and 49 percent identify as nonwhite. Their commitment to diversity and inclusion is evident in their gender fluidity and their articulated openness to—and perhaps preference for—friends from different backgrounds who share their interests rather than their heritage. GenZ highly rate their ability to view the world through others' perspectives and to cooperate with people with different viewpoints (Seemiller and Grace 2019: 30–1).

GenZ's fusion of constructed individualism and social media use also affects their learning style. Multiple studies show that this generation prefers self-education or "intrapersonal learning" to formal instruction (Schweiger and Ladwig 2018: 46, Seemiller and Grace 2019: 23). Its members want to find out things for themselves rather than be told by others. They also prefer to learn experientially, by watching YouTube or Khan Academy videos rather than by reading textbooks.

Because of their informational options, GenZ are also a generation of factfinders. They examine and assess institutional options before making a commitment and strongly believe in institutional transparency (Fruchtman and Schults 2019: 6; Schweiger and Ladwig 2018: 46).

GenZ have a pervasive commitment to social justice. Their major political issues include gay marriage, transgender rights, the "Black Lives Matter" and "#MeToo" movements, the environment, and not surprisingly—given the number of massacres they have observed in their lifetime—gun control. Freedom, self-reliance, equality, fairness, inclusivity, pragmatism, and diversity are major defining traits and values.

According to Pew Research, GenZ are "the least religious generation. About one third have no religion—about the same proportion as among Millennials" (Lipka 2015). Another study reports that "GenZ's ties to religion seem even weaker than Millennials: They are more likely to identify as Atheist or Agnostic (21 percent vs. 15 percent), and most think church attendance is unimportant" (Barna 2018). Nearly half of GenZ do not find religion relevant to their "overall happiness" (Seemiller and Grace 2019: 177). While some in GenZ may participate in or maintain a cultural connection to organized religion, others are finding their own pathway to a sense of spirituality using elements from several religions or creating their own worldviews and practices. Because GenZ live in a culture of unlimited choices, they have numerous platforms for free expression of their beliefs and interests and multiple resources for self-actualization.

Using Technology to Build Jewish Community Connections in GenZ

Research on GenZ is still in its infancy, and there is much to learn about them and their potential impact on the future. This chapter offers a preliminary guide to the range of Jewish connective options available to Jewish GenZ. Which topics attract interest? Which self-understandings are evident? Is this the beginning of a new form of Jewish connectivity and community—of covenantal kinship, so to speak? An initial probe into the range and content of this new form of connection may help to provide the beginning of an answer.

Some basic demographic information helps to shape the context. The vast majority of American Jews are not an immigrant community, and Jewish GenZ are largely third- or fourth-generation American. The Pew Research Center (2018) found that two-thirds of American Jews identify as Jewish culturally rather than religiously. Extrapolating from that report, David Bryfman, CEO of the Jewish Education Project, estimates that more than 70 percent of non-Orthodox Jewish teens likely live in intermarried families, which, he suggests, is the "normative paradigm for most families with Jewish teenagers today" (personal communication). Another estimate is that approximately 75 percent of Jewish teenagers have no connection to a normative range of Jewish youth organizations (Jim Joseph Foundation 2013).

Jewish GenZ connect, engage, and identify themselves through readable, viewable, and interactive content. Every mainstream social media site has established platforms—some unique and innovative—for Jewish groups and with Jewish content.

Jewish GenZ use Facebook, Instagram, Reddit, Twitter, TikTok, Pinterest, Snapchat, LinkedIn, and YouTube to share individual Jewish experiences and create and discover collective ones.

For example, on the account @crazyjewishmom young Jews share primarily comedic text messages about their conversations with their mothers. Such messages include the need to find a nice Jewish spouse, the mother's desire for grandchildren because "I'm not getting any younger," and other comedic and overprotective texts. On food social media accounts people share recipes for the High Holidays or to display their Jewish culinary skills.

Hashtags such as #FirstAntiSemiticExperience, #Strongerthanhate, and #JewishAndProud demonstrate how interactive content helps users respond to hostility to Judaism and Jews. These hashtags have also become a necessary and effective teaching tool. In previous generations, when someone experienced anti-Semitism, it likely was not clear what to do, how to react, or whom to consult. Now, with social media and hashtags about Jewish personal experiences, young Jews can find national and global frameworks and strategies—both individual and collective—for dealing with anti-Jewish hostility and prejudice. These hashtags also can serve to call out anti-Semitic peers on social media. A recent example is an online petition signed by over 150,000 people demanding the expulsion of Penn State students who were photographed with swastikas drawn on their shoulders (Change.org 2020). A new Instagram account, "Jewishoncampus," allows college students to anonymously share their experiences of anti-Semitism on campus with the goal to promote tolerance and diversity.

Snapchat has created banners and special stories for the Jewish holidays, which enable people globally to share how they celebrate them. Snapchat compiles these pictures and posts them for public viewing. One interesting result is that an individual's followers may be exposed to a Jewish holiday about which they otherwise might not have known. TikTok enables users to share their Jewish life with tags such as #Jewish and #JewishCheck, which can range in use from sharing summer camp or school stories to self-deprecating Jewish jokes to anti-Semitic experiences, all with the intention of sharing and relating to their followers. The various Jewish hashtags have been viewed in shared TikTok videos over 500 million times as of July 2020 (TikTok #Jewish). Another example is the game "Jewish Geography," in which people explore mutual connections in one another's community. Once a game played exclusively during personal interactions in shared locations, today's online version facilitates an even more extensive level of interactions and engagement.

GenZ have utilized their obsessive interconnectedness and personal social branding abilities to create a more intimate connection to others. Through one quick search of their contacts or a brief post, Jewish GenZ can often find, for instance, an invitation to Sabbath dinner in a new city, a student they can shadow during a college visit, or someone who might know of a friend looking for a new roommate. Limitations on interactions among Jews once imposed by location or actual face-to-face relationships no longer pertain.

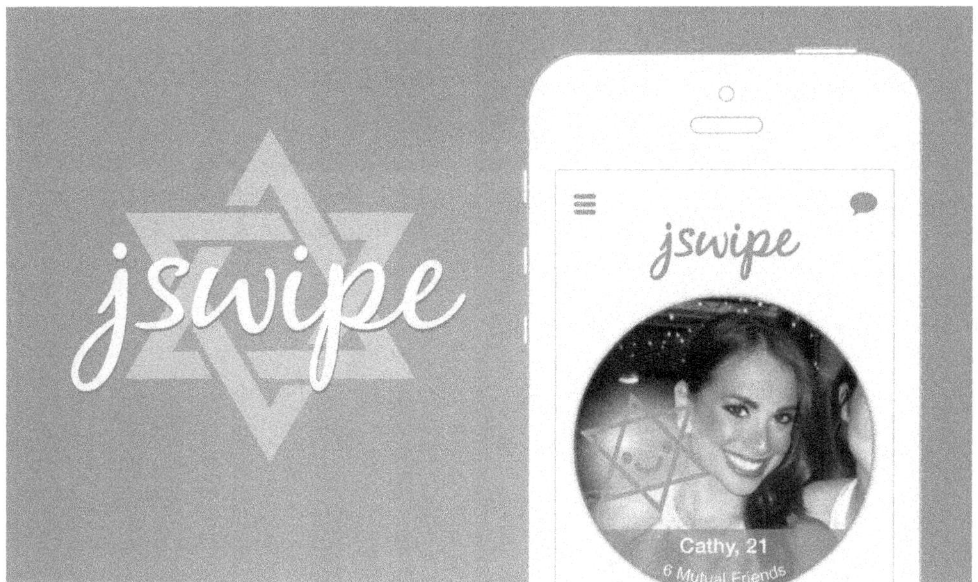

FIGURE 10.2 *The popular Jewish dating app Jswipe.* Source: *Jswipe.*

An exceptionally innovative Jewish social media post is "Eva Stories," which follows the saga of a thirteen-year-old girl murdered in Auschwitz, the Nazi death camp. According to *The Washington Post*, using Instagram "stories"—"short video clips complete with emojis, captions and spoken commentaries—'Eva Stories' garnered close to a million followers within 24 hours of going live" and now has over five million views. The project's creators, Mati Kochavi and his daughter Maya, say the goal "is to raise awareness of the Holocaust in an era of short attention spans and for a generation that is addicted to new media formats." It makes definitive Jewish experience accessible to a new generation in an authentic way (Eglash 2019; Figure 10.3).

Olivia Sher, a journalist for HeyAlma, an online publication that covers "everything from Jewish pop culture to what's happening in the news to personal pieces about identity, feminism, and more," suggests that Jewish social media is "simply our generation's modern-day *shtetl* ('market town')—it is our way of finding a community" (Sher 2020). And that connection can extend beyond friendship. Social media might be a contemporary version of the *shadchan*, the fabled Jewish matchmaker. Jewish dating apps such as "Saw You At Sinai," "Mazel Match," and "Jswipe" have become increasingly popular. According to David Yarus, Jswipe, which he founded, has over one million users, the majority of whom are Generation Z and millennials (JSwipe 2019).

The distinctive character of GenZ's experience is that everything can be personalized and created almost instantly online. One has no need to be a member of any particular

FIGURE 10.3 *A T-shirt for a popular segment of the podcast "campfires and color wars," about people's Jewish summer camp experiences.* Source: © *Campfires and Color Wars.*

community to find what one is looking for. In the words of a Jewish college student, "Who you affiliate with, not what you affiliate with, is the new name of the game" (Fruchtman and Schultz 2019: 7). Another makes the point differently. "Looking at our Judaism as an individualized thing and not the same as everyone else is a really big difference in how we practice Judaism" (Hanau 2019). GenZ are hyperaware and protective of their personal brand, and if Judaism is not part of that brand, while they still care about it, they may not outwardly show it or affiliate with it. However, if Judaism is part of their personal brand, they tend to be vocal and public in their social media presence.

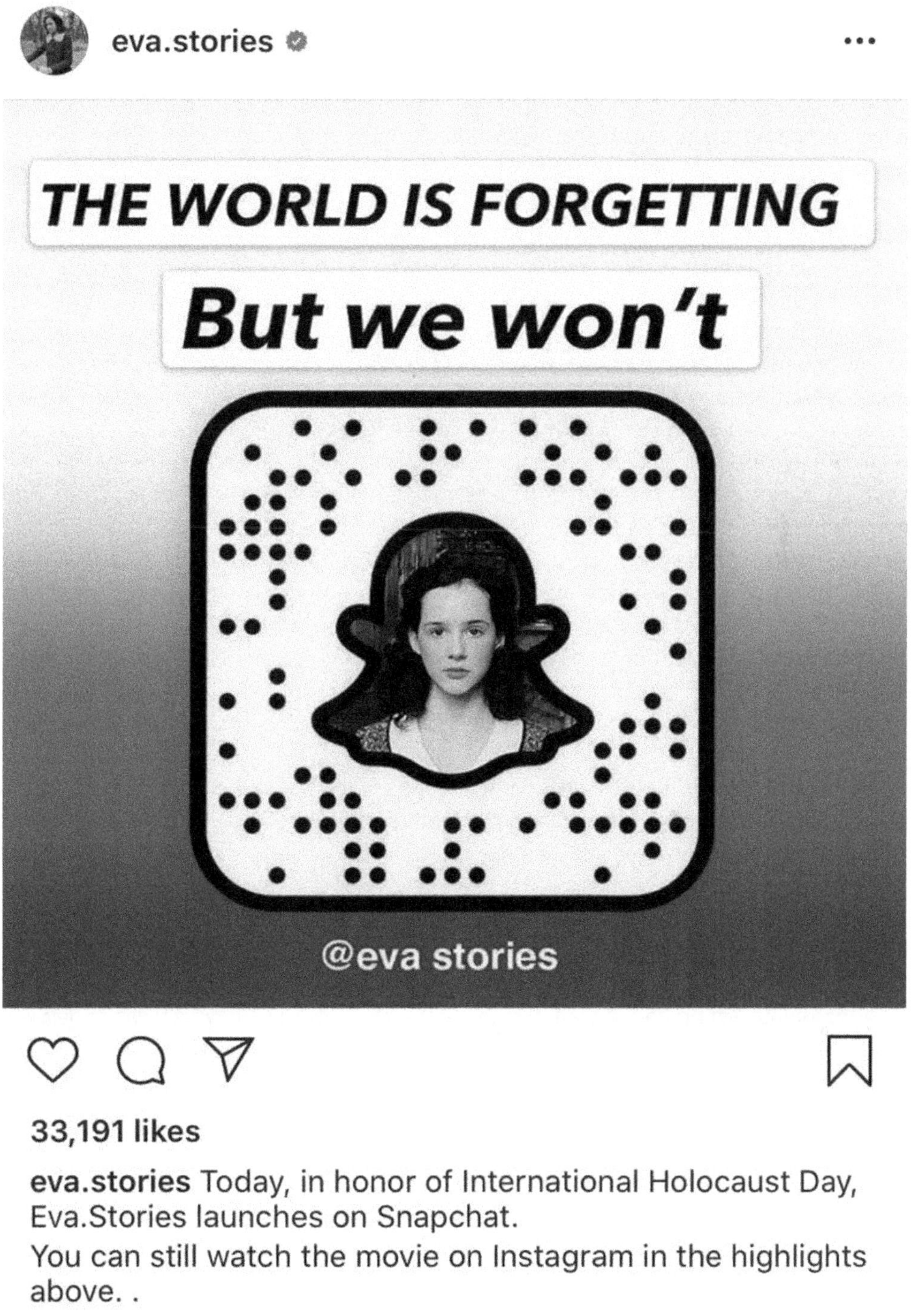

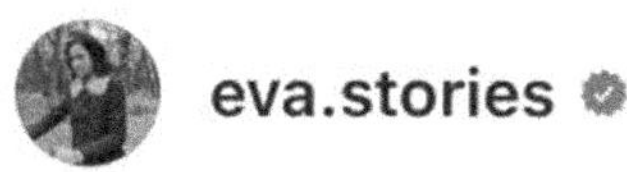

eva.stories
THE WORLD IS FORGETTING
But we won't
@eva stories
33,191 likes
eva.stories Today, in honor of International Holocaust Day, Eva.Stories launches on Snapchat.
You can still watch the movie on Instagram in the highlights above. .

FIGURE 10.4 *An Instagram post of "Eva.Stories," which served as a memorial for international Holocaust Remembrance Day.* Source: © *Eva.Stories.*

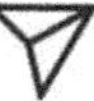

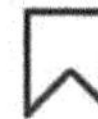

The Expansive Options for Jewish GenZ's Connections vs Previous Generations

Jewish GenZ's use of technology to connect with other Jews has generated a wide array of shared experiences, opinions, interactions, and communities. Historically, Jewish connections were largely constrained by geography or level of religious adherence. By contrast, GenZ's ability to grow their Jewish social network and connections is unlimited. Before the internet, individuals may have found themselves in a Jewish community populated by people with whom they had few commonalities beyond a shared connection to Judaism and geographic proximity. When one's only Jewish options were a local synagogue, youth group, school, or camp, the failure to find friends or feel supported there could be an alienating experience that might negatively affect one's adult connection to Judaism and Jewish organizations. To be sure, the organized Jewish community is no stranger to the internet, but its use has been largely local and institutional (Sheskin and Liben 2015). Today's reality is different. With the ever-expanding internet and social media, the Jewish world, access to Jewish knowledge, and connection to communities of like-minded people are personal and almost infinitely capacious.

To find these varied Jewish affinity communities and virtual "places," one merely has to type an interest or identity into a search engine, or into sites such as Facebook and Reddit, to discover hundreds of people with similar interests and viewpoints also seeking community. In earlier generations, disagreement with the teachings of a rabbi or community leader could create a sense of isolation; for Jewish GenZ, which believes in multiple truths and easily accessible alternative narratives and information, this is not the case. If they dislike a particular message of a sermon, for instance, they can find multiple alternatives online that are more sympathetic.

Significantly, the internet also has opened Judaism and the varied Jewish cultures to a broad and new GenZ audience. For Jews who have decided to live in areas with no local Jewish community, the internet/social media provide an opportunity for them to develop Jewish connections in locations that have few if any other Jews. In all cases, the internet/social media permit Jews to maintain their connections at little to no cost.

Another interesting consideration is that non-Jews now also have access to Jewish resources and Jewish people in ways that, in earlier periods, someone living in an area with no Jews would have found difficult if not impossible.

The propensity of Generation Z to accept the notion of multiple realities and truths has led GenZ to consider themselves social justice activists. This conviction, not surprisingly, has generated a range of opinions on Jewish social issues, particularly surrounding the State of Israel and its policies. There are online debates and arguments about such topics as Israel's legitimacy and history, Palestinian rights within Israel, and the desire by some for an eventual Palestinian State, what constitutes Jewish identity, the range of legitimate Jewish religious practices, gender inequalities within Jewish life, and many more. IfNotNow and Jewish Voice for Peace (JVP) are examples of organizations that gained strong support among GenZ Jews. In partnership with IfNotNow, the #YouNeverToldMe campaign was born "out of a pattern of realizations that the Israel education we received during our youth was one-sided and incomplete." Members of this campaign are "Alumni of different institutions from across the spectrum of Jewish life—Camp Ramah, USY, BBYO, NFTY, Solomon Schechter, Young Judea, URJ, summer camps, and Jewish day schools around the country. We are young adults who proudly identify as Jewish, and, for many of us, we have youth organizations to thank for this" (You Never Told Me n.d.). These beliefs conflict with those of other GenZ groups that reflect the positions of long-standing Jewish community groups and organizations. These divergent perspectives have created tensions on campuses and within organized Jewish life and have often played out on social media discussion boards.

Alternatively, there are groups such as Zioness (2020), a movement primarily managed by and organized for women. Its site claims that:

> Zionism is the movement for Jewish self-determination, the expression of the Jewish peoples' dreams of liberation and empowerment after millennia of Jewish struggles for civil rights and equality in the face of persecution, exile, and genocide. We support Israel's existence as a Jewish and democratic state. [...] *Our Zionism drives our engagement in social action.* As Zionists, we proudly fight for justice and against discrimination for women, people of color, LGBTQ+ individuals, and any other human being whose rights are denied or threatened because of their innate characteristics.
>
> (Zioness 2020, emphasis in original)

GenZ's search for their own truths led to the popularity of "fact finding missions" to Israel, which typically include visiting and meeting with representatives of the State of Israel and the Palestinian territories. These trips aim to provide a wider and more in-depth understanding of the different narratives in the region and typically include conversations spanning an array of experiences and "truths."

Other subgroups within the Jewish GenZ demographic have emerged and gained popularity, which reflects the openness and fluidity of this generation. Examples are people who identify as lesbian, gay, bisexual, transexual, and queer/questioning (LGBTQ) (e.g., Keshet and Eshel), people with disabilities (e.g., Gesher), Jews by Choice and interfaith families (e.g., 18door), and Jews of Color (e.g., Jews in ALL Hues, Be'Chol Lashon). The creation of these different groups allows GenZ to form or celebrate with others their Jewish identity in all of its complexity without conflicting with other aspects of their individual self-identification. The same idea holds true for shared interests and affinity groups. Examples include Jewish art communities (e.g., Jewish Studio Project), Jewish environmentalists (e.g., Hazon), and Jewish musician communities (e.g., Jewish rock radio).

Creating Jewish Identity for GenZ in "Real Life"

Social media even affects Jewish GenZ who had a more conventional engagement with Jewish life as children and teens through camp, synagogue, Jewish education, and Israel trips. As they enter young adulthood, their Jewish involvement is now up to them, not their parents. Thus, if they have an interest in maintaining a connection to Judaism, they generally choose as a starting point a pathway from the internet.

Young Jews who want to have or maintain their Jewish identity and connections are waiting for the institutions around them to catch up to their needs. Many long-standing Jewish organizations and institutions have conducted studies to try to understand what Jewish identity and involvement looks like to GenZ. An additional question is how—and if—to relate online Jewish connections to traditional and established "in-life" Jewish experiences. Currently data are being collected, and more is anticipated (Charles and Lynn Schusterman Family Foundation 2019). Also, organizations are using Instagram and Snapchat to innovate ways to build community.

There also has been an increase in online religious services and *minyanim* (religious quorums) for those whose life or work schedules make it difficult to engage in Jewish religious practices or attend services at a prescribed time. Online sermons and Jewish educational podcasts have become widely accessed. For example, Rabbi Sandra Lawson, also known as the Snapchat Rabbi, has created a Snapchat to spread her messages, teachings, and perspectives. The Jewish Telegraph Agency listed her as among the ten Jews people should follow on Snapchat and one of the fifty Jews people should follow on Twitter (Lawson n.d.). She explains, "I'm always thinking about how to connect with Jews where they already are. You know, the Jews who are not coming to synagogue or the JCC but are still proud of being Jews. I thought Snapchat would be a good place to reach them" (Lawson). When asked what she posts on Snapchat, she responded,

> I'm always trying things. At first, I thought I would just answer people's questions, but the platform is not set up like that. You need to build content and attract followers. So I began creating short *Divrei Torah*, Torah commentaries, on the days when we traditionally read Torah: Monday, Thursday and Shabbat. Each time, I'd talk about the meaning of that week's portion. Sometimes they are long and sometimes they are short.
>
> (Team Be'chol Lashon 2016)

Conclusion

Jewish GenZ have been raised in the internet age and have no experience with a life that is unaffected by, or—in most cases—does not revolve around, connectivity through devices. Because engagement with social media is second nature to them, they instinctively look to it to both support and foster their identities and their choices.

Previous generations gathered in a physical space to create community. Jewish GenZ make their connections virtually—anytime and anywhere. They want to be "moved" or informed or connected by content that comes to them, something largely unavailable to previous generations. But that content is not necessarily Jewish. David Bryfman cogently describes GenZ as a "generation that cares as much if not more about humanity than they do about specifically Jewish life" (Hanau 2019). Liat Cohen-Raviv, executive director at Diller Teen Fellows reinforces that view, "The global world concept has affected Jewish teens in a way we need to be aware of [...]. If we are looking for GenZ to feel more Jewish than anything else, that is unlikely. They have all of these other things they identify with [...]. It is just complicated" (eJP 2015).

In addition, the conventional means of assessing Jewish identity may bypass the ways GenZ define themselves Jewishly. The issue is not with Jewish GenZ but with the questions the older generations are asking them. The Covid-19 pandemic of 2020 might be the unfortunate impetus for many to segue to the next adaptation of Judaism—Virtual Judaism—which GenZ is helping to create. Because the world has been forced to go virtual, it is now possible for Jews to stay Jewish engaged exclusively online. The Jewish world is already reimagining Judaism in this new era with virtual *Brit Milah* (circumcision), *B'nai* and *B'not Mitzvah* (a young adult's first recitation of the Torah in worship), funerals, and *minyanim*. Novel learning opportunities and Jewish communities are emerging across the many social media platforms. MyJewishLearning.com has created a website page called "Daily Guide to Zoom Events, Livestreams and Other Online Resources" to help navigate this new world.

As more and more Jewish identity subgroups are created, GenZ are straying from brick-and-mortar community institutions. The consequence raises a question about the long-term viability of the current structure of the American Jewish community, particularly as it is defined, managed, and measured by its established institutions and organizations. The fast-paced nature of contemporary life means that there could soon be a world in which Jewish children learn about Judaism primarily through lessons they follow on an iPad from a teacher or rabbi on social media. A new Jewish TikTok celebrity could appear who teaches Talmud in one-minute increments. (There are already Christian pastors on the app who give sermons to over 80,000 followers.) What kinds of parents will GenZ Jews be? How will they teach their children about Judaism, when they themselves may be less and less likely to attend Jewish community events? The question is less about how to recreate "the Jewish Community"—as if there ever were a single one—but rather, how—and if—this great diversity, technological progress, and expertise can become the basis to create something new.

Acknowledgments

The authors are grateful to Aiden Pink, Tamar Fenton; Professors Ira Sheskin, Gary G. Porton, and Alan Avery-Peck; Rabbi Lyle Rothman; and Dr. David Bryfman for help and advice on this topic.

Further Reading and Online Resources

Below is an indicative but not comprehensive list of some of the major Jewish GenZ internet and social media. It offers a list of hashtags, websites, videos, organizations, and others, that have a strong internet and social media presence.

I   Political organizations

   A   Israel-related

    1   Aipac.org

    2   Standwithus.com

    3   Jewishvoiceforpeace.org

    4   Ifnotnowmovement.org

    5   Jstreet.org

    6   #younevertoldme

    7   #skipthetrip
This hashtag aims to persuade people to not go on scheduled visits to Israel, primarily Birthright and Congressional visits.

    8   Zioness.org

    9   Womenofthewall.org
"An organization whose goal is to attain social and legal recognition of our right, as women, to wear prayer shawls, pray, and read from the Torah, collectively and aloud, at the Western Wall."

    10 SSImovement.org (Student Supporting Israel)

   B   Domestic politics-related

    1   *Poverty*
      a   Mazon.org

      b   Bluecardfund.org

    2   *Environmentalism*
      a   Hazon.org

      b   Coalition on the Environment and Jewish Life (COEJL.net)

      c   Aytzim.org

    3   *Anti-Semitism*
      a   JewsforJudaism.org
Witty and informative responses and information to refute Christian attempts to convert Jews.

    b Nizkor.org

       A website that teaches how to respond to Holocaust deniers on social media.

    c #jewishandproud

       A recurring hashtag often used in response to anti-Semitic incidents.

    d #neveragain

       A recurring hashtag often used in response to anti-Semitic incidents and during Holocaust memorials.

    e #strongerthanhate

       A hashtag that appeared the after anti-Semitic Pittsburgh attack in 2018.

    f #JeSuisJuif

       A hashtag that appeared after anti-Semitic Paris attacks of 2015.

    g #Togetheragainstantisemitism

       Recurring handle, starting in 2013, used in response to anti-Semitic incidents.

    h Holocaust diary Eva.Stories (Instagram)

    i Jewishoncampus (Instagram)

    j Imthatjew (YouTube)

C Community organizations

    1 *Disability and inclusion*

       a Removingthestumblingblock.com

       b Gesherdr.org

       c Respectability.org

       d Jewishfamilyservices.org

    2 *LGBTQ*

       a Keshetonline.org

       b Eshelonline.org

    3 *Converts and interfaith*

       a Darshanyeshiva.org

       b 18door.org

       c Judaismcourse.com

    4 *Jews of color*

       a Globaljews.org

       b Jewsinallhues.org

II Religious life

  A Synagogues/synagogue organizations

    1 Each synagogue has its own online presence.

    2 Uscj.org (The United Synagogue of Conservative Judaism)

    3 Urj.org (Union for Reform Judaism)

    4 Ou.org (Orthodox Union)

    5 The Office of Rabbi Sacks (Podcast)

    6 Chabad.org

  B Experiential religious groups

    1 JewishstudioProject.org

      "Integrates creative practices from the field of art therapy with learning approaches from the beit midrash (house of inquiry)."

    2 LabShul.org

      "Dedicated to exploring, creating and celebrating innovative opportunities for contemplation, life cycle rituals, the arts, life-long learning and social justice."

    3 OpenTemple.org

      "Open Temple offers Ritual Happenings, Creative Classes, and Mulit-Media portals into Jewish Life, all with a 21st century vibe."

    4 Rebooters.net

      "A premier R&D platform for the Jewish world, that catalyzes their Network of creators, artists, entrepreneurs, and activists to produce experiences and products that evolve the Jewish conversation and transform society."

    5 SaturdayNightSeder.com

  C Schools/campus learning

      Each college religious organization has their own online presence including a social media.

    1 Chabad.org

    2 Aish.com

    3 Hillel.org

    4 MEOR.org

    5 oujlic.org (Jewish Learning Initiative on Campus)

  D Lay learning

    1 Jewishvirtuallibrary.org

    2 MyJewishLearning.com

    3 Sefaria.org

    4 OpenSiddur.org

    5 On the Other Hand: Ten minutes of Torah (podcast)

    6 Judaism Unbound (Podcast)
         Focuses on religious aspects and texts in Judaism.

    7 The Promised Podcast (Podcast)

E Summer Camps
Each summer camp has its own individual online presence both through websites and social media accounts.

    1 Jewishcamp.org

    2 Campfires and Colorwars (Podcast)

III News

  A American

    1 Forward.com

    2 Tablet.com

    3 HeyAlma.com

    4 Jewishcurrents.org

  B Israeli

    1 Timesofisrael.com

    2 Haaretz.com

    3 Jpost.com

IV Culture

  A Cooking

    1 Jewishfoodhero.com

    2 Ok.org—Is it kosher

    3 Breakingmatzo.com

    4 @jewishfood (Instagram)

    5 Jewish moms try each other's brisket (YouTube)

  B Music

    1 Songleaderbootcamp.com

    2 Jewishrockradio.com

    3 Jewishmusicstream.com

    4 Imi.org—Israeli Music Institute

    5 Klezmerguide.com

    6 Yeshiva boys' choir (YouTube)

    7 Maccabeats (YouTube)

C Humor

    1 @crazyjewishmom (Instagram)

    2 @jewthings (Instagram)

    3 @jewishgirlproblems (Instagram)

    4 Schlep (uber parody) (YouTube)

    5 11 Things Jewish Friends Just Get (YouTube)

    6 Jewish Tiktoks

    7 Unorthodox (Podcast)

    8 The Kibitz (Podcast)

D Travel

    1 TotallyJewishtravel.com

    2 Jewishtravelagency.com

    3 BirthrightIsrael.com

E Shopping

    1 SewJewish.com

    2 TraditionsJewishgifts.com

    3 Judaicawebstore.com

    4 Moderntribe.com

    5 Judiaca.com

F MISC

    1 Jewish Internet Guide

    2 JewOrNotAJew.com

V Affinity groups

  A Religious

    1 God Save Us From Your Opinion: A Place For Serious Discussion of Judaism (Facebook)

        A page where people ask serious questions, many of them religious.

  B Interfaith/converts

    1 Jewish parenting for interfaith families (Facebook)

    2 Planning your Jewish interfaith wedding (Facebook)

C LGBTQ

    1 LGBT Jews inclusive and proud (Facebook)

    2 Queer Zoom University Hillel (Facebook)

D Dating

    1 Jdate (application)

    2 Jswipe (application)

    3 SawyouatSinai (application)

    4 MEETJEW UNIVERSITY (Facebook)

E College

    1 ZOOM UNIVERSITY HILLEL (Facebook)

    2 ZOOM UNIVERSITY CHABAD (Facebook)

F Humor

    1 Surely This Will Save Conservative Judaism (Facebook) Meme page where people share funny things relating to the decline in Conservative Judaism's membership.

    2 Jewish Meme Page (Facebook)

Berge, Z.L. and M.B. Berge (2019), "The Economic ABCs of Educating and Training Generations X, Y, and Z," *Performance Improvement*, 58 (5) (May/June): 44–53. https://doi.org/10.1002/pfi.21864.

Cooperman, A. and G. Smith (2013), "What Happens When Jews Intermarry?" *Pew Research Center*, November 12. Available online: https://www.pewresearch.org/fact-tank/2013/11/12/what-happens-when-jews-intermarry (accessed November 16, 2020).

Mather, M. and A. Lee (2020), "Children Are at the Forefront of U.S. Racial and Ethnic Change," *PRB*, February 10. Available online: https://www.prb.org/children-are-at-the-forefront-of-u-s-racial-and-ethnic-change" (accessed November 16, 2020).

Pandit, V. (2015), *We Are Generation Z: How Identity, Attitudes, and Perspectives Are Shaping Our Future*, Dallas, TX: Brown Books.

References

Barna (2018), "Atheism Doubles among Generation Z," January 24. Available online: https://www.barna.com/research/atheism-doubles-among-generation-z/ (accessed November 16, 2020).

Change.org (2020), "Disciplinary Action for Ryann Milligan Penn State Student." Available online: https://www.change.org/p/penn-state-university-disciplinary-action-for-ryann-milligan-penn-state-student (accessed November 16, 2020).

Charles and Lynn Schusterman Family Foundation (2019), "6 Resources All About Gen Z," July 10. Available online: https://www.schusterman.org/blogs/team-schusterman/6-resources-all-about-gen-z (accessed November 16, 2020).

eJP (2015), "Embracing a New Dynamic: 'Generation Z'," *eJewish Philanthropy*, April 27. Available online: https://ejewishphilanthropy.com/embracing-a-new-dynamic-generation-z/ (accessed November 16, 2020).

Engel Bromwich, J. (2018), "We Asked Generation Z to Pick a Name. It Wasn't Generation Z," *The New York Times*, January 31. Available online: https://www.nytimes.com/2018/01/31/style/generation-z-name.html (accessed November 16, 2020).

Englash, R. (2019), "'Hi! My name's Eva': A Teenage Holocaust Victim's Diary Comes to Life on Instagram," *The Washington Post*, May 2. Available online: https://www.washingtonpost.com/world/2019/05/02/hi-my-names-eva-teenage-holocaust-victims-diary-comes-life-instagram/ (accessed November 16, 2020).

Francis, T. and F. Hoefel (n.d.), "'True Gen': Generation Z and Its Implications for Companies," *McKinsey*. Available online: https://www.mckinsey.com/industries/consumer-packaged-goods/our-insights/true-gen-generation-z-and-its-implications-for-companies (accessed November 16, 2020).

Fruchtman, J. and D. Schultz (2019), "The Shift: A Discussion on Welcoming & Engaging Gen Z," *Moishe House*. Available online: https://www.moishehouse.org/the-shift/ (accessed November 16, 2020).

"Generation Z News" (2020), *Business Insider*. Available online: https://www.businessinsider.com/generation-z (accessed November 16, 2020).

Hanau, S. (2019), "Jewish Teens: 'We Don't Want Our Parents' Judaism'," *The New York Jewish Week*, June 5. Available online: https://jewishweek.timesofisrael.com/jewish-teens-we-dont-want-our-parents-judaism/ (accessed November 16, 2020).

Jenkins, R. (n.d.), "How Generation Z Uses Technology and Social Media." Available online: https://blog.ryan-jenkins.com/how-generation-z-uses-technology-and-social-media (accessed November 16, 2020).

Jim Joseph Foundation (2013), *Effective Strategies for Educating and Engaging Jewish Teens*, March. Available online: https://jimjosephfoundation.org/wp-content/uploads/2013/03/Report_and_Appendix_Effective_Strategies_for_Educating_and_Engaging_Jewish_Teens.pdf (accessed November 16, 2020)

JSwipe (2019), *Love Study*. Available online: https://static1.squarespace.com/static/5d8a2beb297c3262d231149c/t/5d93db699ce86b0c4f16e434/1569971057704/JSwipeLoveStudy2019.pdf (accessed November 16, 2020).

Lawson, Rabbi S. (n.d.), "Rabbi, Musician and Activist." Available online: https://www.rabbisandralawson.com/ (accessed December 21, 2020).

Levisohn, J. and A. Kelman (2019), *Beyond Jewish Identity: Rethinking Concepts and Imagining Alternatives* [Kindle edition], Brookline, MA: Academic Studies Press.

Lipka, M. (2015), "Millennials Increasingly Are Driving Growth of 'Nones'," *Pew Research Center*, May 12. Available online: https://www.pewresearch.org/fact-tank/2015/05/12/millennials-increasingly-are-driving-growth-of-nones/ (accessed November 16, 2020).

Magid, S. (2013), *American Post-Judaism: Identity and Renewal in a Postethnic Society* [Kindle edition], Bloomington: Indiana University Press.

Mnookin, R.H. (2018), *The Jewish American Paradox: Embracing Choice in a Changing World* [Kindle edition], New York: Public Affairs.

Pew Research Center (2018), "The Religious Typology: A New Way to Categorize Americans by Religion," August 29. Available online: https://www.pewforum.org/2018/08/29/the-religious-typology/ (accessed November 16, 2020).

Schwieger, D. and C. Ladwig (2018), "Reaching and Retaining the Next Generation: Adapting to the Expectations of Gen Z in the Classroom," *Information Systems Education Journal*, 16 (3) (June): 45–54.

Seemiller, C. and M. Grace (2019), *Generation Z: A Century in the Making* [Kindle edition], Abingdon: Taylor and Francis.

Sher, O. (2020), "How Gen Z Is Using TikTok to Embrace Their Jewishness," *HeyAlma*, January 17. Available online: https://www.heyalma.com/how-gen-z-is-using-tiktok-to-embrace-their-jewishness/ (accessed November 16, 2020).

Sheskin, I.M. and M. Liben (2015), "The People of the Nook: Jewish Use of the Internet," in S. Brunn (ed.), *The Changing World Religion Map*, 3831–56, Dordrecht: Springer.

Team Be'chol Lashon (2016), "Snapchat's Top Rabbi," *My Jewish Learning*, August 11. Available online: https://www.myjewishlearning.com/jewish-and/snapchats-top-rabbi/ (accessed November 16, 2020).

You Never Told Me (n.d.), "Our Open Letter to Fellow Alumni." Available online: https://younevertoldme.org/our-open-letter (accessed November 16, 2020).

Zioness (2020), "About Zioness: A Manifesto for Change and Inclusion." Available online: https://zioness.org/about-zioness/ (accessed November 16, 2020).

Index